STUDIES IN HISTORY, ECONOMICS AND PUBLIC LAW

EDITED BY THE FACULTY OF POLITICAL SCIENCE
OF COLUMBIA UNIVERSITY

Volume CII] [Number 2

Whole Number 232

THE BANK OF THE STATE OF MISSOURI

BY

JOHN RAY CABLE

AMS PRESS
NEW YORK

COLUMBIA UNIVERSITY
STUDIES IN THE
SOCIAL SCIENCES

232

The Series was formerly known as
Studies in History, Economics and Public Law.

Reprinted with the permission of Columbia University Press
From the edition of 1923, New York
First AMS EDITION published 1969
Manufactured in the United States of America

Library of Congress Catalogue Card Number: 78-78008

AMS PRESS, INC.
NEW YORK, N. Y. 10003

PREFACE

THE Bank of the State of Missouri has been singularly neglected by students of American economic development. Founded in the panic days of 1837 and surrounded by paper banks of the worst sort, it continued for thirty years to preach the doctrine of honest money. Its great mission was to set standards. An exaggerated idea of conservatism often prevented it from performing needed business services, but the private banking houses and, in later days, the chartered banks, which grew up to do the work refused by the State Bank, were forced by its example to conduct their business on a higher plane. Its last days as a national bank were clouded by mismanagement; but this should not cause its splendid record as a public institution to be forgotten. In matters of financial policy the bank doubtless made many mistakes, but they were due usually to extreme caution rather than excessive risk-taking. It should be noted, however, that the bank can be judged fairly only in the light of the problems it had to meet. It was a pioneer bank in a new country.

In beginning this study the author was struck by the outstanding fact of the financial conservatism of the state. Missouri's experience was distinctly unlike that of her neighbors. An attempt is made in this dissertation to trace the reasons for the course of this development. Why were there no paper banks in Missouri? The answer to this question is the main thesis of this study. Part of the answer is to be found in the experiences of other states and part of it in unhappy Missouri experiences of earlier days. Accordingly it is necessary to go back to the beginnings of Missouri history in order to see how each banking and currency problem was handled as it arose. The threads of many influences from without the state have been followed. However, external events have been studied only so far as they exerted an influence on local affairs. The method is necessarily historical. Where did the bank come from? What was the extent of its service to the state? Why was it given up? These are some of the questions that have been considered. Thus far the study is conceived of as a contribution to the economic history of the Middle West. However, a serious attempt has been made to analyze the accounts of the bank in order to see just how far it was governed by sound banking principles. Here a departure is made from the historical method and much attention is given to statistical analysis.

The period of Missouri history covered is roughly from 1819 to 1877. It begins with a barter economy. A little later Saint Louis had two chartered banks (1816 to 1822). Both were unfortunate. The state then tried a Loan Office to relieve the pressure following the disturbances of 1819. It too had a stormy career. The result was that Missourians distrusted any and every sort of banking arrangement. Then came the opening of the branch of the United States Bank in Saint Louis with its years of honest service. It was followed by the Cincinnati Commercial Agency—also an honest bank. Thus by 1836 Missouri, in an unusual degree, had seen both good and bad banking, and so was in good condition to consider the building of a state bank. It has been thought necessary to study carefully all of these experiences in order to get the setting for the organization of the State Bank in 1836 and 1837. Then came twenty years of banking monopoly, years of honest banking and of standard setting, but also of much retardation of business. In 1857 the demand for more banking capital became too great to be longer withstood. Accordingly a general banking law was passed creating a number of chartered banks of issue, and removing the State Bank from its position of monopoly to one of mere competition with the rest. The state saw the drift of events and sold out to a private syndicate in 1866. The bank was then nationalized and its character changed to an institution of the "plunger" type. The sale of the state stock really marks the end of the bank as a distinct type. Henceforth, it was merely one of a group of Saint Louis institutions. The story has, however, been carried down to the failure in 1877. This, in brief, is the history which this study has sought to develop.

It should be said in passing that the financial history of Missouri up to 1877 is, to an extent one can scarcely appreciate today, a history of the business and financial interests of Saint Louis. The city dominated the state. To a considerable degree the banking history of Saint Louis was the banking history of the state.

A Note Concerning Authorities

This study was begun in 1916 as a contribution to the history seminar conducted by Professors Jonas Viles and Frank Fletcher Stephens at the University of Missouri. It was expanded later into a sixty-page monograph and presented to the Graduate School of the University of Chicago in 1917 in partial fulfilment of the requirements for the degree of Master of Arts. At the suggestion of

Dr. Henry Rogers Seager the work was continued at Columbia University in 1919. It thus represents a study carried on over a considerable period of time; and it is believed most of the available material has been consulted. The chief sources are federal and state documents and contemporary newspapers. A careful study has been made of the *Journals of the House and Senate of Missouri*, the *Laws of Missouri*, and the *Messages of the Governors* (1819–1877). For contemporary country opinion chief reliance has been placed on the *Missouri Intelligencer*, published at Franklin, Fayette, and Columbia. The State Historical Society at Columbia, Missouri, has a complete file 1819 to date. For Saint Louis opinion *The Missouri Republican*, *The Democrat*, and *The Argus* were largely consulted. Scattered references have been made to other papers both in Saint Louis and in the country districts. *The Bankers Magazine* and certain Philadelphia financial journals have been largely used.

Secondary material is of a scattering nature and highly unsatisfactory. A number of contemporary books on banking and currency problems have been consulted in an effort to get at the serious thought of the day. A great mass of local secondary material is available. It consists chiefly of city directories, gazetteers, city and county histories, and biographies. It is chiefly of a journalistic type and often quite unreliable. Considerable use has been made of it where nothing better could be found. Wherever possible, it has been verified by comparison with other like data and with the sources mentioned above. A statement of the more important authorities quoted will be found in the Appendix.

The following libraries have been consulted and acknowledgment is here made for the many courtesies shown the author by those in charge at each of them: Missouri Historical Society, Saint Louis; Public Library, Saint Louis; State Historical Society, Columbia, Missouri; University of Missouri, Columbia, Missouri; Massachusetts State Library, Boston; Public Library of Boston; Harvard University; Yale University; John Carter Brown Collection at Brown University; the Public Library of New York City; Columbia University; New York University; Public Library of Chicago; Chicago Historical Society; the University of Chicago; and the Congressional Library.

Acknowledgment also is made to Professors Jonas Viles and Frank Fletcher Stephens of the University of Missouri; to Dr. Thorstein Veblen of the New School of Social Research; to Dean L. C. Marshall of the University of Chicago; and to Professors Henry Rogers Seager, H. Parker Willis and other members of the staff at Columbia University for much valuable assistance and criticism. Credit is also due to Alma S. Cable for the reading of the proof.

CONTENTS

PAGE

PART I

THE PERIOD BEFORE 1830

CHAPTER I

CHAPTER II

CHAPTER III

CHAPTER IV

PART II

THE PERIOD OF MONOPOLY

CHAPTER V

CHAPTER VI

PAGE

PART IV

The Final Period

CHAPTER XIX

CHAPTER XX

PART I

THE PERIOD BEFORE 1830

CHAPTER I

Economic Conditions in Early Missouri

For the first three decades of the nineteenth century Missouri was fairly representative of the American frontier. Her people had come for the most part from Kentucky and Tennessee, and so had acquired experience in getting a living under crude and isolated conditions of existence. They were used to trapping and self-sufficient agriculture. Accordingly the necessary adjustments to the Missouri environment were made with no great difficulty. It is the purpose of this chapter to give some description and analysis of the earlier economic life of the state. This should help to get the setting for later financial legislation. It should serve to show how and why Missouri was able for many years to carry on her necessary exchanges without the aid of any sort of organized banking.

Saint Louis had been settled as early as 1764 but had grown slowly. When thirty-six years old it had fewer than one thousand people.[1] However, it became the nucleus of a little frontier settlement, and population gradually spread up and down the Mississippi and westward along the Missouri and its branches. Once away from the rivers it was a wild and unknown country; although, at least, it had been visited by Lewis and Clark, and by Daniel Boone. In 1810 the population of the territory was about 20,000. Then a rapid growth began. By 1820 it had reached 66,000,[2] and by 1830

[1] Conrad, *Encyclopedia of Missouri History* (St. Louis, 1901). Article on "Saint Louis Banking."

[2] Coman, Katherine, *Economic Beginnings of Far West*, vol. ii, p. 56.

slightly more than 140,000. This population was scattered over thirty-two counties and, although St. Louis was the business center, its population, city and county, was under 12,000 excluding slaves. The following table should serve to show something of the scattered state of the population.[1]

FREE POPULATION
(In thousands)

County		County	
Lincoln	3.3	Ralls	3.5
Marion	3.5	Ray	2.4
Chariton	1.5	St. Francis	1.9
Washington	5.6	Perry	2.8
Jefferson	2.3	Cape Girardeau	6.4
Franklin	3.0	Scott	1.7
Gasconade	1.4	New Madrid	1.8
Crawford	1,6	Wayne	2.8
Cole	2.7	Calloway	4.7
Montgomery	3.2	Boone	6.9
Pike	4.9	Howard	8.2
St. Charles	3.3	Cooper	5.8
St. Louis	11.3	Saline	2.1
Ste. Genevieve	1.6	La Fayette	2.4
Randolph	2.4	Clay	4.4
Madison	1.9	Jackson	2.6

This table does not indicate that current histories have exaggerated the importance of St. Louis; but, rather, that it had a remarkable hinterland. In the early days the business of the city was very large in proportion to its population.

The town itself was small. By 1820 it had approximately 600 houses and about 5,000 population.[2] Two years later Shepard[3] reports that paving was being done, and that there were "two-story buildings on the cross

[1] 21st Congress, 1st Sess., *House Document* 263, p. 41.

[2] Shepard, E. H., *History of St. Louis and Mo.* (St. Louis, 1870), p. 63.

[3] *Ibid.*, p. 88.

streets". The amount of building was double that of any former year. There were 46 general stores, 57 groceries, 27 lawyers, 13 physicians, and 5 jewelers. The assessed valuation of the city was $940,000.[1]

And yet this little city carried on a considerable business. Its location was strategic. It was the natural market for the lead mines of the Mississippi Valley. It was the logical outfitting point for the fur trade and for the overland trips to Santa Fé and other western posts. Moreover, it was the local trading center for all of Missouri, much of Illinois and a part of Arkansas. All of this made the dominance of St. Louis inevitable. It is difficult to estimate the amount of trade handled by 1830, but there was a remarkable concentration in St. Louis of all the items mentioned above. At first the local merchants were too cautious to invest in steam-boats, but this was soon overcome and St. Louis became not only a great river port but also a center for steam-boat repairing.[2] By 1826 the reverses of 1819 had been over come and trade, though not brisk, had expanded greatly.

Statehood had come in 1821 under rather stormy circumstances. At this time Missouri was a district of no mean size centering about St. Louis. Important trade relations had been developed with Mexico, the West, and the Southwest.

Mining was by no means the least interest of Saint Louis. It was the lead market of the valley and there were a number of shot towers in the city. Schoolcraft estimated the output of the district at 4,971,000 pounds in 1819. Lead was worth $0.04 a pound in St. Louis. There were 45 mines and about 1130 miners.[3] Salt licks

[1] Edwards, R., and Hopewell, M., *Great West* (St. Louis, 1860), p. 325.

[2] Shepard, *op. cit.*, p. 63.

[3] Coman, *op. cit.*, p. 55.

also added something to local commerce. Salt was worth $1.00 a bushel.[1]

In 1763 the French trading company of Laclede Lequest sent an expedition up the river from New Orleans. Auguste Chouteau was in the group. They viewed the site of St. Louis and returned home. The next year (1764) Chouteau came back with thirty men and built a trading post.[2] This modest beginning was destined to control the richest fur territory of North America. From Saint Louis, as a center, traders penetrated far into the Missouri Valley and explored much of the region between it and the Pacific Coast. It was real pioneer work. The district was a more absolute Indian country than the region between the Alleghenies and the Mississippi at the end of the 17th century.[3]

From 1789 to 1804 the annual fur trade was in the neighborhood of $200,000.[4] In 1808 the following report was made of the St. Louis receipts: deer skins, 158,000; beaver skins, 3,690 lbs.; other skins, 8,000 lbs.; bear skins, 5,100; buffalo hides, 850.[5] Chouteau long continued active in the trade. According to Major Biddle,[6] he had an investment of about $50,000 by 1819 and regularly shipped large consignments to New Orleans. He died in 1829. Another early trader of importance was Manuel Lisa, a Spaniard and Indian agent during

[1] Coman, *op. cit.*, p. 55.

[2] Campbell, R. A., *Gazateer of Mo.* (St. Louis, 1875), p. 517.

[3] Turner, F. J., *Rise of New West* (N. Y., 1906), p. 118.

[4] Knox, J. J., *History of Banking in U. S.* (N. Y. 1903), p. 780 and *Annual Review Mo. Republican*, Jan. 10, 1854.

[5] *Ibid.*

[6] Carr, Lucien, *Mo. A Bone of Contention* (Boston, 1888), p. 128. Major Biddle was a brother of President Nicholas Biddle of the Second Bank of the United States and was quite prominent in St. Louis affairs of his day.

the War of 1812. His honorable character gained the confidence of the Indians and soon his trade was the envy of his competitors. In 1807 and 1808 he made a trip to the present Yellowstone Park and came back with visions of future wealth. He organized a company with $40,000 capital, planned to monopolize the Missouri River trade, and soon had posts 1200 miles up the river. This was the first important business undertaking in St. Louis.[1] Lisa sold his interest in 1819 for $10,000 and the Missouri Fur Company with $70,000 capital took over the business. Its chief base of operations was at Council Bluffs, Iowa, but the furs were shipped to St. Louis. By 1820 the annual Indian trade was about $600,000.[2] About this time William H. Ashley of Virginia organized the Rocky Mountain Fur Company and built a warehouse in St. Louis. Astor's American Fur Company also entered the field and soon the fur trade was at the height of its prosperity. In 1839 the latter company had a warehouse 60 x 35 ft. and four stories high, while the former had one 102 feet long and three stories high. The Hudson Bay Company, however, soon acquired control of the Rocky Mountain district and the Oregon Country, so that St. Louis territory was largely confined to the Missouri Valley. A last St. Louis attempt at Rocky Mountain trade in the late thirties lost $60,000.[3] Also there had been some attempt to secure business in the Minnesota Country, the American Fur Company having entered the field in 1819. However, the competition of the British interests was too keen here also. Chouteau had traded on the upper Mississippi. Eliason records a draft for $1899.33 on P

[1] Houck, L. *History of Missouri* (Chicago, 1908), vol. iii. p. 191.

[2] Edwards, *op. cit.* p. 325.

[3] *Hazard's Register* (Philadelphia), vol. iii. p. 214 (1840–41).

Chouteau and Co., St. Louis, for Minnesota peltry.[1] The inroads of competition and exhaustion of the nearby supplies had caused a considerable decline of the fur business by the thirties, but peltry was still one of the chief factors of St. Louis commercial power.

It was just about this time that a new trade territory developed. The Spanish hold on the Southwest had been weakened by the Mexican Revolution of 1821 and it was now possible to carry on a systematic American trade overland. Congress surveyed a road from Saint Louis to New Mexico and wagon trains began to carry textiles and tinware to Santa Fé and Chihuahua to exchange for horses, mules, furs, and silver. By 1830 this trade amounted to $130,000 a year. Mexican silver coins became an important source of western specie, and the trade contributed largely to the growth of the city.[2]

Aside from this long-distance commerce, Saint Louis early became the distributing center for the rural population of Illinois and Missouri. These were districts of self-sustaining agriculture and trade was not active, yet in the aggregate it added a good deal to the business of the city. Many farmers supplemented their income by trapping, and their catch found a market in Saint Louis. Often attempts were made to take provisions to New Orleans by flat-boat, but the trip was long and dangerous and only the exceptional farmer made it pay. The country was suffering from all the evils of poor transportation. Later when steamboat service was inaugurated business became more active. New houses and much fencing evidenced at least a mild prosperity.

[1] Eliason, "Beginning of Banking in Minnesota," in *Minnesota Historical Society Collections*, vol. xii, 1905-08, p. 691.

[2] Ridgely, W. B., article in *Trust Co.'s*, June, 1904, p. 387, and Turner, *op. cit.*, p. 124.

Crops were good and such products as could be produced at home were plentiful. But all through the period transportation was poor and currency scarce. All of this meant that Saint Louis had much less trade from the back country than would be the case from an equal population to-day. Still the country districts made a substantial contribution to Saint Louis prosperity.[1]

So far it has been the intent of this chapter to show something of the basis of Saint Louis business. The factors were lead, furs, the business of Illinois and rural Missouri, and the Santa Fé trade. It remains to show how this business was carried on before the coming of organized banking. The basic conditions which have been described were those which the first banks had to meet, for Saint Louis had banking institutions during the last fifteen years of this period. However, they will be discussed in later chapters. The rest of this chapter will deal with the earlier methods of exchange. Some attention will be given to currency conditions contemporary with the first banks.

A large part of the early Missouri trade was carried on by means of barter. Coined money was rare. Furs, lead, tobacco and whiskey served as media of exchange and, as late as 1811, most of the business was so transacted.[2] Needles, pins and sheets of writing paper were used for small change.[3] In the country districts the farmers were also trappers. Furs could be marketed more readily than other things and so were adopted as a kind of rude currency. Deer-skin became the stand-

[1] For a discussion of rural conditions in Missouri, see Coman, *op. cit.* p. 39 *et seq.*

[2] Edwards, *op. cit.*, p. 295.

[3] Carr, *op. cit.*. p. 133.

ard. It was the least variable in price and fairly abundant.[1] Sometimes beaver was considered standard. Various kinds of peltry passed current. The range of values was quite large and the various kinds were redeemable in one another at established rates. An early quotation in pounds was: raccoon, $0.125; deer, $0.40; otter, $5.00, etc.[2] Under the Spanish régime notes were payable in peltry unless Spanish-milled dollars were expressly stipulated. $1.00 in specie was regarded as worth $1.25 in peltry.[3] In 1807 Judge J. B. Lucas bought a house in Saint Louis from Pierre Douchoquette for $600 payable in peltries.[4] In fact the city used fur money about as freely as did the country. There was little metallic money used in the fur trade. The influx of several hundred thousand dollars worth of furs each year into Saint Louis was much like the addition of so much currency. It was found inconvenient to use the furs themselves for purposes of exchange so the traders warehoused them in St. Louis and issued receipts. These receipts, or "deer-skin" notes as they were called, passed current all up and down the river.[5] In the Minnesota trade prime beaver at $2.00 a pound was the 1820 standard.[6] In the country districts of southeast Missouri cotton was used. In 1818 New Madrid county petitioned the local governor to declare cotton legal tender at two-thirds of the Nashville price.[7]

The files of the early Missouri newspapers such as the

[1] Conrad, *op. cit.* Article on "Saint Louis Banking."

[2] Ridgely, *op. cit.*, p. 387.

[3] Houck, *op. cit.*, p. 191.

[4] Knox, *op. cit.*, p. 780.

[5] Knox, *op. cit.*, p. 780.

[6] Eliason, *op. cit.*, p. 691.

[7] Houck, *op. cit.*, vol. iii, p. 191.

Missouri Gazette and the *Intelligencer* furnish many illustrations of barter economy. Some selections are given here:

Take notice that about the last of April 1805, I gave my note for $400 to Geo. H. Dougherty to be paid in horses above four and under eight years old, this to forewarn all persons for trading for said note as I am resolved for good reasons not to pay the same unless compelled by law.

JOHN BLOOM
Nov. 11, 1808.[1]

The subscriber has just opened a quantity of bleached country linen, cotton cloth, etc. . . . which he will sell on very low terms. He will take in payment furs, hides, whiskey, country-made sugar, and beeswax. Saint Louis. Jan. 3, 1810.[2]

Dry goods, groceries, liquors, iron, steel for cash or pork.

B. PRATTE.[3]

Notice to farmers—Owing to the pressure of the times and the want of capital we will receive meat, tobacco, etc. on a commission basis paying cash when we can get it.[4]

Duff Green of Franklin advertises that he would receive the following in payment of debts (pork, corn, wheat, tobacco, beans, peas, onions, beeswax, potatoes, lard, butter, tallow, flax, tow linen, linsey, deer-skin, furs . . . "in fact any sort of produce."[5]

A number of such advertisements may be found in almost

[1] *Mo. Gazette* (St. Louis), Dec. 21, 1808.

[2] Quoted from a St. Louis paper as a typical advertisement in Edwards, *The Great West*, p. 295.

[3] *Mo. Gazette*, Jan. 11, 1809.

[4] *Mo. Intelligencer and Boone's Lick Advertiser* (Franklin), Nov. 11, 1819.

[5] *Ibid.*

any issue of the local papers, indicating a general and acute shortage of money.

While these seem representative of prevailing tendencies, the country was not wholly without currency and specie. During the Spanish régime silver had been imported from Spain to pay troops stationed at Saint Louis. One shipment of $12,000 is recorded.[1] Later the Santa Fé trade caused the influx of a good deal of silver. It was relatively plentiful in 1820 in Saint Louis, Saint Charles and Ste. Genevieve, and consisted of Mexican, Central American and Spanish coins. Some English, French, German and Spanish gold was also in circulation.[2] The "lost and found" column of the *Intelligencer* shows that coin was not wholly absent: "$100 reward for recovery of a small trunk containing $800 specie except about $50 in Bank of Missouri notes."[3]

The Missouri Intelligencer, published at Franklin, an inland town opposite the present site of Boonville, throws much light on general business conditions. It has already been quoted to show something of barter conditions and of the presence of at least limited amounts of specie. It also gives evidence of considerable use of paper money. In the issue of July 23, 1819, the Franklin stores announced that they would receive Missouri and Illinois notes for merchandise. The Boggs and Rector store included those of North Carolina, South Carolina, Georgia, Tennessee and Kentucky. In the issue of March 11, 1820, a reward was offered for the recovery of a purse containing $55 in Bank of Missouri notes. Editorially the *Intelligencer* protested against the flood

[1] Knox, *op. cit.*, p. 781.

[2] Address of Lon V. Stephens in "Banking and Resources of Mo.," at World's Congress of Banks and Financiers, Chicago, 1893.

[3] *Mo. Intelligencer*, Nov. 11, 1820.

of counterfeit small notes and advised against the use of bank paper in denominations less than $5.00.[1] The Land Office at Franklin announced that it was now receiving notes of certain designated city banks in payment for government land.[2]

Putting together such evidence as we have, it seems clear that by 1820 the country districts of the state were far from a complete dependence on barter. They were, however, quite as far from having sufficient currency and specie for the necessary transaction of their business affairs.

Purposely no discussion so far has been included regarding ways and means of banking. By this time Missouri had a bank but she had developed it after trying a good many makeshift banking arrangements.

The first banking was done by certain traders. Flatboat men going up and down the river often made collections and transferred funds.[3] The following is an illustration of the method:

Bill of lading—shipped to Peter Povenchere of the town of St. Louis, merchant, on board the boat Jas. Madison, whereof Charles Quincy is master, ready to depart for Louisville, Kentucky, 6 packs of deer-skins, marked and numbered . . . and a bbl. of bear's oil which I promise to deliver unto Mr. Francis Tarascon, merchant of Louisville, Ky. I acknowledge also to have of said Peter Povenchere a note of Peter Menard on Louis Lorimer, inhabitant of Cape Girardeau, for 1000 lbs. receiptable deer-skins, said note transferred to my order; and I bind and engage myself to ask of said Louis Lorimer the payment of said note and if I reclaim it to deliver to said Francis Tarascon the 1000 lbs. of deer-skins to-

[1] Oct. 7, 1820.

[2] *Mo. Intelligencer*, Mar. 11, 1820.

[3] Knox, *op. cit.* p. 780.

gether with the six packs and bbl. of bears oil now received.[1]

A man going on a trip sometimes offered to carry funds or make collections. An example is shown by the following advertisement which appeared in the *Missouri Gazette* of January 1, 1809:

The subscriber to set off to New Orleans, Washington, Philadelphia, and New York next February. Will return May or June. Offers agency to the public in commercial or confidential line.

The Saint Louis fur companies themselves often undertook to carry on banking functions for their customers, making loans, cashing drafts, and selling exchange.[2] In 1764 Auguste Chouteau adopted the plan of entering the value of the skins which he purchased in a book in livres. Then he threw the bale of furs into his warehouse and the customer had a credit against which he could trade. The livre existed only on the book. He had no French coins. The accounts were all kept in money terms, so it was not simple barter. After about 1770 there was some Spanish coin in circulation, but fur money was the thing generally used. Maxent Laclede and Company had had a monopoly, but some competition developed. The merchants got together and decided that fur money would be understood unless "hard money" was stipulated and that furs of first quality should be valued at 40 cents a pound, second quality 30 cents and third or inferior grade 20 cents. Quality was protected by a proclamation of Governor Cruzat requiring an examination before weighing. The balance of trade usually favored St. Louis and capital was rapidly

[1] Quoted by Ridgely, *op. cit.* p. 387.

[2] Eliason, *op. cit.* p. 676.

accumulated. A trapper would be given a receipt for his season's catch and this receipt would pass current by indorsement. It was called a "bon" and was redeemable in so much in furs on demand. When furs were shipped to New Orleans or Montreal, drafts were drawn on the buyer who accepted them and made payment by sending needed supplies.[1] This method with various refinements incident to increasing use of specie developed into the typical St. Louis private bank. Certain respected business men gradually took on banking functions. In 1808 Wilkinson and Price advertised that they had bills of exchange on the government for sale. And in newspapers of the city, 1810–19, begin to appear notices of brokers and merchants doing certain work incident to banking.[2]

Meanwhile business methods had been changing rapidly. The increasing volume of business made the makeshifts just described seem woefully inadequate. Saint Louis had reached the stage of organized banking. Her earlier experiments are described in chapters III and V. Here it may merely be said in passing that by 1821 barter was of declining importance. Notes of the Bank of Missouri, notes of the U. S. Bank, and those of chartered banks of other states were becoming numerous. Private banking was not in favor. The General Assembly of 1821 passed an act prohibiting the circulation of the notes of private banks and conferring exclusive rights on the notes of the U. S. Bank and those of Missouri chartered institutions. The penalty for violation was a fine of $100 to $300 or a year in jail or both at the discretion of the court.[3]

[1] Stevens, W. B., *St. Louis the Fourth City* (St. Louis, 1909), pp. 287-290.

[2] Houck, *op. cit.*, vol III, p, 191.

[3] *Mo. Intelligencer*, Jan. 15, 1821.

CHAPTER II

National Conditions Affecting Early Missouri Banking

Business in Missouri reached a point where banking institutions became necessary at a time when national finances were much unsettled. The charter of the First United States Bank expired in 1811 and renewal was refused. It had been conceived by Alexander Hamilton as a method of securing permanency to the national government by making provision for the war debt and thus forcing the respect of foreign powers. His masterful arguments overcame constitutional objections and induced the investment of much overseas capital in the bank. His expectations were fully justified. The bank did its full share in making the new government respected abroad and in addition paid satisfactory returns on the capital. The dividends averaged 8⅓ per cent.[1] Albert Gallatin, Secretary of the Treasury, had submitted a report to Congress asking for a renewal of the charter and highly commending the management. He argued that the bank had done its full duty. The fight, however, did not turn on questions of management. The old question of constitutionality was revived. At this stage of American history, states-rights ideas were much in evidence. Moreover, it was contended that state institutions could do all the national bank had

[1] Goddard, T. H., *General History of Banks in Europe and U. S.* (New York, 1831), p. 94.

done and that no local control would be lost. Another motive was also present: The bank had many British stockholders and the operation of the Embargo and Non-Intercourse Acts had caused hatred of all things British. Representative Derba of Kentucky made a speech in Congress in which he claimed the stock was owned by George III.[1] What seems more fundamental is that all the cheap-money forces fought the recharter, picking up such arguments as happened to come to hand. The fight was hard and when the final vote came Vice-President Clinton had to cast the deciding ballot. He voted against the bill and the charter was lost.[2]

The liquidation of the bank not only left the country without banking facilities, but it caused about $7,000,000 of specie to be sent back to Great Britain in payment for stock owned in that country. This was just a year before the outbreak of the War of 1812.[3]

With the national bank out of business and public opinion favoring local institutions, it is not surprising that many state charters were granted. An attempt was being made to fill the gap. Local banks, operated within their own borders under state charters, was the solution offered. Between 1811 and 1814, one hundred and twenty state banks were organized with a total capitalization of nearly $30,000,000, much of which was paid for by loans on the security of the stock. The circulation of the country during this time increased from $22,000,000 to $45,000,000.[4] This occurred during

[1] C. C. Plehn, Article in *Bulletin American Institute Bank Clerks*, June 1, 1903.

[2] Spalding, E. G., *One Hundred Years of Banking* (Buffalo, 1876). Address.

[3] Albert Gallatin, *Considerations on Currency and Banking in U. S.*, p. 44.

[4] *Ibid.*, p. 44.

a war that ruined our foreign commerce and coastwise trade. Little provision was made for regulation of the note issue, and that meant an unregulated banking business, for deposit banking was still quite unimportant.

The War of 1812 put a heavy strain on these state banks. The government soon found they were too weak to be depended upon for necessary war finance. By 1814 most of them, outside of New England, had found the pressure of war too great and had suspended. Their notes went to a discount, but were still used. There was little specie left in the country and when general suspension came there was nothing better. It was either use these notes or "shut up shop."[1] Grave financial disorders ensued. The government had funds to the amount of $9,000,000 in ninety-four of the state banks. These funds were tied up just when they were most needed for war purposes. The interest on the national debt was defaulted.[2] The government was forced to sell its paper at a heavy discount to secure necessary war funds and so the cost of the war was largely increased.[3]

After the war there came a speculative period culminating in the Panic of 1819. The finances of the country were still in the hands of the suspended banks. The several states began to look about for a remedy and the most common answer was more state banks. The makers of our federal constitution had "hard money" ideas. States were forbidden to issue bills of credit, but they circumvented the law by creating private corporations with virtually that power. In many cases the state became a direct partner. The national bank idea was taken over by the state and re-enacted on a local basis. As early as 1810

[1] Callender, G., *Economic History of U. S.* (Boston, 1909), p. 565.

[2] Spaulding, *op. cit.*, p. 22.

[3] Hepburn, A. B., *Contest for Sound Money* (N. Y. 1903), p. 78.

Vermont, Delaware, Kentucky, and North Carolina had organized banks wholly or partially owned by the state.[1] In many cases the capital was only partly paid up and it was no uncommon thing for the shareholders to borrow back all they had put in.[2] The denominations of the circulation often were made small on the theory that demands for redemption would thereby be less frequent. Many of the banks were located in inaccessible places to further hinder presentation. Public opinion seemed to sustain this kind of banking. The debtor classes, as always, wanted cheap money. It was not considered good form to ask for specie, and tar and feathers sometimes were used to dissuade those who persisted. Moreover, as time went on, the state banks loaned more and more heavily on real estate paper. Under the credit system of selling public lands the purchaser had only to pay down 25 per cent. No lots were sold of less than 160 acres. The result was that men put all their money into the initial payment and trusted to bank loans for the balance.[3] In 1814 the sales of public land amounted to only 864,536 acres; by 1819 it had increased to 5,475,648 acres, a total which was not to be reached again for fifteen years.[4] Everybody was trying to find a remedy for the economic disorder.[5] Numerous state plans were put forward, but the problem was a national one and could be met only on a national scale.

[1] Hepburn, *op. cit.*, p. 74.

[2] Bullock, C. J., *Essays on Monetary History of U. S.* (Boston, 1907), p. 83.

[3] Turner, *op. cit.*, p. 136.

[4] Simons, A. M., *Social Forces in American History* (N. Y., 1911) p. 161.

[5] It was during this time of speculation and suspension that organized banking was attempted first in Missouri. The Bank of St. Louis opened in 1816. See chapter iii.

In 1814 Dallas was appointed Secretary of the Treasury and he at once began an agitation for currency reform. In 1815 he asked for national banking legislation, holding that it was not to be expected that the state institutions could or would meet the issue. They were finding suspension profitable.

Finally in 1816 the charter of the second United States Bank was approved by Congress. The authorized capital was $35,000,000, one-fifth of it to be owned by the government. It was provided, however, that the bank might open when all of the government stock and $8,400,000 of the private stock had been paid in. The cheap-money interests had fought the project bitterly, and their influence no doubt accounts for some of the weak points in the charter. Only $2,000,000 coin and $13,872,610 bonds were actually paid in, the balance being represented by stock notes.[1] There was no charter limit on the amount of capital to be assigned to each section of the country and, as a result, the debtor regions in the West and South soon had the larger part of its business. Sixteen of the twenty-nine branches were west of the Mississippi or south of the Potomac.[2] However, the great purpose of the bank was to bring about the same sort of note redemption in the West as had already been accomplished for New England by the Suffolk Bank.

The early days of the national bank were days of dishonesty and bad management. In 1818 its loans were $43,000,000, largely either directly or indirectly on speculative real-estate investments. A Congressional Committee of Inquiry on the question of the bank's solvency reported that it was not in a failing condition; but the

[1] Plehn, *op. cit.*, *passim*.

[2] Wildman, M. S., *Money Inflation in U. S.*, p. 104.

fact that forty members of Congress were stockholders doubtless tempered the report.[1] At any rate drastic reorganization was deemed necessary and the bank imported $7,000,000 specie at a cost of $800,000.[2] This together with a policy of retrenchment enabled it to save itself—but the panic was on.

Taking a broad view, the Panic of 1819 was a part of the collapse following the wars of Napoleon. The industrial boom caused by the Embargo, the War of 1812, excessive internal improvements, and Western land speculation were all factors of weight. Senator Benton laid the whole blame on the oppression of the United States Bank.[3] At any rate the storm broke when it tried to force the state banks to resume specie payments. The currency was in a deplorable condition. Western notes were quoted at from 10 per cent to 60 per cent discount and Southern notes from 1 per cent to 25 per cent. The Bank of Tennessee at Nashville had suspended in 1819. The Missouri banks were also in trouble. In 1821 President Cheves stated that he was unable to find any bank in Tennessee, Indiana or Illinois that he considered sound.[4] In fact few Western or Southern banks even made a show of specie payments from 1819 to 1822. The states that passed stay laws were in the worst condition because the United States Bank was afraid to venture into territory where obstacles were set deliberately to prevent collection of debts. It refused to accept the notes of non-specie-paying banks in payment of public

[1] *Niles Register*, Feb. 27, 1819.

[2] Berkeley, W. A., *The Money Question* (Grand Rapids, 1876), p. 127; *Report of U. S. Comptroller of Currency, 1876*, pp. ix and xxxiii; and Hildreth, Richard, *History of Banks* (Boston, 1837), p. 64.

[3] Simons, *op. cit.*, p. 160.

[4] Catterall, R. C. H., *The First Six Years of Second U. S. Bank* (Ph. D. thesis, Chicago, 1902), p. 83.

dues and restricted the circulation of such banks by sending their notes home for redemption. As it kept its own notes as far as possible out of what it considered dangerous territory, the South and West were left with no sound currency.

Now why did the United States Bank take such drastic measures? It had been founded to end the condition of suspension and the Congressional investigations had convinced the bank early in its career that the only safe thing to do was to follow the charter. Moreover, the policy of receiving the notes of suspended banks indiscriminately meant that it might be unable to meet its own obligations in specie. It could not afford to suspend. The penalty was twelve per cent.

The bank had discounted too liberally on Western landed security, holding over $6,500,000 of Western paper in 1819. It pressed for the payment of the big debt and of course became unpopular. It did not attempt to expand the national currency, but rather to limit it to the amount that could be supported by the specie reserves. The notes of the national bank, being uniform, were in demand for long-distance payments and were purchased with state bank notes. In this and other ways large amounts of such notes were accumulated in the branch offices. The weekly settlement which was demanded caused the state banks to look to their reserves and to withdraw excess notes from circulation. This forced contraction explains much of the opposition to the bank and why it was so largely a Western development.[1] When the paper state banks began to fail, the national bank was held responsible. Richard Hildreth, however, comes nearer to the truth when he says that

[1] See Wildman, *op. cit.*, pp. 104-109.

they had no one to blame but themselves, for they had little capital except the cupidity of the public.[1]

Kentucky perhaps affords the best example of the paper banking of the time. She had chartered forty-three independent banks by a single act of her legislature and by 1818–19 all had suspended.[2] Their charters were repealed and the Commonwealth Bank of Kentucky organized without stockholders, and under the management officers elected by the legislature. The circulation was assigned to counties in proportion to their taxable property and was to be loaned to needy citizens on real estate mortgage security. The only real capital was an appropriation of $7,000 to pay for the printing of the notes. An issue of $2,000,000 was put out. Any debtor who tendered these notes and met with a refusal had his debt automatically extended for two years.[3] This circulation was declared unconstitutional,[4] but the reply of the state was merely to oust the judges. Kentucky experienced the worst evils of inflation. A fifty to seventy-five per cent discount was not uncommon for Commonwealth Bank notes. Kentucky, however, was not alone in her attempts at debtor relief. The West was desperate. The records of nearly all the Western and Southern legislatures are filled with stay laws, loan-office plans, and other legislation of a similar nature. The Missouri Loan Office was one of this group of experiments.

The panic had left a path of widespread ruin. If there had been no domestic troubles the depression would

[1] Hildreth, Richard, *History of Banks*, p. 68.

[2] *Ibid.*, p. 71.

[3] Turner, *op. cit.*, pp. 138–139.

[4] See *11 Peters* 348.

[5] See chapter iii, Section C.

have been severe. The European war (1793–1815) had made business for American merchants. The farm products of the Mississippi Valley had found markets abroad. The general peace ruined this business. Moreover, the close of the War of 1812 stopped the government demand for many products. Land, which had been bought at speculative prices, could not be sold and money could not be secured to pay the interest on the mortgages. The national bank had determined to save itself at all costs, and so was calling loans and foreclosing mortgages in every quarter. It came to own most of Cincinnati and 50,000 acres or more of Kentucky and Tennessee land.[1] It soon acquired the name of "Monster" and was attacked by all the debtor states. All sorts of legislation against the bank were tried. It was generally charged with deliberately attempting to collect all the specie of the country into its own coffers. In 1817 Maryland levied a tax of $15,000 on the branch at Baltimore and Tennessee placed one of $50,000 on the branch at Nashville. Illinois barred it from the state altogether. Kentucky taxed each of its two branches $60,000.[2] Ohio made a $50,000 levy and denied the bank the right to plead a case in the state courts.[3] A decision of the United States Supreme Court denied the right of the states to levy such taxes and thus saved the bank from utter ruin.[4] However, the lawlessness of the frontier asserted itself and the bank found it very difficult to get justice.

By 1822 the currency was in much better condition; but there was still depression and falling prices. Trade

[1] Wildman, *op. cit.*, pp. 107–108.

[2] *Ibid.*

[3] Simons, *op. cit.*, p. 163.

[4] Wildman, *op. cit.*, p. 108.

and industry showed little activity and did not recover fully until about 1830. The state banks of the West mostly had given up the struggle and anti-bank feeling had prevented the organization of new ones. The United States Bank accordingly had little Western competition.[1]

The West and South, however, were far from satisfied with the service rendered by the bank. They usually owed the East and accordingly notes issued in the South and West were sent East regularly to pay balances. In August 1818 it was determined to stop this by supplying the debtor sections with branch drafts which were redeemable only in Philadelphia. The note issues were withdrawn then as rapidly as possible from these districts.[2] The branches did not always follow the rules laid down by the mother bank, and often bad banking was carried on. Communication was difficult and, if a branch board of directors chose to defy the home office, as they sometimes did, redress was slow in coming. The branch policies often were quite at variance with those announced in Philadelphia. This lent color to the later charges of President Jackson that the bank had failed to establish a uniform and sound currency.[3]

Before attempting to discuss the troubles with Jackson it will be well to glance at the published statements of the bank.

On October 1, 1822, the following report of its condition was made to Congress:[4]

[1] See Hildreth, R., *History of Banks*, pp. 78 to 80.

[2] Root, L. C., in *Sound Currency*, Sept. 1, 1897, p. 12.

[3] Catterall, R. C. H., *Successes and Failures of First and Second U. S. Bank* in *Academy Political Science Proceedings*, vol. i, no. 2, Jan., 1911.

[4] Goddard, T. H., *General History of Banks in Europe and U. S.* (N. Y., 1831), pp. 98 to 106.

Assets (Investments)

U. S. 5 per cent Stock	$11,000,000.00
U. S. 6 per cent Stock	2,020,469.27
Personal Loans	26,236,150.88
Loans Secured by Bank Stock	5,974,725.80
Mortgage Loans	8,000.00
Due from State Banks at Interest	739,918.76
Real Estate Taken for Debt.	587,102.38
Due from State Banks Current Account.	910,950.97
Paid on Account Bonus and Premium 5 per cent Stock.	1,180,880.00
Banking Houses at Cost	834,922.15
State Bank Notes	664,642.56
Specie	3,346,434.22
	$53,504,196.99

Liabilities

Capital paid up	$34,892 139.63
Circulation	5,456,891.90
Deposits	6,776,492.74
Unclaimed Deposits	129,741.28
Due to Banks	1,964,898.36
Reserve for Losses	3,743,899.00
Profit and Loss.	51,897.07
Interest July 1 to Sept. 30.	388,237.01
	$53,504,196.99

The suspended debt was $10,418,306.66, all considered good except $3,743,899.00 for which a reserve had been provided. These losses were chiefly in Ohio and Kentucky and other Western states. On April 1, 1819 Ohio and Kentucky debts were $6,351,120.80. By August 30, 1822 there had been a reduction to $5,389,477.18. The report concludes that it is the policy of the bank to be indulgent with the suspended debt account if security is arranged, and that on the whole the loans are as good as those of other banks in their respective communities. The loans of the different branches were not given separately but Boston had only $95,000. Evidently the bank was not doing much business in the Northeast;

but the figures given show something of the difficulties the bank had to meet in the West.

The statement of August 1, 1831, shows something of the growth of the business:[1]

Investments

Funded Debt		$3,490,681.06
Personal Loans		41,585,298.70
Mortgage Loans		19,700.00
Domestic Bills		14,409,479.72
Foreign Bills		121,214.60
Bank Stock		777,458.07
Mortgages		140,958.63
Bills Chargeable to Contingent Fund		3,452,976.10
Real Estate		2,491,892.99
Due from Banks		621,523.08
Expenses		259,383.50
Banking Houses		1,160,455.54
Notes of State Banks		2,080,442.33
Specie		11,545,116.51
		$82,165,578.89

Liabilities

Capital paid up		$35,000,000.00
Circulation		22,399,447.52
Deposits		16,368,085.89
Public Deposits	$7,252,249.42	
Private Deposits	9,115,836.47	
Due to Individuals in Europe		168,372.72
Unclaimed Deposits		251,766.03
Interest		614,685.07
Profit and Loss		1,750,048.51
		$82,165,578.89

The circulation of the bank had never been excessive. The statement here given is about the maximum before 1836. Prior to 1824 it had been below $6,000,000 and the specie holdings were usually in excess of the circula-

[1] Dean, Sydney, *History of Banking and Banks* (Boston, 1884), p. 164.

tion.[1] From 1819 to 1829 the specie varied between $2,000,000 and $6,000,000 and the deposits between $5,000,000 and $15,000,000.[2]

As early as 1829 there had been signs of a coming storm. The bank charter was regarded as a political privilege and therefore legitimate "spoils". Jackson was accused of being unfriendly to the bank in order to get the support of state bankers and capitalists who owned none of its stock. It was intimated that he wanted to crush it so that he could start a new one and see that his friends acquired stock.[3] All of this may have been partisan talk. It may have been that Jackson was sincere in his opposition. He was a product of the West and had seen much more bad than good in banking. At any rate in 1829, or six years before the expiration of the charter, he sent a message to Congress, saying:

> The charter of the Bank expires in 1836 and its stockholders will most likely ask for a renewal of their privileges. Both the constitutionality and the expediency of the law creating the bank are well questioned by a large portion of our fellow-citizens, and it must be admitted that it has failed in the great end of establishing a uniform and sound currency.[4]

The cabinet disagreed and there were stormy sessions. The Bank felt able to defy all enemies and so begged for no favors. Nicholas Biddle, president, used more force than judgment in presenting the Bank's side of the case. There were lengthy Congressional investigations and majority and minority reports presented. The

[1] Hepburn, *op. cit.*, p. 95.

[2] Spaulding, *op. cit.*, p. 30.

[3] Hildreth, R., *Banks. Banking and Paper Currencies* (Boston, 1840), pp. 84 and 85.

[4] Quoted in Spaulding, *op. cit.*, p. 31.

Majority Report suggested that the bill be tabled until the public debt had been put in better condition; the Minority Report recommended that the charter be renewed. After much discussion the recharter bill was passed, but was vetoed by President Jackson.

The charter failed largely because the bank question had become a matter of partisan politics. The reasons advanced by Jackson were far from convincing. In a report made to the House of Representatives in 1830 Congressman McDuffie said that the bank had not met justice at the hands of the President as regards his statements about the uniformity and soundness of its notes:

> On the whole it may be confidently asserted that no country in the world has a circulating medium of greater uniformity than the United States; and no country of anything like the same geographical extent has a currency at all comparable on the score of uniformity.

The report went on to say that the state banks had been forced to resume, at least to the extent that one could always get sound money. North Carolina alone had inconvertible paper and even there the depreciation was slight.[1] The branch drafts were objects of heated attack. Senator Benton attempted to discredit them, claiming that for the outlying states payment in Philadelphia meant total inconvertibility. The South and West had no gold with which to redeem the notes, hence they were furnished with drafts. Because of this, Senator Benton said that the bank had not furnished a uniform and sound currency.[2]

[1] McDuffie's Report, *House of Representatives*, Apr. 13, 1830, Committee of Ways and Means. Of course his statements about uniform currency refer to the note issue and not to the system of branch drafts.

[2] Speech of Senator Benton on the "State of the Currency", U. S. Senate, Jan. 20, 1832.

Not content with the failure of the charter, Jackson next announced his intention of taking the government deposits from the bank on the ground that they were not properly secured. On the evidence of the Verplanck Investigation, which reported that the bank had assets of $80,000,000, to meet $37,000,000 of debts, Secretary McLane of the Treasury department refused to obey Jackson's order to stop depositing in the national bank. He was thereupon replaced by Mr. Duane who proved no more tractable. At last Roger B. Taney was made Secretary of the Treasury and the President's will was done. The Finance Committee of the United States Senate objected that the money was safe and should not be taken away from the bank, but Jackson was determined on his course.[1]

After the removal the bank was still able to show a satisfactory statement:[2]

November 1, 1834.

Investments		*Liabilities*	
Discounts	$34,667,828.24	Notes	$15,968,731.90
Mortgages	87,591.29	Government Deposits—Treas.	429,465.07
Domestic Bills	11,086,373.07	Government Deposits—Public Officers	1,837,168.66
Foreign Bills	2,727,782.11	Private Deposits	6,741,752.24
Real Estate	3,024,788.45	Capital	35,000,000.00
Due from State Banks	427,102.89		
Specie	15,910,045.31		
	$67,931,511.36		$59,977,117.87
		Surplus	7,954,393.49

From this statement it may be noticed that the removal

[1] For a discussion of the removal of the deposits see Spaulding, *op. cit.*, pp. 31-41, and Gilbart, J. W., *History of Banking in America* (London, 1837), p. 23 *et seq.*

[2] Gilbart, *op. cit.*, p. 24.

of deposits was not entirely accomplished by the end of 1834. The bank was by no means ruined but the psychological effect was bad. It accepted a charter from the State of Pennsylvania and continued in business. The changed national conditions restricted its sphere of influence and the panic of 1837 gave it a blow from which it never recovered. It failed in 1841.

Meanwhile state banks were being organized to take over the business given up by the national bank and to secure a share of the coveted distribution of government deposits. In the issue of May 2, 1835 *Niles Register* said, "The banking capital of the United States has increased $50,000,000 to $60,000,000 since it was determined that the Bank of the United States should be put down"; and again in the issue of July 25, 1835, "We have perhaps added $100,000,000 to our banking capital." Within seven years after the veto, 304 new banks had been organized with a capital (largely paper) of $145,000,000.[1]

It is very difficult to study Western banking and finance of this time without going afield from purely banking problems. The Western states very generally demanded paper banks, or at least some legislation in mitigation of the debtor classes. The West was a country deeply in debt, and in need of capital. Internal improvements, cheap transportation, and currency expansion seemed essential to prosperity. The crying need was for markets. Turner[2] quotes an Ohio pioneer of 1830 to the effect that it required one man and a team four days to take a load of thirty-five or forty bushels of wheat thirty-five miles to the river. Wheat was worth $0.50 a bushel delivered at the river. The

[1] Dean, *op. cit.*, p. 171.

[2] Turner, *op. cit.*, p. 106.

farmer really got about $0.30, but he could not get cash. He had to take his payment in trade at high prices. This would have been as apt an illustration ten years earlier. An understanding of these and other similar difficulties of living in the pioneer West goes far to explain the mental attitudes shown toward the political and financial questions af the day.

As early as 1822 Missouri had begun to show signs of recovery; but she had been through with much the same experiences as her neighbors. She had some hard lessons in banking and was to receive some others that were more pleasant. The United States Bank opened a branch in St. Louis just about the time the Jackson troubles started. It gave the state good service, but, of course, inevitably stirred up political factions. It closed with the parent bank and Missouri was left again without banking facilities. The emergency was met by the Commercial Bank of Cincinnati—a second satisfactory experience.

Chapter IV treats of these experiences in some detail. It must be kept in mind, however, that Missouri was but a segment of the nation and that her problems can be understood only in the light of national conditions. This is the justification for this chapter. It should help to explain Missouri history previous to 1835. In tracing the attempts of Missouri to provide banking facilities adequate to meet the national conditions here discussed, it will be seen that she was feeling her way gradually toward honest banking.

CHAPTER III

Early and Unfortunate Ventures in Banking and Currency

A. *The Bank of Saint Louis*

The Territorial Legislature of 1813, acting on the petition of Auguste Chouteau and a group of representative Saint Louis business men, authorized the organization of a bank of issue, to be called the Bank of Saint Louis.[1]

The new bank was not backed by commercial adventurers but by the leading business men of the territory. Its aim was to advance the business interests of the city. The legislature seems to have passed the charter bill with little opposition. Currency conditions were bad. The territory had no banking enterprises and it must have been evident to every member of the legislature that economic organization had reached a stage where a local banking institution was badly needed. In Chapter I it has been shown how great the need had become. The people were tired of primitive and makeshift currencies. St. Louis had 2200 people, and the Territory of Missouri, 58,260.[2] Fur, peltry, and lead were being exported in large amounts and payment was being made to the Indians in varied commodities.[3]

[1] Geyer, H. S., *Digest of Laws of Missouri* (St. Louis, 1818), p. 86.

[2] Knox, *op. cit.*, p. 781.

[3] An interesting discussion of the need for the bank is found in James Cox, *The Old and New in Saint Louis* (St. Louis, 1894).

It seemed as if the bank had everything in its favor. The plan was welcomed by the town of Saint Louis. There was no competition. However, a pioneer bank was certain to meet difficulties: the people were unused to banking practice; business turnover was slow; and there had been little education in the prompt discharge of obligations.

Data are hard to secure on the actual conduct of the bank; but the charter has been preserved and so it is possible at least to learn something of the banking ideas of the time.[1]

The charter was to expire August 1, 1838. It provided for a bank of issue with a minimum capital of $150,000 in shares of $100 par value. This was to be exclusive of any stock which might be taken by the territorial government. Books were to be opened in Saint Louis, Saint Charles, Cape Girardeau, Ste. Genevieve, Mine a' Breton, and New Madrid, Missouri for the receipt of subscriptions and were to remain open until one-half the stock had been subscribed, after which time the president and directors might sell stock in any manner not forbidden by the charter. This provision of opening the books in several places was a common practice at this time, due largely to fear of domination by capitalistic classes; but, in this case, the reason seems to have been the necessity of combing the territory for available capital. The capital stock was not to exceed $450,000 without the consent of the legislature.

The management was vested in the hands of a board of thirteen directors, elected by the shareholders for a term

[1] The material for the discussion of the charter has been taken from Geyer, *op. cit.*, p. 86 *et seq.* (complete copy of charter) and Dewey, D. R., *State Banking Before the Civil War* (National Monetary Commission).

of one year. All directors were required to be residents of Missouri Territory, nine of them of St. Louis, and the other four preferably of Ste. Genevieve. A meeting could be called only by giving sixty days notice. Proxy voting was allowed. The president and any six directors constituted a quorum for the transaction of business. The president was to be chosen by the directors from their own number. The territory made no stock subscription but reserved the right to take not more than 150 shares, unless the legislature should by resolution change the amount.

The charter was to become invalid if the bank was not opened by December, 1817. It could be opened when one-half of the stock was subscribed. Payment for stock was due on demand of directors, and in any proportions by giving sixty days notice. The penalty for failure to meet this requirement was forfeiture of stock. However, the charter itself contained no requirement that the stock should be paid for in specie.

There were several provisions relating to control by the shareholders. Votes for directors were assigned according to a sliding scale. Owners of from one to ten shares had one vote for each share; owners of from ten to thirty shares had one vote for each five shares; and owners of over thirty shares one vote for each ten shares; provided, however, that no person could have more than seventeen votes. Moreover, residence in the United States and American citizenship were qualifications for voting. Not more than one-fourth of the stock could be sold outside of Missouri and Illinois; and non-residents of these two territories could not have more than one-fourth of the votes. The owners of 800 shares could call a special meeting at any time by giving the required sixty days notice.

The charter was not without protection for the creditors of the bank. There was no limit on the circulation except that the total debts of the bank were not to exceed double the paid-up capital and surplus. In case this limit was exceeded the directors, voting for the excess, were to be held personally liable. Real-estate holdings were limited to the banking house, except that real estate might be taken to secure a debt previously contracted. The bank was not to engage in merchandising. The notes were secured only by the general assets. They were invalid unless signed by both the president and the cashier, and were assignable by indorsement. Dividends were payable semi-annually out of profits and, if a false dividend were declared, directors authorizing it were to be held individually liable. The bond for the cashier was fixed at $10,000, and for all other employees at $5,000. Loans were to be secured by at least one indorser, except that lead, peltry, or furs might be accepted as collateral in place of indorsement, provided they were actually deposited in the bank or within one mile of it. Such collateral could be sold on ten days notice to pay the debts of the borrower. The interest rate was limited to six per cent, payable in advance.

The main office was located in Saint Louis; but branches without issue privilege could be opened in Missouri at places to be chosen by the directors, provided that Ste. Genevieve should have the first branch and that none should ever be located nearer than fifty miles of St. Louis nor of any other branch.

From this analysis of the charter it is clear that no provision was made for specie payment, either of stock or circulation. There was little control of the issue function and no requirement concerning publicity of accounts. Before condemning the charter for secrecy, it should be said that state legislatures were very slow to demand reports from chartered banks. Massachusetts had little publicity of bank accounts until 1838; and New York required no regular reports until 1824. The First United States Bank was required to make regular returns to Congress, but only two were ever published.[1]

Subscription books were opened at the places designated in the charter; but on September 20, 1813, it was announced that the necessary amount had not been secured.[2] In December, 1814, books were again opened, this time at Saint Louis, Saint Charles, Ste. Genevieve, Herculaneum, and Mine a' Breton, Missouri Territory, and Kaskaskia and Cahokia, Illinois Territory.[3] This time $100,000 was asked for and on July 11, 1816, it was announced that the subscription had reached $134,900.[4] It had taken three years to secure this amount in Saint Louis and the nearby towns of Missouri and Illinois. This, too, was merely a promise. It was not paid up. The delay of three years had caused great impatience; and a movement to start a second bank was already under way.[5] Missourians were also becoming interested in the project for a second national bank; and the congressional delegate from Missouri had asked for a Missouri branch.[6] The slowness in starting the Bank of

[1] Dewey, *op. cit.*, p. 131.

[2] Jones, Breckenridge, Article in Centennial no. of *Missouri Historical Review*, Jan., 1921, "A Hundred Years of Banking in Missouri", pp. 345-392. This recent article by Mr. Jones, a prominent St. Louis banker, contains much newspaper material on the Bank of St. Louis and the later Bank of Missouri.

[3] Edwards, *op. cit.*, p. 309.

[4] Jones, *op. cit.*, p. 353.

[5] Stephens, *op. cit.*

[6] Jones, *op. cit.*, p. 358.

Saint Louis is an eloquent commentary on the scarcity of local capital available for investment.

Pursuant to the charter provisions for payment for stock, a 15 per cent call was made on September 20, 1816, payment to be made the following November. Ten per cent was called for December 24, 1816, one-half to be paid in specie; three 5 per cent calls were made the following spring and summer. The final call of 60 per cent was not asked until September, 1817.[1] Although the charter made no specific requirements as to the method of payment, the directors ordered that it must be made in gold, silver, approved paper of the Banks of Cincinnati, Vincennes, Richmond, the State Bank of Tennessee, the Banks of Kentucky, and such other bank paper as was accepted by the United States Government in payment for land and taxes.[2] Evidently the bank in its inception did not aspire to "Wild Cat" methods.

The bank opened on December 13, 1816. It was very popular. The sudden influx of new currency, however, caused an unnatural expansion; it was not long before a good deal of speculative paper was in the portfolio and the circulation was regarded as excessive.[3] Some of the notes have been preserved. The following is an example:

> The President, directors, and company of the Bank of Saint Louis promise to pay $5.00 to —— or Bearer on demand.
> Saint Louis, Mo. Territory. June 18, 1817
> S. Hammond, Pres. John B. Smith, Cash.[4]

[1] Jones, *op. cit.*, p. 354.

[2] *Mo. Gazette*, Oct. 5, 1816, quoted in Dewey, D. R., *State Banking Before Civil War*, p. 21.

[3] Pope, J., Address, "Part Which Banks of Mo. Have Played in Commercial Development of State", *Proc. Mo. Bankers Association*, p. 84 *et seq.*, 1905.

[4] Conrad, *op. cit.*, article on "St. Louis Banking".

The notes were printed privately according to the design selected by the bank. The fur interests of the city were symbolized by a cut—a trap with a beaver caught in it. The following advertisement from a Missouri newspaper illustrates the character of the notes:[1]

Notice to Banks,
S. T. Toncray, engraver of Shelbyville, Kentucky, will engrave plates and furnish paper for all denominations of notes in a style as difficult to counterfeit as any and 50 per cent cheaper than Philadelphia prices. Water-marked paper used.

Little information is available as to the amount of business done by the bank. However, the land offices for Missouri, Illinois, and Arkansas had been located in Saint Louis; this, with other business centering in the city, must have assured the bank a reasonable future, provided good management could be obtained.

The bank, however, did not have a fortunate career. Those connected with it were not trained bankers and made many mistakes. However, it should be emphasized, that those responsible for it were the best business men of Saint Louis and the purpose of the bank was to care for legitimate business. The commissioners who originally opened the bank included the following names: Thomas Brady, Bartholomew Barthold, Samuel Hammond, Rufus Easton, Robert Simpson, Christian Wilt, Auguste Chouteau, J. B. C. Lucas, C. B. Penrose, Moses Austin, Risdon Price, Bernard Pratte, and Mona Lisa. Hammond had been territorial governor; Easton was the delegate to Congress; Chouteau and Lisa were the leading fur traders of the city; Lucas later was a political opponent of Senator Benton, while Pratte and several others were prominent local merchants. Moses Austin,

[1] *Mo. Intelligencer*, Mar. 26, 1821.

later of Texas fame, was prominent in the affairs of the bank.[1] Only five of the group (Hammond, Pratte, Price, Austin and Simpson) ever became directors.[2] Samuel Hammond was elected president and J. B. G. Smith, cashier. Thomas H. Benton was a stockholder, though not a director, and seems to have been a leader of the more conservative element. His experiences in this bank, doubtless, had their influence on his later "hard money" ideas; and it may be stated here, that subsequent Missouri banking history cannot be understood if Benton is left out of it.

The St. Louis newspapers contain a good many articles relating to the bank, but most of them give little real information about its condition. Although no published statements were made, President Hammond once asserted that the loans at no time exceeded $224,000.[3]

The bank lasted two years, but it was in trouble most of the time. It advanced large sums for real-estate speculation and issued more notes than it could carry safely. Seemingly President Hammond was somewhat inactive and the cashier did not realize the danger of currency inflation. The panic of 1819 gave an excuse for failure, but internal dissensions in the directorate already had given the bank its death blow. The cashier, J. G. B. Smith, had issued notes with only his own signature, although the charter required that the president should also sign them. He had then gone to Kentucky and made large real-estate loans. The directors voted to honor the notes and accept the loans, but the incident was not closed.[4] On February 11, 1818, Mr. Pilcher, a

[1] *City Directory of St. Louis*, 1816.

[2] *Ibid.*, 1818 and 1819.

[3] Jones, *op. cit.*, p. 364.

[4] Pope, *op. cit.*, p. 84 *et seq.*

director, offered a resolution to remove J. G. B. Smith as cashier and replace him with T. W. Smith. The resolution was adopted. Three directors promptly resigned. Several stockholders, not directors, hearing of the trouble, held an informal meeting and decided to take charge of the bank. Lieutenant James McGunnegle, Daniel Bissell and Thomas H. Benton were members of the group. They locked the building and demanded the keys to the safe. The directors, of course, refused, whereupon a stockholders' committee of five took charge of the premises and refused to admit any member of the board. The bank remained closed for several days until the directors could institute court proceedings to regain control; then it re-opened and began to redeem its circulation. After paying out $14,000 in specie it closed again. Internal troubles and the condition of the business seemed to call for liquidation. In fact there seemed no other honorable way out; and the directors showed no disposition to avoid their obligations. The officers, however, made capital of the action of the stockholders' committee and asked for time. The bank was allowed to re-open; but it was too weak to exist and finally closed in the summer of 1819.

It is certain that the losses of the stockholders were heavy, but the record is scanty concerning the redemption of the notes. The deposits probably were small. It is certain that the assets were applied to the payment of the debt; but numerous suits filed in the St. Louis courts indicate that the settlement was not satisfactory. The files of the *Gazette* for 1818 and 1819 contain many references to the troubles of the bank; but the papers carry no records of a final settlement. From the available evidence it seems fair to conclude that not all the notes were redeemed. It was, however, in no sense a paper bank. Its failures were largely due to inexperience and struggles for control inside the bank. At least one is left with the impression that the banking field was considered worth fighting over. This first bank gave St. Louis and Missouri a lesson in the caution and training necessary to successful banking; but it also gave an insight into the utility of banks in the transaction of business. Saint Louis was not left without a bank. O'Hara, the cashier of the Bank of Saint Louis in its last days, announced the opening of a private banking house soon after the final closing in 1819. There was one other chartered bank left. The Bank of Saint Louis had not been able to maintain its monopoly. The Bank of Missouri was in the field. Its career is another story of misfortune, but it left its imprint deeply on Missouri politics and finance.[1]

B. *The Bank of Missouri*

The delay in the organization of the Bank of Saint Louis had caused a good deal of dissatisfaction among certain of those interested in the project. The list of commissioners, who opened the subscription books for the Bank of Saint Louis, contains a number of names which did not appear on the directorate when the bank was opened. Nor are they mentioned in the accounts of the later career of the institution. Prominent among

[1] Secondary accounts of the last days of the Bank of St. Louis are available in Stevens, W. B., *Saint Louis the Fourth City* (St. Louis, 1909), p. 291 *et seq.*, and Edwards, R., *The Great West*, pp. 309 and 310. Some contemporary information is given in the *City Directory of St. Louis* for 1821. This article states that Moses Austin left St. Louis in disgust at his losses in the bank wreck and went to Texas. Mr. B. Jones, in the article previously cited, has given an admirable account based largely upon the early files of the *Saint Louis Gazette*. The author had only a limited opportunity to consult these files and so has quoted on several occasions from Mr. Jones' article.

those left out were Auguste Chouteau and Mona Lisa, representatives of the local fur-trading interests.[1] It seems that much of the dissatisfaction with the Bank of St. Louis came from the fur interests. They represented the type of local business most in need of better banking facilities. Together with some of the more adventurous element of the city, they were able to arrange a kind of partnership with the purpose of petitioning the legislature for a charter for a second bank. Probably little banking business was transacted under the partnership contract. Shepard gives a somewhat different interpretation to the motives for organization, ascribing it to a feeling of elation at banking prospects and a desire to share some of the fruits of the venture.[2] However, there is no doubt that the leaders of the movement were disgruntled promoters of the Bank of St. Louis. Whether this action was responsible for it or not, the original group hurried their plans and succeeded in opening for business first.[3]

Auguste Chouteau and others presented a petition to the Third Territorial Legislature, asking that the existing partnership be changed to a corporation and that it retain the name of Bank of Missouri which had been previously used.[4] There seems to have been some opposition to the measure, for although discussed early in the session, it was not passed until January 31, 1817.[5]

[1] See *City Directory of St. Louis* for 1817, 1818 and 1819 for lists of directors.

[2] Shepard, *op. cit.*, p. 57.

[3] The Bank of St. Louis opened Dec. 13, 1816, and Bank of Mo. in spring of 1817 (as a chartered bank).

[4] Geyer, *op. cit.*, p. 74.

[5] The Secretary to the Governor is authority for the statement that on the first ballot there were only three negative votes (quoted in Geyer's *Digest*, *op. cit.*, at end of charter).

The name Bank of Missouri was retained. The legislature again showed interest in a proposal for partial state ownership (as with the Bank of Saint Louis), by reserving the right to add $100,000 to the stock of the Bank, such stock to be paid for from the state treasury. The option was to remain in effect ten years.[1] However, the right was never used.

J. P. Cabanne, Charles Gratiot, and three others were appointed to act as a committee to receive subscriptions for stock.[2] The original subscription of $78,500 was taken by 83 individuals and firms. A complete list is quoted in Edwards' *The Great West*.[3] The largest block was thirty-one shares, taken by Thomas Riddick. Auguste Chouteau subscribed for thirty shares; L. W. Boggs, ten; Alexander McNair, first governor of Missouri, ten; J. B. C. Lucas, ten; etc. All eighty-three subscribers were residents of Saint Louis. Many of the names reflect French extraction. It was planned to sell more stock as rapidly as possible. The Bank of Saint Louis had $100,000 capital and the new bank wanted to be larger. The French influence persisted; for, at a later date, it was reported that Frenchmen held 276 out of the 780 shares owned in Saint Louis.[4] The stock was paid for on calls by the directors, partly in specie and partly in the notes of other banks of issue. The latter were, however, all converted into specie by the management of the bank.

The charter was modeled closely on that of the Bank

[1] *Laws of Missouri, 1804–24*, pp. 278 and 532 *et seq.* (state publication).

[2] Stevens, W. B., *St. Louis the Fourth City*, p. 292.

[3] P. 310.

[4] Carr, *op. cit.*, pp. 133 and 134.

[5] *Missouri Intelligencer*, July 16, 1821.

of Saint Louis, but was much more detailed and contained additional provisions looking toward the protection of its creditors.[1] The authorized capital was $250,000 in shares of $100, exclusive of such stock as the territorial government might subscribe later. The legislature was to consider propositions for increase of the stock on petition of the bank. It was required that $5.00 be paid down on each share at time of subscription, such payment to be forfeited unless $20.00 additional were paid before February 1, 1817.[2] The remaining three-fourths was payable, on call of the president and directors, on ninety days previous notice, provided that no call of more than $25.00 a share could be made. The charter did not require that these payments be made in specie.

Management was entrusted to a board of nine directors elected by the stockholders for one year. The president was named by the board from its own membership. He and any four directors constituted a quorum for the transaction of business. In case of illness the president might name any director as his proxy. Citizenship both of the United States and of Missouri and ownership of stock (the amount not specified) were qualifications for directors. In fact all stockholders were required to prove American citizenship.[3] There was a sliding scale in the voting privileges of stockholders, much like that of the Bank of Saint Louis. It provided one vote for each share up to four shares; one vote for each two shares from four to twenty shares; one vote for each four

[1] The charter is quoted in full in Geyer, H. S., *Digest of the Laws of Mo.*, 1804-24 (State Printer).

[2] Applying of course only to the original subscription.

[3] This seems to have been a reflection of the opposition to the Bank of the U. S. on account of its foreign stockholders.

shares from twenty to forty shares; one vote for each six shares from forty to one hundred shares. No stockholder could have more than fifty votes and could not vote at all until he had owned stock sixty days. Only those living outside of Saint Louis were allowed to vote by proxy. Regular meetings of the shareholders were held in May of each year after eight weeks newspaper notice; and special meetings might be called at any time by the owners of 500 shares.

There were certain provisions safeguarding the public. The interest rate on discounts was limited to six per cent. The negotiability of all drafts was established by law. The directors were entitled to inspect the books at any time. In addition a report was to be made to each session of the legislature, setting forth the condition of the bank. If this revealed any evasion of the law, the legislature could require reform or, failing in this, might revoke the charter. Directors were required to serve without compensation and were forbidden to borrow more than $3,000 each from the bank. Shares were transferable but transfer was not to be made on the books until the seller had discharged all his indebtedness to the bank. Dividends might be declared semi-annually. But any director present at dividend meeting who failed to protest was held individually liable if capital was impaired by such dividend if the directors had knowledge of such impairment. Loans were limited to twice the paid-up capital. Total debts were limited in the same manner except that deposits were not to be included in the debt. In case of excess the directors were personally liable. All circulation was redeemable in specie on demand under a penalty of 5 per cent for each month of suspension. Moreover, the territorial courts were ordered to entertain suits for the collection of such bills. The bank was prohibited from owning boats or engaging in any trade except in bullion, bills of exchange, and stocks or merchandise pledged. Real estate could be owned only for an office unless taken to secure a debt previously contracted in good faith. However, once owned, there was no provision requiring its sale. The president and cashier were elected by a majority vote of the entire membership of the board. Neither the cashier nor any of his assistants were allowed to own stock in the bank. This rule did not apply to the president. Bonds of from $6,000 to $10,000 were required of all employees.

The territory retained an option on stock by providing that 10,000 shares or less might be subscribed for at any time within ten years, such stock to carry the same voting privileges as private stock and to be paid for out of any funds in the treasury. In return for the charter it was agreed that there should be no tax exemption; and that, upon request of the legislature by joint resolution, loans should be made to the territory to an amount not to exceed one-half of the paid-up stock owned by it, provided ninety days notice were given of intention to apply for a loan.

The main office was located in Saint Louis but the purchase of $40,000 stock by any county made it obligatory for the bank to open a branch in such county within six months. The branches, however, were to have no issue rights.[1]

The charter was to expire in 1838 but might be sooner given up by vote of owners of two-thirds of the stock. Six months time was given the petitioning group to qualify under the charter.

[1] One branch was established at Ste. Genevieve.

The legislature seems to have profited by the experience secured in making the charter for the Bank of Saint Louis. At least this charter shows a tendency to throw somewhat greater safeguards about the creditors of the bank. It is clearly an expanded copy of the older charter; but it instituted a penalty for suspension of specie payments and provided for rudimentary government inspection. At this time Saint Louis and, in fact, all of Missouri were seeing the results of bad currency which was coming over the border from other states. If a new bank was to be started, it clearly was not desirable merely to add a little more to the stream of fluctuating and unsatisfactory bank paper. That this bank fared worse than the Bank of St. Louis gives evidence of the great weight the personal equation has in banking policy.

The bank of Missouri opened for business under its new charter early in 1817 in quarters in the basement of Auguste Chouteau's home on Main Street.[1] Chouteau was elected president. He was the richest man in town and his connection with the bank doubtless gave it considerable prestige. He, with Mona Lisa, was able to turn most of the fur business of the town to the bank.[2] Chouteau himself seems to have been active in the management. The first cashier was Lilburn W. Boggs, afterwards governor of Missouri.[3]

The times were unfavorable for safe banking. Saint Louis was just getting over the depression which followed the War of 1812 and was pretty thoroughly inoculated with the idea of getting rich out of speculation in public lands. This era of speculation lasted just long enough, for the community to get badly involved and the

[1] *St. Louis Republic*, July 12, 1908, Centennial Edition.

[2] Ridgely, *op. cit.*, p. 387.

[3] Knox, *op. cit.*, p. 782.

bank was left to struggle with the panic conditions of 1819. Nevertheless, it had a large paid-up capital and the support of a large element of the wealthier class and in its earlier days seemed to prosper.[1] It never, moreover, made an effort to secure the support of working men. It paid little attention to their wants and, when the tide of unpopularity came, this worked against it.[2]

In 1819 the bank moved to a new brick building at 6 North Main Street.[3] Banking hours were from 10 to 2 except on Sundays, January 1st, July 4th and Christmas. Loans were made only on Tuesday and Thursday, but application had to be made the day previous. By 1821 Chouteau had resigned on account of advanced age and had been succeeded by Thomas F. Riddick. Lewis Bompart was now cashier. Two bookkeepers were employed. The board of directors included President Riddick, Thomas H. Benton (then a lawyer with offices on Washington Avenue), Joseph Phillipson, Thomas Brady, Henry Von Phul, James Kennerly, Michael Tesson, Thomas Hempstead, and A. L. Langham.[4]

Notes were issued in denominations of $1.00, $3.00, $5.00, and $20.00. The following is a copy of one of them:

The President, Directors and Company of the Bank of Missouri promise to pay $1.00 on demand at their office of deposit and discount in Ste. Genevieve to Wm. Shannon or bearer.

Auguste Chouteau	St. Louis, Oct. 1, 1818
President	John Dales, Cashier.[5]

[1] See Pope, *op. cit.*, p. 84.

[2] Edwards, *op. cit.*, p. 310.

[3] *City Directory of St. Louis, 1819.*

[4] *City Directory of St. Louis, 1821.*

[5] Conrad's *Encyclopedia of Missouri History*, Article on "Saint Louis Banking".

At first the notes were well received. In 1819 John Wiggins and Richard Venebles advertised that they would pay a premium of one per cent for Bank of Missouri notes.[1] The Franklin Land Office in Central Missouri accepted its notes in payment for public lands. Ste. Genevieve Branch notes were taken also.[2] However, before the failure the notes of the bank were in bad repute, as is indicated by the following letter published during the contest for the State Bank in 1836:

> How will the proposed State Bank be made to pay its debts? The old Bank of Missouri was required to pay specie on demand under a penalty of 5 per cent per month, but its notes passed current at 50 cents on the dollar, etc.
>
> (signed)
> Corbin[3]

Much of the prosperity of the bank was due to the fact that it held large federal deposits. Late in 1817 it had begun to receive land-office money. *The Missouri Intelligencer* of July 16, 1821 reports that the bank had deposits of $700,079.05 in 1819, of which only $72,973.00 was to the credit of individuals. The Missouri, Illinois, and Arkansas land offices in Saint Louis accumulated large amounts of money which had to be taken care of by such facilities as were afforded. There was no branch of the United States Bank in Saint Louis; so it was difficult for the government to make use of the Saint Louis banks. It was decided finally to let the Bank of Missouri keep a permanent deposit of $150,000, in pay-

[1] *Mo. Intelligencer*, May 28, 1819.

[2] Under the charter, section 19, branches did not have the right of issue; but this was avoided by issuing Ste. Genevieve notes at Saint Louis, signed by the president and cashier of the mother bank and making them payable at the Ste. Genevieve office.

[3] *Mo. Argus* (St. Louis), June 24, 1836.

ment for which it was to convert the various state bank notes which were received at the land office into acceptable funds and to remit them to a branch of the national bank.[1] This new contract forced the Bank of Missouri to demand specie in its dealings with other banks. It thus won the everlasting enmity of nearby institutions such as the Bank of Edwardsville, Illinois. Bad relations with other banks no doubt contributed to the undercurrent of unfavorable comment which grew up in Saint Louis in 1821 and so added to the troubles of the bank.

The progress of the bank can be best seen from its published statements. Although the legal requirement was only that reports be submitted to the legislature, they were published regularly in the local newspapers.

In 1819 the paid-up capital was $250,000, deposits $773,662, circulation $135,000, loans $447,941, and specie holdings $252,562.[2] The cash reserve against deposits and circulation was 27.7 per cent. The large deposits mostly represented federal funds from the land office.

The next year showed a radical change as indicated by the following incomplete statement (000.00 omitted):[3]

Cr.		*Dr.*		
Debts due (Loans)	$367	Capital		250
Real Estate	15	Home Office	$210	
Eastern Notes	25	Ste. G. Br.	40	
Specie	189	Deposits		256
		Circulation		141

The decrease in deposits is to be accounted for chiefly by the change in the government contract. The cash reserve at this time was very large. Deposits varied

[1] Jones, *op. cit.*, quoting from *Report of Secretary of Treasury*, 18th Congress, first session, pp. 444, 525, 545, 551, 565.

[2] Pope, *op. cit.*, p. 84.

[3] *Mo. Intelligencer*, Sept. 30, 1820.

very little after the first big slump. The *Missouri Intelligencer* reports them:[1]

1819	$773,652
1820	255,258
1821	255,562

On July 2, 1821, loans were $393,000, deposits $256,000, specie $106,000, while an investment account of $86,000 had appeared.[2] In the issue of July 21, 1821, the *Missouri Intelligencer* carried a complete statement for June 1, 1821:

Cr.		*Dr.*	
Loans	$393,983.01	Capital	$250,000.00
Cash	109,531.47	Deposits	255,562.94
Collections	13,619.02	Circulation	79,402.00
Real Estate	19,713.70	Profits	7,667.43
Branch capital	40,000.00		
Owed by other banks	15,785.17		
	$592,632.37		$592,632.37

L. Bompart, Cashier. T. F. Riddick, President.

This is the last statement published before the closing of the bank. Since September, 1820, there had been a rapid rise in loans and an even more rapid fall in specie and circulation. This statement, however, tells little of the true condition of the bank which was to be revealed by the investigations following its failure two months later.

The final chapters of the bank's history illustrate well the speculative tendencies of the times. The incoming settlers of Illinois and Missouri brought considerable money with them. As business opportunites were scant

[1] *Mo. Intelligencer*, July 16, 1821.

[2] *Ibid.*, Aug. 22, 1821.

and markets unsatisfactory, they turned to real-estate investments. Government land could be bought for $2.00 an acre; but, as only 25 per cent had to be paid down, $80 would buy a quarter section. Moreover, the government was inclined to accept the notes of most of the chartered banks in payment. Everybody expected to get rich out of the new settlers. The banks kept expanding their issues to meet the speculative demands. When panic conditions came and the United States Bank exerted pressure to maintain specie payments, the failures were many. In the St. Louis trade territory the fur business helped to tide over 1819. The troubles mostly came in the period of depression which followed.[1]

In the city of Saint Louis speculative conditions also prevailed. City lots sold at unheard-of prices. Two brick churches (one, a Catholic church, 130 feet long) were started on Market Street. Neither were ever finished. A fine theatre building was erected on Chestnut Street. It was never used. The banks were quite reckless in their credit extension. Money seemed plentiful in Saint Louis all through 1817, although the burden of supplying funds for the purchase of government land had begun to be felt. The exportation of lead and furs, however, held up well and brought in a large supply of funds available for investment. The Bank of Missouri was being operated in a manner little better than that of the average Western bank of the time, and this in spite of the fact that the directorate represented the better business elements of the city. However, they seem to have caught the fever of speculation. Late in 1817 there occurred a duel between Benton and Lucas involving

[1] For a discussion of land speculation in the upper Mississippi Valley see Scharf, J. T., *History of St. Louis City and County* (Philadelphia, 1883), p. 1370 *et seq.*

certain of the affairs of the bank. The feeling engendered by this weakened the bank. The building boom continued. Wealthy men from the East came to Saint Louis, and, for a time, helped to keep up the supply of capital. Colonel Justis Post brought in $100,000 in cash, bought land, and built a country house and a mill near Saint Louis. The Bank of Missouri saw a chance to bolster up its slender resources, sold him some stock, and elected him a director. He did not prove to be an asset to the bank. After a quarrel with the management he sold his property for what it would bring and moved to Illinois; but not until he had used his influence to the detriment of the bank.[1]

By 1820 Missouri had asked for statehood and was engaged in a violent discussion of slavery questions. This emphasized the unbalanced state of the public mind and so reacted to make business even more unsafe. The over-expansion was now making itself felt. Settlers had ceased to come and the papers carried many announcements of sheriff's sales. The bubble had burst with resulting business stagnation. The Bank of Missouri, however, never had failed to redeem its obligations and, in spite of a good deal of unfavorable street gossip, seemed to retain a large degree of public confidence.[2]

The legislature of 1821 appointed a committee to study the causes of the existing business stagnation and to ascertain if the Bank of Missouri had violated its charter. It was common talk that the bank held much questionable paper; and the recent statements had shown rising circulation, and falling deposits and specie holdings. The report of the committee was brought in on June 15,

[1] For this and other incidents relating to the course of St. Louis speculation see Shepard, *op. cit.*, pp. 57-62.

[2] Dewey, *op. cit.*, p. 79.

1821, but after discussion it was decided not to print it, so one can only guess what facts were brought out.[1] *The Missouri Intelligencer* of August 22, 1821, states that the investigation of the committee forced the liquidation of the bank. At any rate specie payments were suspended on August 4, 1821, and the directors decided to liquidate the business. A statement was issued by the president to the effect that all debts would be paid, that no incorrect banking had been done, and that the failure was due wholly to the suspension of banks in other states. Figures for deposits and circulation were given out as follows: public deposits $152,000, private accounts $42,000, outstanding note circulation $84,000.[2]

After the failure it began to appear that the causes lay chiefly within the bank itself. The management had been of the worst type, although public confidence had been kept up by maintenance of specie payments. Investigations were instituted by the legislature in 1822, but they are hard to check with previous reports because the business of the branch at Ste. Genevieve was not included. It appeared that $108,795 of the $210,000 capital stock of the mother bank had been paid in by the directors with "stock notes", that they had borrowed $79,569 on real-estate mortgage security, and $60,075.86 on their personal notes. In addition they had indorsed paper to the amount of $37,310. From this statement it is seen that the board of directors owed the bank $285,869.86 or $75,869.86 more than the capital stock. The

[1] *House Journal, 1st General Assembly Mo.* Extra Session, pp. 40 and 63.

[2] *Mo. Intelligencer*, Aug. 22, 1822. This issue contains a very full account of the legislative investigation made by the General Assembly in 1822. Most of the material relating to the condition of the bank is taken from this source.

total loan account was only $443,869.68 and this amount included bills of exchange to the amount of nearly $25,000. The liabilities were given as follows:

Capital (Mother Bank)	$210,000.00
Circulation	84,301.00
U. S. Deposits	152,407.65
Individual Deposits	42,611.01
	$489,319.66[1]

It seems clear that much of the trouble of the bank was caused by excessive loans to directors. It must be said, however, that the members of the board were business men of good standing in Saint Louis. Their paper was perhaps as good or better than the average offered by other customers of the bank. The charter, however, forbade any director to borrow over $3,000.00 and this had been clearly violated.[2] When trouble came this fact left them without defense.

It must be emphasized that the actions of the directors did not constitute the only reason for the failure. If they had borrowed nothing banking would have been a difficult business in Saint Louis at this time. Moreover, there is reason to believe that the United States Bank exerted a weakening influence. General Duff Green, writing in 1866, states that one of the first acts of his public life was to examine and report on the causes of the suspension of the Bank of Missouri. He states that it and the Bank of Edwardsville, Illinois, were forced to convert the notes of each other into specie to be sent by

[1] *Mo. Intelligencer*, Aug. 22, 1822, and *21 Niles*, 38. Secondary accounts of the failure are given in Sumner, W. G., *History of Banking in all the Leading Nations*, vol. i, U. S., p. 162, and Pope, *op. cit.*, p. 84.

[2] Section viii.

the same steamer to the United States Branch Bank at Louisville. The constant demands for specie caused ill feeling between the banks. He says in part,

The Bank of the United States was but a part and a weaker part of the financial system. The specie which the Bank of the United States took from the South and West was remitted to London to help the Bank of England to resume specie payments. It reduced the value of the land one-half and the government forced the purchasers to relinquish their purchases for which they were unable to make payment and meant the loss of more than one-half the sums previously paid.[1]

This, of course, was a local view. It merely meant that pay-day had arrived and put an end to the land speculation. Of course it hurt the bank.

The failure caused a run on the nearby Bank of Edwardsville, Illinois. It was forced to suspend.[2] Fifty-four thousand dollars of government deposits were lost.[3]

The liquidation of the Bank of Missouri was prolonged and one can only estimate how large the losses were. *Niles Register* says the customers of the bank lost at least $150,000.[4] *The Jeffersonian Republican* (Jefferson City, Missouri) in the issue of March 12, 1836, is authority for the statement that the circulation was redeemed at fifty cents on the dollar.[5] No report of the final settlement is available. However, something is known about the outcome of the debt to the government. Up

[1] Duff Green, *Facts and Suggestions* (N. Y., 1866), p. 80.

[2] Dowrie, G. W., *Development of Banking in Illinois* (University of Illinois Studies in the Social Sciences), vol. ii, no. 4, p. 17.

[3] Garnett, C. T., *State Banks of Issue in Illinois* (University of Illinois Studies, 1898), p. 5.

[4] 30 *Niles*, 282.

[5] Quoted in Jones, *op. cit.*, p. 391.

to February, 1823, only $38,854.78 of the $152,407.65 federal deposit had been paid.[1] The bank transferred certain notes from its portfolio to the government in satisfaction of its claim, but in 1837 $84,544.57 of them were returned as still unpaid although suits had been brought and judgments rendered.[2]

The Bank of Saint Louis had closed in 1819. Now the Bank of Missouri was in liquidation and St. Louis was left without banking facilities except for some private agencies which issued notes of extremely uncertain value. Two important results grew out of these failures. For a long time Saint Louis lost interest in local banks. She preferred even to go back to a state of barter. The heavy borrowings of the directors of the Bank of Missouri gave rise to the opinion that banks were instruments whereby the rich could defraud the poor. Much political capital was later made of this. Good came out of it, however, for it took seventeen years to overcome the feeling and Missouri escaped most of the wild banking practice which obtained between 1820 and 1840. The other great result was the education of Senator Thomas Hart Benton. Before leaving the Bank of Missouri an attempt will be made to trace his connection with it.

Statements regarding Benton are so biased by political considerations that it is all but impossible to get at the truth. It is at least a matter of record that he was a director of the Bank of Missouri and had, like the others, borrowed heavily from it. He had also been a stockholder of the Bank of Saint Louis. It is doubtless true

[1] *House Document 27*, 23rd Congress, 2d Session, *Report of Secretary of U. S.*, on "Public Money", Dec. 15, 1834.

[2] *American State Papers*, vol. v, p. 624, quoted in Jones, *op. cit.*, pp. 390 and 391.

that his experiences with banks while in Saint Louis had much to do with his later "hard money" proclivities. When he became convinced of the evil, political and economic influence of the Second United States Bank, he worked unceasingly for the defeat of the recharter bill. He argued that it flooded the country with its notes, thus causing speculation, and that it could manufacture a panic on demand by drawing them in. This with its loans to members of Congress placed it in a position to control elections. Benton professed to have no confidence in any bank of issue; but, judging from his conduct as a bank director, the fear of the political power of the national bank was his strongest motive. When Missouri wanted to charter a state bank he fought the idea with all his might, and when he saw that the movement could not be stopped he turned his attention to making it as safe as possible, Likely, much of the conservatism of the State Bank was due to his influence.

Something of Benton's dealings with the Bank of Missouri can be inferred from the following quotations from various sources. J. B. C. Lucas in a letter to J. W. Taylor said:

> It appears by unquestionable evidence that Thos. H. Benton, Senator from Missouri, who was one of the directors of the Bank of Missouri when it failed, is indebted to the bank to the sum of $13,000. Much involved . . . to a greater amount than he is able to pay.[1]

Niles Register remarks that ugly stories were afloat about Senator Benton's connection with the Bank of Missouri; that at any rate he was on the board and so could not be wholly absolved from responsibility for a

[1] *Lucas' Letters, 1815-1836* (St. Louis, 1905, published by his grandson, J. B. C. Lucas).

failure which caused a loss of $150,000 of customers' money.[1] *The Missouri Republican* in its fight against the State Bank plan in 1837 copied the following editorial from the *Washington City Reformer* of August 26, 1837:[2]

Colonel Benton was a director of the old Bank of Missouri. By charter no director of the bank could borrow more than $3,000 from it. He was entitled to borrow this much for his services. As editor of *The Enquirer* he fought other banks and got public deposits for the Bank of Missouri. When these amounted to $180,000 the directors divided them up, and broke the bank. These facts are known in Saint Louis and when the Branch Bank of the United States was established, the directors refused to discount Benton's paper. He began to fight. He urged Jackson to remove the deposits, obtained the office of the Cincinnati Commercial Agency for Saint Louis, and put its direction in charge of his political partisans. Public deposits reached $2,000,000. His partisans put through the state bank charter to start a bank by money borrowed on state bonds. The directors were partisan. He borrowed $1,000,000 from the Secretary of the Treasury and got $2,000,000 government deposits; so with $3,000,000 public money he goes to Missouri to speculate in public lands and laugh at the ruin which overwhelms the country. But let us see. He denounces the banks with his breath and builds them up with his facts. When he was writing anti-bank articles, he was helping to draft the Bank of Missouri charter.

C. *The Loan Office*

The failure of the Bank of Missouri and the subsequent legislative investigation brought economic conditions in the state sharply to the attention of the General Assem-

[1] 30 *Niles*, 282.

[2] *Mo. Republican* (St. Louis), May 12, 1837.

bly. As has been brought out in connection with the Bank of Missouri, general business conditions were highly speculative. Merchants were liberal in granting credits. Land was purchased without much thought of price or location. Carr records the sale at auction of a piece of land whose only description was that it was located about thirty miles north of Saint Louis.[1] Full advantage was taken of the liberal terms offered by the national government. The crisis of 1819 had slowed down immigration from the East; so the market for land dwindled. Bank notes of uncertain value from other states had driven out most of Missouri's specie. The panic of 1819 had ruined the banks, so that the people were left with no means of payment except notes of little or no value. There was no money to pay taxes or to complete payments on land which had been purchased. Even, if a man owed only a little he might be unable to pay. The government at Washington saw the plight of the West and extended the time of payment on public land installments. The state legislature also wanted to help and, in its first session after statehood, ways and means of relief were considered. It was this state of affairs which furnished the motive for the Loan Office Act. Missouri conditions were merely those of the Middle West of the time. The Loan Office Act itself was not a peculiar or isolated bit of legislation. It was merely a part of the attempt of the West to afford relief to its people. The records of legislation in other states of the section show many stay laws, loan offices or paper banks.[2]

The General Assembly of 1821 first considered the establishment of a state bank. The opposition, how-

[1] Carr, *op. cit.*, p. 133.

[2] Carr, *op. cit.*, pp. 136 and 137.

ever, was too great, and besides no well-thought-out banking plan had been formulated. A compromise plan was proposed and passed on June 27, 1821.[1] It was an attempt to do two things: (a) to furnish a satisfactory currency; (b) to enable citizens to borrow necessary funds at a fair rate of interest. The plan was briefly as follows: The state was to be divided into five districts with a loan office (not called a bank) in each one. The local management was entrusted to boards of three commissioners to be elected by the General Assembly. The state auditor and state treasurer were empowered to issue certificates to the amount of $200,000 in denominations ranging from $0.50 to $10.00. These were to be assigned to the several districts in proportion to population, to be loaned in amounts of $1,000 or less on real estate security of at least double the amount of the loan or $200 or less on personal property. The rate of interest was fixed at 6 per cent in advance and repayments were not required in amounts larger than 10 per cent semi-annually. The plan was entered into with a good deal of caution, it being provided that 10 per cent of the notes were to be withdrawn from circulation each year until all were retired. The original idea seems to have been merely to make temporary provision for the extraordinary circumstances of the time. The governor was given power to borrow specie subject to the approval of the General Assembly, such loan to be used as a redemption fund. Only $2,000 actual cash was appropriated. This was to be used for expenses of organization. The

[1] For text of the act see *Laws of Mo., 1804–24*, p. 760 *et seq.*, and 831 to 865 scattered references. Secondary aceounts giving the main features of the plan are available in Sumner, *op. cit.*, vol. i, U. S., pp. 161–162, and in *Sound Currency*, April 15, 1895, Article on "The States as Bankers".

state revenue from the salt springs and the faith and credit of the commonwealth were pledged for the redemption of the certificates.

The state agreed to accept these certificates in payment of all dues to itself, including taxes, and provided that all its civil and military officials should be paid with them. Furthermore they were to draw interest at 2 per cent from date of issue until redeemed. Persons holding leases on the state salt springs were required to sell salt for certificates and any ferry-man refusing to take them was to lose his license. It was expected that these measures would insure their circulation as currency. The form of the certificate was as follows:

> This certificate shall be receivable at the Treasury or any of the loan offices of the state of Missouri, in the discharge of taxes or debts due the State, for the sum of $5.00, with interest for the same at the rate of two per centum per annum, from this date, first day of September, 1821.
>
> Wm. Christy,
> Auditor of Public Accounts
> Nathaniel Simonds,
> State Treasurer.[1]

Offices were opened at Charitan, Franklin (Boonville), Saint Charles, Cape Girardeau, and St. Louis. The people showed a disposition to give the plan a trial. *The Missouri Intelligencer* gives evidence that the certificates circulated in the country districts. Note the following advertisements:

[1] A. J. McCulloch, *The Loan Office Experiment in Missouri, 1821-36, University of Mo. Bulletin*, vol. xv, no. 24, Social Science Series, August, 1914, p. 8. This is perhaps the best account of the Loan Office.

Will take loan office money at fair price for plows, hoes, and blacksmithing.

W. O. Short [1]

150,000 brick for loan office certificates at par.[2]

However, not every one in Franklin was disposed favorably toward the experiment. At a political dinner two toasts were offered: (a) "To the Loan Office, established by the desertion of every principle of moral and political honesty"; and (b) "To our uninvited representatives—may they learn to prefer the wishes of their constituents."[3] A few days earlier one of these representatives, Duff Green, had felt called upon to explain why he voted for the Loan Office. He had been sent to the legislature on an anti-bank platform. He said in substance, "It was not a question of good or bad currency but of currency or no currency. Shall the sheriff take money or plows for taxes? Our gold and silver are disappearing daily. The Loan Office isn't like a bank. No one man can monopolize it. The state is a kind of friend, helping all the needy until by farming they can pay their debts.[4]"

Considering the wild finance of neighboring states, Missouri handled this credit venture in a remarkably conservative manner. Although the original authorization was for $200,000, the issues were made quite slowly. There were, however, certain abuses. It was the intention of the original bill to use the certificates only for emergency aid to citizens, but later the treasurer was authorized to use them to pay outstanding auditor's

[1] *Mo. Intelligencer*, Oct. 16, 1821.

[2] *Ibid.*

[3] *Mo. Intelligencer*, July 16, 1821.

[4] *Mo. Intelligencer*, July 9, 1821.

certificates.[1] Only the payment of salaries was originally contemplated, but by 1822 ordinary state expenses were being met in this way. An additional issue of $50,000 for this purpose was arranged. On December 29, 1821 a $50,000 loan was made to N. Bliss for the construction of an iron works, and in 1822 one to another party for a grist mill.[2] Data relating to the actual conduct of the system is very meagre, but it is certain that the legislature regarded it in no sense as a permanent solution. The next session instituted means for restriction. It was enacted on November 27, 1822 that no more certificates should be issued or loaned. The Bliss Iron Works grant was repealed. Loans were ordered called in at the rate of 10 per cent a month. Finally it was provided that a debtor might be discharged on payment of four-fifths of his indebtedness.[3]

In the meantime, in the case of Mo. *v.* Lane, the Saint Louis Circuit Court had declared the Loan Office Certificates to be bills of credit and therefore unconstitutional. The state had loaned the certificates in exchange for promissory notes of customers. These notes, the court said, could not be collected if the debtor chose to plead the unconstitutionality of the law. In discussing the case the judge of the lower court said: "Kentucky had the start of Missouri in the paper money system. She sent her money here and spent it. We determined to adopt a system to exclude Kentucky commerce. We did it."[4] After this decision the certificates depreciated

[1] *Laws of Mo.*, 1804-24, p. 863.

[2] Sumner; *op. cit.*, p. 163.

[3] *Ibid.*, p. 163. *Laws of Mo.*, 1804-24, pp. 940 and 1011.

[4] Mo. v. Lane, St. Louis Circuit Court, Feb., 1822, reported in *Sup. 22 Niles, 128.* The stand of the court was later confirmed by U. S. Supreme Court in the case of Craig *v.* Mo., *4 Peters U. S.*, 410.

from 35 per cent to 50 per cent.[1] All who had become indebted for them were in a position to repudiate their obligations. In the face of this certain loss it is greatly to the honor of the state government that no attempts were made to evade redemption. In 1829 Governor Miller was instructed by the legislature to borrow $70,000 to redeem the certificates still outstanding. Twenty thousand dollars for this purpose was furnished by the United States Branch Bank in Saint Louis.[2]

It is difficult to be certain how large the total issue was. The state treasurer had records for $184,788. According to the auditor $188,647 were redeemed. This may indicate either bad accounting or counterfeiting. There may well have been both. The state had handled the institution in an easy-going way. In fact it was not until the court decisions showed just how untenable her position was that she decided to pay all the costs and close up the deal.

The message of Governor Miller on November 16, 1830, gives the clearest available statement of the case:

> By act of the legislature of January 23, 1829 the executive borrowed $70,000 to redeem outstanding auditors' warrants and Loan Office Certificates. The duty has been performed. This was a great thing for the state. It has enabled her to withdraw to a great extent a species of paper which at all times has been below par and which at no period of its existence answered the purpose to any considerable degree of a circulating medium. The state lost at least twenty-five per cent. Large money lenders came out ahead by buying up warrants at 25-50 per cent discount.
>
> The United States Supreme Court after two years deliberation held that the state could not recover debts due her for

[1] Sumner, *op. cit.*, p. 162.

[2] *Mo. Intelligencer*, July 17, 1829.

loans which were secured by promissory notes and mortgages. This caused great loss.

The outstanding debts are

$42,896
$20,000 interest from 1822 to 1830.

$62,896.

This amount is due from the Loan Office and will likely never be paid. Thus ends a system which has been a losing game to all except borrowers, shielded by the Supreme Court and the discount bankers.[1]

In 1833 the auditor reported that of the $47,020.00 due to the state on October 1, 1830, only $3,612.00 had been paid. The remaining $43,408 was regarded as worthless.

In this chapter Missouri's first three attempts to solve her banking and currency problems have been discussed. All three were failures. She had never had a successful banking venture. So it is small wonder that many of her people were afraid of any sort of a banking proposition. These experiences gave her caution when the task of making the State Bank was approached. If she had had no other teaching, the State Bank might have been delayed longer than it was, but she was destined to experience a little good banking—just enough to make her sure that banks were useful if properly controlled. The first of these happier experiences was the Branch Bank of the United States in Saint Louis.

[1] *House Journal, 1st Session, 6th General Assembly Mo., 1831*, p. 7 *et seq*. The message has been quoted only in substance.

CHAPTER IV

Some Early Experiences in Sound Banking

A. *The Branch Bank of the United States.*

The closing of the Bank of Missouri in 1821 again left the state without a bank. There was no machinery for long-distance payments except thru the accommodation of certain local merchants who had established Eastern credits. In time this practice developed into a kind of private banking, for Saint Louis was not destined to have another bank for eight years.

As early as 1827, the Bank of the United States was asked to consider Saint Louis as a location for a branch office, and Mr. T. Cadwalader was sent out to look over the ground and report on the possibilities for a profitable business. His report is a very interesting document. It gives essentially the following data:

The chief business of the city is the selling of dry goods and groceries which are purchased in Philadelphia and New Orleans. The retail trade amounts to about $750,000 a year, in addition to $150,000 in sales to the Indians. Fur exports are $500,000 a year, but three-fifths of this trade is controlled by the Astor interests and can be expected to furnish little business for a bank. The other important export is lead, but this is quite speculative. The city has a population of 5,000 and is growing. Twenty new houses were built last year. The river trade is increasing. There is little business in bills of exchange, except in the shipping of furs. There are no local banks, nor have there been any since 1821. A new bank could not expect to carry a loan of more than $100,000 to $200,000. Such a small volume of business would not pay.

On the basis of this analysis he gave as his opinion that the location of a branch in Saint Louis would be inexpedient at this time.[1] The officials evidently relied on his report, for no action was taken.

The bank, however, watched the growing prosperity of the city, and two years later did open a branch office there. John O'Fallon, a young Saint Louis business man who had become wealthy by a wife who owned $100,000 of local real estate, was installed as president. He developed into a banker of marked ability and left a deep stamp on the subsequent banking policies of the city. Sympathy with the ideals of the mother bank was secured by placing on the board of directors Major Thomas Biddle, a brother of Nicholas Biddle, president of the United States Bank; and by appointing as cashier H. S. Cox, a former official of the Philadelphia office.[2] The local interests of the city were protected fully. Ten out of the twelve members of the first board were residents of Saint Louis.[3] Besides those mentioned they included such men as Pierre Chouteau, John Mullanphy and Peter Lindell.[4] It was a remarkable board of business men; and in the four short years of the life of the branch it was to impress firmly on the city the principles of sound and conservative banking. The fine spirit of the board is exemplified by the attitude of Peter Lindell. Although inclined to take speculative risks as an

[1] Report of T. Cadwalader, investigator for U. S. Bank, in *Petition for a Branch Bank in Saint Louis*, March 17, 1827. Document in N. Y. Public Library. The text quoted above is adapted from this report.

[2] Edwards, *op. cit.*, p. 340, and Ridgely, *op. cit.*

[3] Shepard, *op. cit.*, p. 93.

[4] *City Directory of Saint Louis*, 1829.

individual, he was ultra-conservative as a director, regarding his place on the board of directors as a trusteeship. On one occasion a merchant came to him and asked that he recommend the renewal of a $5,000 loan at the bank. Lindell thought it was not a gilt-edge note, so he paid it himself and made a personal loan to the merchant.[1]

The bank was well received. The management was such as to inspire confidence, and before long it became common knowledge that it was being run on much more conservative lines than had been the case with either the Bank of Saint Louis or the Bank of Missouri. Since 1821 the people had become accustomed to a great shortage of currency and had learned to be afraid of such bank notes from other states as found their way into the town. Mexican, French, and Prussian silver were present in limited amounts and were highly valued.[2] Accordingly at first they were a little afraid of the notes of the Branch Bank. This fear, however, soon disappeared. The new bank proved a great aid to the town and, although it attempted to do little business in the country districts, some sub-offices were established. Life in the country was simple; and the small stock of specie brought in by the settlers enabled them to supplement barter, and so to get along in some manner without banking facilities. Saint Louis itself developed a good deal of prosperity. From 1820 to 1830 the population had grown slowly. In addition to the banking handicap, the old French families had been moving to the country, and the hunters were drifting farther westward.[3] The census of 1830 showed a growth of only 2,000 above the previous one. The next decade was to record a 10,000 increase. In the early thirties there was considerable build-

[1] Stevens, *op. cit.* (St. Louis, 1909), p. 294.

[2] Shepard, *op. cit.*, p. 95.

[3] *Ibid.*, p. 95 *et seq.*

ing of stores and warehouses in St. Louis and not a little paving was done. Likely much of this increased activity is directly traceable to the influence of the Branch Bank.

Something of the amount and kind of service rendered by the bank can be seen from its published statements.

On August 1, 1831 O'Fallon reported that his office had but $848.14 in the suspended-debt account and that all of this would likely be collected. It included $342.75 loans on personal security, $500.00 bills of exchange, and $5.39 interest.[1] The highest suspended debt it ever reported was $2712.00 in July, 1834.[2] The loans were largely discounts on personal security, but some advances were made on stocks and bonds, as is evidenced by the following report of March 12, 1832:[3]

Loans on Stocks	*St. Louis Branch March 12, 1832*
Louisiana State Bank	$4,980
Missouri State Stock	5,000
Illinois State Stock	52,500
Missouri Stock Loan	10,000
	$72,480

The office was not opened until late in 1829; so the year ending January 1, 1830 showed net profits of only $595.83. For January 1, 1831 this was increased to $19,949.11, and for January 1, 1832 to $30,464.25.[4]

No small part of the prosperity of the branch was due to the public deposits made necessary by land office, army post, and Indian dealings. They were, as listed:

[1] *House Report, 21st Congress*, Report of Committee on Ways and Means, no. 358, p. 193.

[2] *23rd Congress, 2nd Session, Senate Document 17*, Dec. 18, 1834.

[3] *21st Congress, 1st Session, House Report 358*, Committee on Ways and Means, p. 193. This is a rare document. A copy is in possession of N. Y. Public Library.

[4] *Ibid.*, p. 536.

January 1, 1832	$371.417.86
February 6, 1832	211,571.96
October 15, 1832	161,019.00
July, 1833	160,550.77, *etc.*[1]

Individual deposits ran somewhat higher than Mr. Cadwalader had estimated:

February 6, 1832	$219,572.63
October 15, 1832	221,426.00
July, 1833	281,480.00[1]

The circulation was usually above $800,000.

Comparative statements, more or less complete and taken from the reports of the parent bank to Congress, are given here:

Accounts	*Feb. 6, 1832*[2]	*Oct. 15, 1832*[3]	*July, 1833*[4]
Discounts on personal security	$599,012	$580,000	$478,414
Discounts on stock other than of banks	77,980	27,500	....
Domestic bills of exchange	72,971	88,936	83,789
Due from U. S. Bank and offices	447,890	1,093,403	....
Expense account	1,020	2,299	....
Notes of Bank of U. S. and other branches	1,061,315	616,930	....
Specie	147,970	163,411	285,138
Circulation	844,955	834,410	....
Interest account	9,444	18,391	....
Unclaimed dividends	84	....	....
Due to Bank of U. S. and offices	1,114,009	1,321,357	....
Due to state banks	8,952	16,710	....
U. S. deposits by U. S. Treasurer	181,555	121,691	160,550
Deposits of public officers	30,016	39,328	....
Individual deposits	219,572	221,426	281,480

[1] Compiled from statements quoted elsewhere in this chapter.

[2] *22nd Congress, 1st Session, House Report 460*, p. 267, and *21st Congress, 1st Session, House Report 358*, Committee of Ways and Means, p. 193 *et seq.*

[3] *22nd Congress, 2nd Session, House Document 8*, Letter of Secretary of Treasury, December 11, 1832.

[4] Quoted from reports to Congress in Pope, "Part which Banks have Played in the Commercial Development of the State," p. 89.

Certain other reports were rendered relative to the volume of business transacted. These deal chiefly with bills of exchange, branch drafts, and transfers of specie.

During 1830, $200,000 of London and Paris exchange was sold. The volume, however, was only one-half as great the next year.[1]

In 1832 the following report of total exchange transactions was made:[2]

Domestic Bills purchased	$273,000
Domestic Bills collected	457,000
Branch drafts	795,000
Notes of U. S. Bank received	1,212,000
Transfers for U. S. Treasury	600,000
	$3,337,000

At this time the amount of bills of exchange on hand was $51,001.04. They were payable in eight different cities, thus showing something of the varied business connections of Saint Louis.[3] Exchange rates varied from par to 1%.[4]

[1] *22nd Congress, 1st Session, House Report 460*, p. 208.

[2] *23rd Congress, 2nd Session, Senate Document 17*, Dec. 18, 1834.

[3] Philadelphia, $400; Washington, $250; Cincinnati, $4,650; New York, $10,756.06; Baltimore, $4,080; New Orleans, $8,775; Louisville, $19,-417.99; and Pittsburg, $2,671.99 in *21st Congress, 1st Session, House Report 358*, p. 39.

[4] *Ibid.*, p. 34. Exchange rates for which drafts are sold and bills purchased. St. Louis office:

City	*Drafts Sold*	*Drafts Purchased*
Bank of U. S.	Par a ½	......
Boston	1	......
Hartford	1	......
New York	1	½
Baltimore	¾	½
Washington	....	1
Richmond	1	......
Nashville	....	¾
New Orleans	Par a ½	½
Louisville	Par a ½	½
Lexington	Par a ½	½
Cincinnati	Par a ½	½
Pittsburg	⅓	½

Little specie was transferred to or from the Saint Louis Branch. Usually it did not exceed $1,000 or $2,000 a year.[1] The branch drafts which Benton fought so bitterly, however, were used in considerable volume. On March 26, 1832 the books showed an issue of $318,000, of which amount $86,765 was in the vaults of the bank, thus leaving $231,235 in circulation.[2]

The figures which have been presented here indicate the kind of service the United States Bank was giving Saint Louis. The city appreciated the bank, and the storm which swept it out of existence was not made in Saint Louis. As the tide of political feeling rose, the people began to take sides on the bank question and it became a favorite topic of discussion in the state press. However, it is much to the credit of the Saint Louis Branch that it largely escaped censure. The argument turned on the larger issues of the bank as a national institution.

The Missouri Intelligencer perhaps published more political news relative to the bank fight than any other paper in the state. It was a country newspaper in a district friendly to Jackson, but its editor favored the United States Bank and made full use of his opportunities to plead its case. One gets the impression that the interest of the average Missouri farmer in the bank contest was much less than is indicated by the large amount of newspaper space used. The editors were engaged in spreading propaganda. As late as September, 1831, a reader wrote to *The Intelligencer* that the United States Bank was of little interest in Boone County, and that it had caused no party division.[3] However, the various candidates thought it worth while to make statements about their stand on the

[1] *House Report 460, 22nd Congress, 1st Session*. p. 205.

[2] *Ibid.*, p. 57.

[3] *Mo. Intelligencer*, Sept. 24, 1831.

bank question. General Ashley, candidate for Congress and a director of the Saint Louis Branch Bank, in a letter to the chairman of the Committee of Correspondence of Calloway County said:

I am in favor of rechartering the bank. It is indispensable for commerce . . . . and for the transactions and financial operations of the United States Government. The Bank must be powerful in order to be useful. Its notes are good anywhere. Its influence has forced the local banks to be more honest. Bank failures and depreciated paper are seldom heard of. Drafts have but ¼ of 1 per cent exchange charges. Deposits are safe.[1]

His opponent, Colonel R. W. Wells, was against the bank, but adopted a policy of saying as little about it as possible. L. W. Boggs of Saint Louis, in his candidacy for governor, opposed the bank on constitutional grounds, but admitted that its service to the country had been great. He could not hope to gain St. Louis support without being fair to the Branch Bank. His opponent, Dr. Bull, favored the recharter bill.[2] James McLelland, candidate for lieutenant-governor, advocated the recharter, but believed no branch should be put in any state without its consent.[3] Beginning with the issue of July 30, 1831 *The Intelligencer* carried a sub-title: "The Union, Internal Improvements, Domestic Manufactures, The United States Bank, and Real Reform". From this time on it fought hard for the bank, never missing a chance to copy favorable editorials from other papers or to discourse on the evils of state banking. In the issue of January 26, 1833, after the struggle had been definitely lost, it delivered a last broadside with an editorial on "The

[1] *Mo. Intelligencer*, Sept. 24, 1831. Adapted from letter published in full in this issue.

[2] *Ibid.*, June 2, 1832.

[3] *Ibid.*, May 5, 1832.

Bank Mania". The more important points are given here:[1]

In anticipation of the prostration of the Bank of the United States, Alabama has organized a state bank with $2,000,000 capital and Tennessee one with $3,000,000 capital. The governors of Kentucky and Ohio both recommend state banks. Applications have been made for several new Pennsylvania charters where the Bank of the United States has long been the faithful guardian of business and prosperity. When it shall be laid low, the country will be overrun with a flock of vultures in the shape of state banks and all this for a blind and vindictive hostility.

In Saint Louis the feeling became personal. Senator David Barton and Pettis, a candidate for Congress, made a fight on the United States Bank. Pettis, in particular, had a good deal to say about the integrity of Nicholas Biddle. His brother, Major Thomas Biddle, went to the hotel and whipped Pettis with a "cowhide". The controversy ended in a duel. The men fought with revolvers at a distance of six feet and both were killed.[2] The tragedy caused more comment in the Saint Louis papers than the bank question itself.

The election results showed that rural Missouri, at least, was pro-Jackson. R. W. Wells was nominated for Congress by twenty-six votes to General Ashley's eight. *The Intelligencer* made the claim that Wells was not fundamentally opposed to the bank, but that he fought it merely because it was a part of the Democratic platform.[3] In the presidental election the state, outside of St. Louis, voted for Jackson; but the bank was so vital to St. Louis that Clay carried

[1] Adapted from a lengthy editorial.

[2] Shepard, *op. cit.*, p. 99.

[3] *Mo. Intelligencer*, Oct. 8, 1831.

the city.[1] Jackson, however, received all four of the electoral votes.[1]

The state government took an official interest in the bank question. As early as 1831 the House of Representatives appointed a committee to inquire into the legality of placing a state and county tax on the Branch Bank at Saint Louis.[2] The tax was never levied, but, whether on account of the recognition of the services of the bank, or because of an adverse report of the committee, it is impossible to say. Governor Miller was outspoken in his views. He declared the United States Bank was subversive of free institutions and accordingly impossible.[3] L. W. Boggs had lost the race for governor; and the new executive, Daniel Dunklin, in his first message urged the people, "To fight the United States Bank, for it is only intended to show us the insignificance into which we are dwindling as the general government encroaches".[4] On December 28, 1832 he announced that he had approved a resolution asking Missouri's senators and representatives to oppose the recharter of the national bank.[5]

In the issue of July 31, 1831 *The Intelligencer* announced with glee that the re-charter bill had been passed by both houses of Congress and that General Ashley had voted for it. The following week the veto message was published in full with editorial comments of no uncertain tenor: "The veto is a high-handed measure which will produce a whirlwind from one end of the country to the other. That such an ignorant man as Jackson should attempt to expound the

[1] Pope, *op. cit.*, p. 89, and Shepard, *op. cit.*, p. 110.

[2] *House Jour., 6th General Assembly Mo., 1831*, p. 70.

[3] *Ibid.*, p. 73.

[4] *House Journal 6th General Assembly Mo. 1831*, "Message of the Governor," p. 30.

[5] *House Journal 7th General Assembly Mo. 1832-33*, p. 151.

Constitution is almost unbelievable ".[1] A few days later this additional comment appeared: " The people of the West owe the United States Bank $30,000,000. To call this loan means ruin, and all on account of the ignorance of a single individual ".[2] A good deal of space was used for some weeks in copying indignation editorials from other newspapers and in censuring Senator Benton for his support of Jackson. The President's statements about the solvency of the bank was denounced as most vindictive and derogatory to the high station of the President of the United States.[3]

The veto was received with divided feelings in Saint Louis. The business interests of the city, of course, were greatly disappointed; and at a mass-meeting, presided over by Dr. William Carr Lane, resolved that, " We receive the President's veto with mortification and regret ".[4] A committee, composed of Pierre Chouteau, Edward Bates, and five others was appointed to draw up resolutions commending the bank and censuring Jackson.[5] The President, however, was not without friends in Saint Louis and they were just as outspoken as the other group. A meeting at the City Hall approved the veto message as an act

That will be the death blow to an institution which from its enormous capital would have such a controlling influence as not only to crush at pleasure every moneyed institution but would insinuate its tendencies of corruption into our Congressional halls and sway the councils of the Republic. . . . The stand taken by General Jackson against the moneyed powers of Europe and America is a mark of patriotism and

[1] *Mo. Intelligencer*, July 31, 1832.

[2] *Ibid.*, Aug. 4, 1832.

[3] *Ibid.*, Jan. 1, 1833.

[4] Conrad, *op. cit.*, article on " St. Louis Banking."

[5] Shepard, *op. cit.*, p. 106.

firmness not surpassed since the light of liberty dawned upon our country.[1]

The removal of the deposits caused much local interest. *The Intelligencer* said:

We are curious to know whether the President will withdraw the deposits from the Saint Louis Branch and how he will pay out public money for Indians at this point as there is no other bank in Missouri. In fact we expect to see little hard money.[2]

Early in the next year this same journal printed the McDuffie speeches in Congress concerning the removal of the deposits, and copied notes from other Missouri newspapers on the national depression.[3]

In line with the policy of the home office the Saint Louis Branch began at once to restrict its business, and the contraction caused a considerable amount of adverse comment. *The Intelligencer* said: "We have been friendly to the United States Bank but now we do not hesitate to condemn it. The contraction was excessive and vindictive." [4] Missouri, however, must have escaped most of the national distress. The Saint Louis Branch was officered by local men interested in the business development of the city, and it made the necessary contraction as painless as possible. The files of *The Missouri Republican* (1832 to 1834) contain hardly a word about the removal of the deposits or subse-

[1] Edwards, *op. cit.*, p. 344. The author was unable to find any record of the minutes of either of these meetings. The quotations given in the secondary authorities do not agree so one can be sure of little that transpired except that one group strongly condemned and the other as strongly praised the action of the administration. See also Davis and Durrie, *History of Mo.* (St. Louis, 1876), p. 105.

[2] *Mo. Intelligencer*, Nov. 2, 1833.

[3] *Ibid.*, Feb. 1, 1834.

[4] *Mo. Intelligencer*, Feb. 10, 1834.

quent hardship. *The Intelligencer* had much to say about national aspects but hardly a hint of local hardships. This, though, is not surprising, for the bank had little influence in the country districts. On April 26, 1834 *The Intelligencer* published an article copied from an Illinois paper (whose name is not given), stating that Mr. Amos Lane had said in the House of Representatives that Indiana, Illinois, and Missouri had felt no presure in consequence of the action of the President. It took exception to this statement in these words:

> We freely admit that the pressure here has been very slight compared to the experiences of other states, but there is pressure in Illinois. There is no price and no market for one of the great staples of the country. Wheat will not now be taken in payment of goods by the merchants. . . . In the meantime, pushed by Eastern creditors our merchants collect and remit all the funds they can obtain. This pressure will prevent the usual immigration to the state. We look toward the future with much solicitude.

This statement no doubt applied to some extent to Missouri conditions.

The Branch Bank at Saint Louis began to make plans for liquidation. The president, John O'Fallon, handled it in masterly fashion, and in the final accounting closed the books with a loss to the government of only $125.00.[1] The statement of June 30, 1837 shows how far the liquidation had proceeded on that date:[2]

Bills of exchange	$227,517.00
Due from the Bank of U. S.	392,099.00
Due from state banks	55,019.00
Due to Bank of U. S.	674,792.00
Deposits	723.00
Loans	263.00

[1] Shepard, *op. cit.*, p. 95.

[2] *25th Congress, 2nd Session, Senate Bulletin 21*, p. 230. Statement of St. Louis Branch, June 30, 1837.

The closing of the Branch Bank again left Saint Louis without a bank, a condition she had been in several times before. Good service had been rendered and, although political considerations had prevented full recognition of its usefulness, Saint Louis was never willing to be without a bank again. Measures were instituted at once to secure some sort of a substitute for the closing institution.

B. *The Cincinnati Commercial Agency.*

The substitute found was a branch of the Commercial Bank of Cincinnati, Ohio. As soon as definite decision was made to close the branch of the United States Bank, the Commercial Bank of Cincinnati entered into a contract with the Secretary of the Treasury of the United States, by the terms of which the bank was to become the depositary of public funds for Illinois and Missouri and to perform all other government work that had been cared for by the Branch Bank of the United States. It further agreed to open an office in St. Louis with full discount powers and to transact a general banking business. The contract also provided that the notes of all specie-paying banks in the West, with one or two exceptions, would be received on deposit.[1] Announcement was made in *The Missouri Republican* that the St. Louis office would open on June 15, 1835 to buy and sell bills of exchange, discount paper, and accept deposits.[2]

The Agency was well received in Saint Louis, for it seemed to offer at least partial relief from a bad situation. The newspaper comments, not only in Saint Louis but in the country districts, were favorable without exception. It had evidently won the confidence of the government and

[1] *Mo. Intelligencer*, May 9, 1835, copied from *Mo. Republican* of May 5 1835.

[2] *Ibid.*, May 23, 1835, copied from *Mo. Republican.*

that was enough to insure it a fair trial. The land-office and army-post business would give it a stake worth responsible care. Moreover, John O'Fallon had recommended it as worthy of patronage and was trying to turn business to it. In November he announced that it had purchased the accounts and business of the Branch Bank.[1] It rendered fair service from the first. Exchange was sold at ½ of 1 per cent premium, or about the rate formerly charged by the Branch Bank.[2] In fact it seemed as if an effort were to be made to continue the business along the old lines.

The business available for a banking house was increasing constantly. The report of the local wharfmaster for 1835 showed a river business double that of 1831. The ciy was also increasing in population. It had 15,000 people in 1836.[3]

The Agency was amply able to carry on the work it had undertaken. The home office in Cincinnati made the following statement of condition in January, 1834:[4]

Resources		*Liabilities*	
Specie	$75,967.20	Capital paid up	$1,000,000.00
Notes of other banks	52,574.00	Profits	47,790.30
Due from banks	63,918.61	Circulation	325,892.00
Real estate	2,000.00	Due to banks	16,631.37
Loans	1,282,981.09	Deposits	89,127.23
	$1,477,440.90		$1,477,440.90

In 1836 the Saint Louis office reported specie holdings

[1] *Mo. Intelligencer*, Nov. 7, 1835, and Edwards, *op. cit.*, p. 359.

[2] *Ibid.*, July 11, 1835.

[3] St. Louis at this time was little more than a river trading point. It had no public school, park, theatre, or library. It had no bank except the office of the Agency. See Shepard, *op. cit.*, p. 114.

[4] *House Document 498, 23rd Congress, 1st Session*, Condition of State Banks 1834.

of $513,859.06 and government deposits of $1,978,383.94.[1] So long as the government contract lasted, it had sufficient funds to maintain a big banking business, irrespective of conditions in Cincinnati. By 1837 the specie had decreased to $409,553, total deposits were $2,262,900, and the loan account stood at $1,398,811.[2] On March 3, 1837 the *Missouri Republican* published the following figures for the home office: capital, $1,000,000; circulation, $750,000; loans, $4,000,000; and public deposits, $2,500,000. This last item included the Saint Louis deposits but the branch loans were not listed. At this time the Saint Louis loan was $650,000. Evidently the home office had greatly expanded its business on the basis of the Saint Louis government deposits.[3]

In order to discuss adequately the history of the Agency it will be necessary to anticipate somewhat the course of legislation in Missouri. A state bank had been chartered in 1837 with monopoly privileges. In order to make this effective it was necessary to get rid of the Agency. Even before the State Bank was chartered, the legislature had shown hostility to the existing banking arrangements and a bill providing for their expulsion had been introduced. The Jefferson City correspondent of *The Saint Louis Argus* had reported that prospects for its passage were favorable.[4] Saint Louis had been watching the proceedings of the legislature with much interest. In December, 1836 ex-mayor William Carr Lane offered a resolution in mass-meeting requesting that no action be taken relative to the expulsion of the Agency unless a state bank were first chartered.[5] The

[1] Spaulding, *op. cit.*

[2] Pope, *op. cit.*, p. 89.

[3] *Mo. Republican*, March 11, 1837.

[4] *Mo. Argus*, Jan. 13, 1837.

[5] Stevens, W. B., *Saint Louis the Fourth City*, p. 299.

business interests of the city had learned something about the utility of banks. The expulsion bill did pass, but not until provision had been made for the state bank. The legislature showed little regard for vested rights. The Agency was forced to leave the state although it was fiscal agent and depository for the federal government under a contract which had not yet expired.[1] Sentiment in St. Louis for the most part supported the stand of the legislature. The Agency had been welcomed in the city, but largely because there was nothing better available. It had been prosperous and, although the service given had been satisfactory, local pride was hurt. St. Louis was making money for Cincinnati. Why not perform the service herself and stop paying tribute to a rival city?

However keenly the Agency may have felt toward the injustice of the law, there was nothing to do but obey it; and on May 23, 1837 the following notice was made public:[2]

> Persons having notes due in June or July (renewable), may renew by paying 10% and interest before the board meets 9 a. m. May 29th for 90 days or four months. Depositors have been notified by advertisement to call for their balances. If not called for they will be transferred to Cincinnati. We close at the end of the month in obedience to law.
>
> W. C. Anderson, agent.

The next week announcement was made that the local debt had been transferred to Cincinnati and payment would be expected on reasonable terms. It offered to accept 5 per cent installments. *The Missouri Republican,* commenting on the plan to force payment, said: " This closing act of the Agency deprived it of respect. Few people will regret its disappearance. It had no interests in common with us ".[3]

[1] *Mo. Republican,* Feb. 8, 1837.

[2] *Ibid.,* May 25, 1837.

[3] *Ibid.,* June 2, 1837.

The debt referred to here was only a small part of its portfolio, for the newly organized State Bank had purchased most of its $550,000 debt three months earlier. The Agency, not being in a position to drive a hard bargain, decided to take the best offer it could get and leave the state without a contest. During the negotiations, however, it had threatened to transfer all its specie to Cincinnati and force payment on every note as it matured unless its terms were met. The State Bank agreed to accept its deposits, to assume all its local obligations, and to purchase its building and furniture at a cost valuation. The Agency, on its part, agreed to send no more specie to Cincinnati and to cease all business in the state.[1]

Missouri had passed through a varied banking experience. She had seen all the inconveniences of barter and the dangers of "wild-cat" currency. She had issued none of the latter herself, but her neighbors had supplied the deficiency. There had been two local banks in St. Louis but both had failed, due largely to the inexperience of their managers. There had been a period of makeshift private banking. The Loan Office had been tried as an experiment in debtor relief and it had ended in disaster. So far there had been little in her history to develop a sentiment favorable to banks. Then in 1829 had come the Branch Bank and, after its closing, there had been two years of the Cincinnati Agency. The former was clouded by political considerations and the latter suffered the disadvantage of being an alien from a rival city; yet both gave honest service and taught St. Louis and the state that banks could not well be dispensed with. Now all of these were out of the way, leaving nothing behind them but some lessons of experience. The new State Bank was to have a clear field—a chance to demonstrate what it could do to serve the state.

[1] *Mo. Republican*, March 11, 1837.

PART II

THE PERIOD OF MONOPOLY

CHAPTER V

THE DEMAND FOR A STATE BANK

THE State Bank of Missouri was not organized by a group of impulsive politicians who wished to get for the state a share of the federal business to be distributed after the closing of the United States Bank; neither was it organized to provide a place to invest Missouri's share of the Surplus Revenue of 1836. Both of these factors no doubt had their influence, but the demand for a state bank was much more fundamental than this. Banking questions had been considered pretty constantly since 1813. The earlier experiences, described in chapters III and IV, were attempts at solution of local banking problems. The attitude of those in authority was always one of caution. The first constitution, adopted June 12, 1820, reflects the unhappy experiences connected with the failure of the Bank of Saint Louis.[1] It provided that the General Assembly might incorporate one banking company, and no more, to be in operation at the same time, such bank to have not more than five branches, only one of which could be established at any one session of the General Assembly. The maximum capital authorized was $5,000,000, and one-half of this was to be reserved for the state.[2] The Senate Finance Committee reported a bill for the organization of such a bank November 13, 1820, but it met with scant

[1] See Wetmore's *Gazetteer of Mo.* (St. Louis, 1837).

[2] *Constitution of 1820*, art. vii, quoted in *Mo. Intelligencer*, Aug. 12, 1820.

favor.[1] It was to require seventeen years of discussion to put this constitutional provision into effect.

One of the first acts of Alexander McNair, first state governor, was to call a special session of the General Assembly for June, 1821 to consider the financial situation of the state. McNair's connection with the Bank of Missouri gave him a peculiar interest in financial problems.[2] No one seemed to know just what action was contemplated; but rumor had it that an attempt would be made to organize a state bank under the constitutional authority of 1820. The governor himself was silent. The newspapers at once began to make conjectures and it became evident that sentiment was divided largely on town or country lines. Saint Louis wanted a bank; the rural districts were skeptical. *The Intelligencer* voiced the feelings of the latter, and on April 20 submitted three reasons why a state bank should not be established: (a) Missouri had no money and could only get it by a loan at 5 per cent or 6 per cent so where would the profit be? (b) a bank would chiefly aid the president and directors for they would have the first chance to borrow the funds; and (c) collections could be made only at the end of a law-suit and that would be an expense to the state.[3] Later, it characterized the bank proposition as a machine without capital for the purpose of making money without the aid of gold,[4] and argued that it would encourage extravagant buying outside the state. The thing to do was rather to live simply and work for economic self-sufficiency.[5] Copious extracts were taken from the Kentucky newspapers

[1] *Senate Journal, 1st General Assembly Mo.*, 1820, p. 114.

[2] See Sec. C of chapter iii for a discussion of the problems demanding solution.

[3] *Mo. Intelligencer*, April 20, 1821.

[4] *Ibid.*, May 21, 1821.

[5] *Ibid.*, July 9, 1821.

to show how banking was ruining the credit of the state and forcing the people to labor to enrich a bank aristocracy.[1]

The arguments presented seem to have carried conviction. The citizens of Franklin called a mass-meeting at the court house, protested against the special session on account of the cost, and resolved that, " In the opinion of the meeting, the establishment of a state bank at this time, so far from promoting the good of the community, would only lead to the support of a host of bank officers, speculators, and swindlers at the expense of the honest and industrious part of society.[2] In Howard and Chariton Counties mass meetings were also held, and a specie bank condemned. It was suggested that, if the state must have a bank, the solution might be to invest $500,000 in the stock of the fast declining Bank of Missouri and amend the charter so specie payments could be suspended. The notes could then be made legal tender.[3]

Meanwhile Saint Louis business interests, speaking through the *Missouri Gazette,* were demanding that the special session charter a bank. Their plan provided for a capital issue of $500,000, the whole amount to be owned by the state. St. Louis was to have the home office, but branches were to be located at Franklin and Jackson. The executive heads and boards of directors of all three offices were to be appointed by the legislature. The method outlined for securing the capital was to borrow $500,000 on the credit of the state at 6 per cent interest and on this security to issue $900,000 of circulation. It was thought that the bank might be opened with safety at once, but that its currency should not be redeemable until the loan was floated. Loans were to be limited to 90 days, not more than $2,000

[1] *Mo. Intelligencer,* May 14, 1821.

[2] *Ibid.,* May 21, 1821.

[3] *Ibid.,* June 4, 1821.

to any one person, interest rates at 10 per cent, and no loans except on real-estate collateral to double the amount of the loan.[1] Commenting on this proposition, *The Intelligencer* suggested that the directors would soon borrow all the money, break the bank, and leave the farmers to pay the bills.[2] Saint Louis was looking for an easy way out of debt, but as yet had little comprehension of the principles of sound banking.

When the legislature met it soon became evident that no bank bill could be passed .The Saint Louis plan was rejected without ceremony. The final outcome was the Loan-Office Bill, discussed in chapter IV, section C. The Loan Office now became the all-absorbing topic and little was heard about a state bank for ten years. The files of *The Intelligencer,* 1824 to the end of 1829, contain nothing to indicate that it was being discussed. The Loan Office, however, was a serious attempt to face existing financial questions and, while it was a total failure, the attempt and the discussion aroused by it had a large place in moulding the character of the later legislation.

After 1829 the presence of the Branch Bank in Saint Louis tended to keep down the demand for state legislation, but it also had the effect of producing an unprecedented demand when it became known that the Branch was to be closed. Saint Louis was never again to be willing to depend on forwarding houses and makeshift private banks.[3]

[1] *Mo. Gazette,* May 2, 1821.

[2] *Mo. Intelligencer,* Oct. 9, 1821.

[3] The forwarding house had indeed rendered a service not to be despised between 1821 and the opening of the Branch Bank. The following advertisement is typical: *Mo. Intelligencer,* Nov. 6, 1830.

"The undersigned are prepared, having extensive warehouses at the steam-boat landing, to receive, store, or forward every description of goods. Liberal advances will be made on consignments for sale or shipment.—Keen and Page."

Late in 1832 *The Intelligencer* again took up the bank fight. Governor Miller had shown a disposition to favor a state institution to replace the closing United States Branch Bank. *The Intelligencer* argued that the people had had their Bank of Saint Louis, Bank of Missouri, and Loan Office, so could not be expected to be willing to try another experiment.[1] A week later it expressed fear that the new legislature might be led astray, but insisted that the people strongly opposed a bank. The editor said he had just returned from a trip over a large part of Howard, Boone, and Cooper Counties, and had kept his ears open. He reported considerable interest and anxiety, but great disapproval. He pledged his paper to fight all such swindling institutions.[2] In placing a valuation on this evidence, it should be remembered that *The Intelligencer* was an organ of the United States Bank and so opposed to any and all state banking legislation. At any rate, early in the next year, its Jefferson City correspondent wrote that the friends of the bank were rallying and rapidly gaining force due to the widespread fear that there would be no reliable media of exchange after the Branch Bank closed. The stock argument was that a state bank would be the best way to meet the emergency. *The Intelligencer,* commenting editorially on this letter, admitted the ruin that would be wrought by Jackson's action, but refused the remedy and characterized the new state banks now being discussed in Missouri and other states as vultures ready to pounce upon the people once the United States Bank was gone.[3] Not enough evidence is available for positive statements on the rural bank sentiment at this time. Occasional mass meetings were

[1] *Mo. Intelligencer*, Dec. 8, 1832.

[2] *Ibid.*, Dec. 15, 1832.

[3] *Ibid.*, Jan. 12, 1833.

held in the state. One in Randolph County indorsed the proposed bank, while another at Fayette opposed it.[1] Meanwhile the Seventh General Assembly had convened in Jefferson City and legislation was being planned. Although Governor Miller was supposed to be in favor of a state bank, he tried to avoid making political enemies, and in his message merely said: "It has been suggested that a state bank be established. Whether that is wise or not, I will leave to your judgment .If it is done, school money may be put into it as follows:

$40,000	3 per cent Fund
63,000	Seminary and Saline Funds
36,000	School Funds
$139,000	

It should be a good investment". He did, however, take occasion to say that the United States Bank was subversive of free institutions.[2]

The Senate took no action on the bank question except to send one of its members, William Carr Lane, to Saint Louis to interview representative business men on the feeling in Saint Louis.[3]

In the House the discussion centered on the proper means of investing the state funds. A select committee was appointed to investigate the matter. It recommended a bank. The amount found available for investment differed from the governor's estimate by $21,000.[4] However, it was stated that some bonds were yet unsold, so the total might reach $150,000. The committee reasoned as follows:

[1] *Mo. Intelligencer*, Jan. 12 and 26, 1833.

[2] *Senate Journal, 7th General Assembly, Mo.*, 1832-33, p. 198.

[3] *Mo. Intelligencer*, Feb. 2, 1833.

[4] Principal of state funds, $39,000 Seminary; $23,000 Saline; and $56,000 3 per cent fund.

(a) There was no pressing need requiring the expenditure of the state funds. Therefore they were available for investment of the proper sort.

(b) These funds should not be left unemployed. To allow state money to lie idle meant, in fact, to withdraw it from the circulating media of the country; and there was no room for loss, since it was almost certain that the United States Bank would not be rechartered.

(c) Except for United States Bank notes currency circulating in the state was unworthy of use. It consisted largely of the issues of banks outside of the state which had filtered in and, of course, could not be regulated effectively.

On the basis of these facts the committee recommended a state bank founded on specie capital, insisting that such a bank, if prudently managed, would surely show a profit. The state could borrow the school funds with little risk, but should pledge their repayment with 6 per cent interest. As the new bank would likely make from 7 to 10 per cent, this should be easy. Numerous reasons were advanced why the bank should be profitable. There were no adequate facilities existing within the state or near it. A bank would serve all of Missouri and most of Illinois. It would have no competition. Moreover, there was not enough massed capital to make a dangerous run possible. The notes would be returned in small amounts by individuals and, owing to the scarcity of coin, would be used in trading and not often presented for redemption. The need for a government fiscal agency to care for the Indian business, should the Branch Bank close, was emphasized. Moreover, it was pointed out that the fur business and the Santa Fé trade would insure the bank a profitable business in exchange. The initial capital suggested was $500,000, it being thought that not more could be profitably used at once because the Branch

Bank might be expected to remain open until the expiration of the charter. The capital could be increased as the demand arose. In order to bring in outside funds and to insure credit away from home, it was suggested that some of the stock be sold outside the state. It was argued that a specie-paying bank was particularly desirable at this time; for, with the disappearance of the United States Bank, irredeemable notes would flood the state. Probably a state bank could not prevent this entirely, but at least it could set standards. The management problem was not expected to be difficult because it was pointed out that the Branch Bank had been run successfully for four years by Missourians, and in addition there were many people in the state familiar with the principles of sound banking. The committee evidently was trying to recommend a safe plan. To guard against insolvency and to keep the notes on a specie basis, it was suggested that one-half the capital be paid in gold and silver before opening and the rest within one year in the same manner. Circulation was to be restricted to the amount of the paid-up capital for the first two years, after which time it might exceed that amount by 50 per cent. It was thought, however, that the legislature might safely be given the right to suspend this rule in case of emergency. Protection for the state's interests could be secured by at least five state directors to be appointed by the legislature, and by state examinations with power to recommend judicial proceedings of liquidation in case of violation of the charter. Eight private directors were recommended in order to attract investment. The committee strongly recommended that an act embodying these provisions be drawn up and passed at once; for, if left undone for two years, capitalists would have found other use for their money, and the advantage of getting started before the confusion, inevitably to follow the closing of the United States Bank, would be lost. Moreover, in such a time of confusion, well considered legislation would be all but impossible.[1]

The opposition, however, was too strong. The report, by a vote of 28 to 20, was referred to the next General Assembly, and an appropriation to print copies for general distribution was refused.[2]

Meanwhile Daniel Dunklin, a strong supporter of the Jackson policies, had been elected governor by a majority of 1100. Inauguration took place before the adjournment of the legislature.[3] In his address he urged an unceasing war on the United States Bank.[4] During the campaign he had fought the state-bank idea, so it seemed likely that he would not support any banking legislation.[5] At any rate the matter was dropped and the legislature adjourned without having done more than discuss the problem.

For a short time after the adjournment there was little agitation of the bank question, but Jackson's removal of the deposits from the United States Bank started the discussion all over again. By November, 1833 a peristent demand had arisen for a special session to reconsider the bank bill. *The Intelligencer* ventured the prediction that, unless a new United States Bank were chartered, the states would all try banking experiments and all go bankrupt.[6] On the 16th of November it quoted two other papers (*The Republican* and *Courier*) as demanding a special session, but insisted that public opinion was anti-bank and that the

[1] "Report of Select Committee to consider Proper Means of Investing State Funds by Chartering a Bank or Otherwise," *House Jour.*, 1832-33, *7th General Assembly Mo.*, pp. 258-261.

[2] *Mo. Intelligencer*, Feb. 16, 1833.

[3] Rader, Perry S., *History of Missouri* (Columbia, Mo., 1898), p. 217.

[4] *Senate Journal, 7th General Assembly Mo.*, p. 30.

[5] *Mo. Intelligencer*, Dec. 7, 1833.

[6] *Ibid.*, Nov. 9, 1833.

regular session a year hence should be awaited.[1] However, doubt began to creep into the mind of the editor and he stated, "If the people want a state bank, let their will be done, but we doubt it".[2] *The Missouri Republican* refused to consider the issue dead, and reported that a petition for a state bank was being circulated among the merchants and was being largely signed.[3] It was not long before all the papers were much concerned. *The Salt River Journal* demanded a special session. *The Palmyra Courier* thought a state bank with five branches judiciously located would give facilities to all customers at fair rates and argued that the prevailing high interest rates were evidence enough of the need for a bank.[4] *The Missouri Republican* was not certain of the wisdom of a special session, for it believed nothing would come out of it.

We ought to find out how the legislature stands before we say too much. They have previously been uniformly and pertinaciously opposed to all banks. At last session, so far as we can ascertain, about one-half of the members of the House were opposed to banks "in toto". There was another and less honest portion who saw the advantages of the bank and would support it if they could make it a political machine. The rest were real friends and wanted to fill the gap left by the loss of the Saint Louis Branch of the United States Bank. This last group introduced a bank bill and aimed to vote against it if it got into politics. Is it reasonable to suppose that any bill could be passed under such circumstances? Has the Senate been more friendly and is there any indication of a change in either house? The only hope is to elect a different sort of a legislature.[5]

[1] *Mo. Intelligencer*, Nov. 16, 1833.

[2] *Ibid.*, Nov. 30, 1833.

[3] *Ibid.*, Nov. 22, 1833, copied from *Mo. Republican.*

[4] *Ibid.*, Dec. 7, 1833.

[5] *Ibid.*, Dec. 14, 1833, copied from *Mo. Republican.*

The Palmyra Courier kept on discussing the subject in every issue. It supported Saint Louis, arguing that the rural districts had had no such chance as Saint Louis to speak with authority on the utility of banks; that paper banks had caused all the trouble; that they were no argument against honest institutions; and that, since Society required a paper circulation, the State should be required to manage the banks and keep them sound.[1]

There seemed to be much sanity in the contention of *The Republican* that a special session would be ineffective. There was no doubt of the hostility of the governor, nor that he had had the support of the majority of the lower house. The Senate had not come to a vote on the question, but it had shown no pro-bank sentiment. Worse yet, the friends of the bank in both houses were uncertain just what kind of an institution they wished to have. The excesses of the Illinois banks had done much to encourage anti-bank feeling.

The discussion finally became so heated that Governor Dunklin wrote an open letter to the *Jeffersonian Republican* (Jefferson City) explaining his refusal to convene the Assembly in special session. He said in part:

The state bank question was up last session and a majority of the representatives acting under the full conviction that the charter of the United States Bank would not be renewed, refused to charter a state bank. Since that time nothing has happened but the removal of the deposits, which gives foundation for a special appeal to the Assembly. I do not see what that has to do with it. It may force the federal government to provide places of deposit in some of the states, but that is their business, and we as a state have nothing to do with it. The framers of the federal constitution never designed that the fiscal operations of the government should

[1] *Mo. Intelligencer*, Dec. 14, 1833 copied from *Palmyra Courier*.

be dependent on state legislation. To call a special session is to indirectly censure the government for the removal of the deposits. Except for that act there would have been no demand for a special session. I am unwilling to believe that the people of the state, after receiving the President's veto upon the bank bill with acclamation, are disposed to censure the act. There is no evidence to induce the belief that a majority of the people of the state wish an extra session. A full persuasion rests on my mind that a very respectable proportion of them are opposed to all banks; and their objections based on former Missouri experience seem well founded. Our first trial was the Bank of Saint Louis, 1816, and the last the Loan Office, created by the extra session of 1820; and during these years we discover no improvement in this system of legalized swindling. Another fact discreditable to banking is the inducement it holds out to mankind to commit crimes of forgery and counterfeiting money which is more aggravating by falling on those least able to bear it. The laboring class from inexperience are usually the sufferers. We must not lose sight of the heavy losses which commodities sustain from failures of banks. . . . I do not wish to be understood as saying that safe banking is not possible. A bank is useful in a wealthy state where many people have no active use for their money, but Missouri is not in such a condition. Our people have but little capital, and that is rather equally distributed. Those who have money can invest it more profitably than in State Bank stock. Small loans can be made privately on good security at 10 per cent. Why then invest in bank stock which will pay 5 or 6 per cent? It is better for people to pay high interest rates than to take the risk of running a bank, etc.

He argued that a note issue would do nothing toward making money plentiful for cash must be kept on hand for redemption (he seems to think 100 per cent). Aside from this he expressed doubt that the legislature would pass a bank bill if called together, for all the present arguments were presented then and yet only twenty voted for the bank. More than that, these twenty were divided hopelessly regarding the sort of a bank they wanted. Some thought the state should elect a majority of the directors, others thought it should be a people's bank. Some wanted to make the shareholders jointly and severally liable for the debts of the bank, others wanted a corporate limitation. The argument that a bank was necessary to provide a suitable investment for the Seminary fund was becoming of less importance, for 3 per cent of it had been distributed to the counties and a part of it had been applied to the payment of the state debt. The sum available would be at least $80,000 less than when the legislature adjourned. More than that the cost of a special session would be too great.[1]

Commenting on this letter, *The Intelligencer* said it contained ample reason to convince any unprejudiced mind of the impolicy of convening the legislature at this time for the purpose of establishing a state bank. It, however, took violent exception to his statement about the veto: "If the governor means by the people receiving the veto with acclamation a few noisy office-seeking politicians we do not controvert him; but if he means a majority of the yeomanry of the state, we demand proof. Our congressional elections are the only criterion and they show the opposite.[2]

The state press was somewhat divided on the bank question. St. Louis papers showed the greatest interest and usually favored a state bank. *The Intelligencer* was the most active of the rural opposition sheets. It is difficult to say just how the sentiment was divided. *The Intelligencer* made the claim that much of the agitation was in the minds of the editors and that, outside of Saint Louis, a large percentage of the people had not taken sides.[3] *The Jeffer-*

[1] *Mo. Intelligencer*, Jan. 14, 1834. Copied from *Jeffersonian Republican.* The last part is adapted, the letter being too long for reproduction in full here.

[2] *Ibid.*, Feb. 18, 1834.

[3] *Ibid.*, Dec. 4, 1833.

sonian Republican was quite active, but its capitol-city location may go far to explain that. On May 9, 1835 it printed what was probably an inspired article, stating that nothing could induce Governor Dunklin to call a special session except a vote at the polls next election with the question put as to the sort of a bank wanted. The Governor came in for a great deal of personal recrimination. He was accused of being a tool of the United States Bank and of "uniting with it in an effort to crush the West by refusing the aid of a state bank for their relief.[1] *The Intelligencer* refused to make such a charge but expected to see only ruin come out of the existing financial arrangements.[2]

At least enongh newspaper comment has been given to show that the bank question was being largely discussed and would surely be an issue in the coming legislature.

When the Eighth General Assembly met, interest in the state-bank question was intense. Governor Dunklin made known his attitude in his opening message. The section dealing with the bank is essentially as follows:

Of course many of you are here feeling that your constituents demand a state bank. I am opposed to the whole system of paper money as inexpedient. If the stockholders are not made individually responsible for redemption, there is grave danger. Organizing a company to issue paper money brings up grave constitutional questions regarding the power of the state to emit bills of credit. I think it at least should include bank notes. Chartering a bank will not help, for a state cannot do indirectly what it is prohibited from doing directly. The Bank of the United States is being much discussed now. In September, 1833 the public deposits were removed and put in state banks. Some thought this made it

[1] *Mo. Courier*, Jan. 24, 1834.

[2] *Mo. Intelligencer*, Feb. 1, 1834.

necessary to have a bank in the state and petitioned the Assembly. It would help the government and relieve business pressure. But banks issuing paper money are not the safest depositories for gold and silver. The government must take care of its own money. It is not the duty of any state to establish a bank for the convenience of the general government if contrary to its own interests.[1]

The governor's message made it clear that he would actively oppose the passage of any legislation looking toward the establishment of a bank of issue. After some days of fruitless discussion, the Senate voted to ask him for advice on the proper investment of the school funds. He replied that a bank made free from imposition on the people would in his opinion be satisfactory. He proposed that a bank be chartered with all privileges, except note issue, arguing that the business of exchange and government deposits would insure a profit of more than 5%. He also implied that he would not oppose a bank of issue if shareholders were made individually liable for the circulation.[2]

The suggestions of the governor met with scant favor. The friends of the bank were not at all agreed as to the details of the proposed charter, but all wished it to have the issue function and felt that the imposition of individual liability would prevent the sale of private stock. As it seemed quite certain that the governor would veto any bill contrary to his suggestions, the prospects for a state bank were not bright. The shortage of currency, however, was becoming alarming and many people were talking of emigrating. *The Intelligencer* constantly commented on the dearth of specie, and the untrustworthiness of such currency as did exist.[3] This condition of affairs spurred the

[1] Message of Gov. Dunklin, *Journal Senate Mo., 8th General Assembly*, 1834-35, pp. 17-22; also reported in *Mo. Intelligencer*, Nov. 22, 1834.

[2] *Mo. Intelligencer*, Jan. 31, 1835.

[3] See particularly Jan. 31, Feb. 21, and May 2, 1835.

friends of the bank idea to attempt to override the opposition of the governor.

Early in January, 1835 Mr. O'Neil of Saint Louis introduced a bill providing for a bank of issue with a capital of $1,000,000 in 10,000 shares of $100 each. The state was to take one-half the stock and the rest was to be sold within the state if possible. In case of failure to sell $500,000 stock in the state, subscription books were to be opened in New York. The circulation was to be limited to the amount of the capital stock, and made redeemable in gold or silver. The shareholders were to assume individual liability for circulation proportional to the amount of stock held. In case of suspension state deposits might be removed.[1] This bill was evidently an attempt on the part of Saint Louis business interests to meet the governor half way.

This bill, however, did not secure the support of the friends of the governor and, after a conference, another bill was introduced. It provided for a bank of discount, deposit and exchange, but without the issue function.

The capital was to be $1,000,000, entirely owned by the state. In addition to the $150,000 in the various school funds, the governor was empowered to borrow $850,000 by means of a bond issue, running not to exceed thirty years, at not to exceed 5% interest. This would provide a capital of $1,000,000. The profits from the $850,000 bond-issue stock were to be credited to the common school fund and those from the $150,000 to higher education.[2]

The bill was referred to the committee of the whole, and on February 9, 1835 it reported in favor of the general idea of a state-owned bank for the sole purpose of maintaining a sound currency. The plan of putting all profits into the

[1] *Mo. Intelligencer*, Jan. 24, 1835.

[2] *Senate Jour., 8th General Assembly Mo.*, 1834-35, p. 235.

school fund was also indorsed. It was estimated that a net addition of $50,000 should thus be made annually to the fund. Saint Louis was suggested as the proper location in order to assist in caring for federal business. No agreement, however, could be reached on the details of the plan of organization; South Carolina, Georgia, and Mississippi were cited as examples of what might be done.[1]

Not considering this a satisfactory outcome the bill was referred to a select committee of five members. An amendment was offered and passed by a vote of 15 to 9 to divert the profits from the school fund to the state treasury and to use them for general state expenses, thus reducing taxation. On March 11, 1835 the committee was ordered to make a report and, upon refusal, the bill was postponed indefinitely by a vote of 14 to 5.[2] On March 21, 1835 a bill was passed providing for a bank without issue rights to be exclusively owned an controlled by the state.

The governor had been able to force his ideas on the Senate, but he was to lose in the House.[3] Meanwhile the House had began consideration of a bank bill. On December 31, 1834 a resolution was passed affirming the constitutional right of the General Assembly to establish a state bank and declaring that it was deemed expedient to establish one at this time.[4] The House plan provided for a bank with a capital of $800,000 in $100 shares. One-half was to be sold to private in-

[1] *Mo. Intelligencer*, Feb. 21, 1835.

[2] *Senate Journal, 8th General Assembly, Mo.*, p. 295.

[3] *Mo. Intelligencer*, March 21, 1835.

[4] *Constitution of Mo.*, 1820, art viii, "The General Assembly may incorporate one banking company and no more to be in operation at the same time. The bank to be incorporated may have any number of branches not to exceed five, no more than one to be established at any one session of the Assembly. The capital stock must not exceed $5,000,000, one-halt to be reserved to the state."

dividuals to be paid for in installments in the current money of the United States.[1] The other half was to be reserved for the state to be paid for at its option either like the private stock or by an issue of bonds bearing 6 per cent interest payable semi-annually. The state might sell its stock at any time, provided not more than $100,000 were sold in any one year. Management was to be in the hands of twelve directors representing both state and private stock in proportion to the shares owned by each. All must be citizens of Missouri and of the United States; and, in case of removal from the state, sale of stock, or bankruptcy, their offices were to be declared vacant. The term was two years. The legislature was to elect the president from the membership of the board. Numerous provisions were provided to increase the safety of the institution. No loans were to be made on the security of the stock and directors were to receive no discount privileges not enjoyed by any other customer of equal financial rating. Notes of denominations less than five dollars were prohibited. Dividends were to be paid only from profits and were not to exceed six per cent until the surplus should equal 2 per cent of the capital. An annual statement was to be published and, in addition, full reports were to be made to each house of the legislature each session. It was also provided that an examination committee of the legislature might have access to the books at any time. In case of suspension of specie payments the entire assets were to be placed in the hands of trustees for the benefit of creditors. The notes of the bank were not given exclusive monopoly rights; but only notes of the United States Bank or of state banks in denominations of $20.00 or above were to be allowed to circulate in the state. The state agreed to receive its notes for all debts

[1] This would have allowed payments in state bank notes.

due to itself and to deposit its funds in the bank. In payment for this the bank was to furnish free transfer of public funds and to act as fiscal agent for the state. An assessment of twenty-five cents a share was to be made in lieu of all taxation. It was to be allowed to open as soon as $200,000 private stock had been sold and fully paid. The charter was to expire January 1, 1855, but two years were to be allowed for liquidation. There were no definite reserve requirements or limitation of the amount of issue. Little was said about the type of loans to be allowed. The bank was to be an asset currency institution but without any carefully worked out scheme of regulation of the assets. It is probably unfair, however, to apply stringent criticism to this and other plans of the Eighth Legislature, for they were usually merely preliminary drafts and did not reach the stage of final passage.

This bill met no better fate than those of the Senate. It was referred to a committee on December 10, 1834. On January 12th the committee reported that nothing had been done. On the 16th it reported that work was being done but was not yet completed, and asked for more time. The extension was granted, and on January 21, 1835 it reported that, in the judgment of the commitee, it was inexpedient to establish a bank of discount, deposit, and circulation at the present session. The report was accepted by a vote of 36 to 25.[1]

At this juncture private parties in Lexington and Mayville petitioned for charters for independent banks, but were refused.[2]

The Burch Bill, embodying the ideas of the governor, having passed the Senate, was now introduced into the

[1] *House Journal, Eighth General Assembly, Mo.*, 1834-35, pp. 96-97-98 for full report of the attempted legislation.

[2] *Mo. Intelligencer*, Jan. 24, 1835.

House. It was rejected without ceremony on the first reading.[1]

On April 11, 1835 the legislature adjourned, no bank legislation having passed either house. There is little doubt that the active opposition of Govenor Dunklin was responsible for the failure. In the light of subsequent developments, however, it will be important to recall that Missouri had seriously attacked the banking and currency problem as early as 1835.

Saint Louis business men at once began to plan along other lines. An attempt was made to get the State Bank of Illinois to open an office on the river opposite the city. As an inducement the merchants offered to purchase a large block of stock.[2] The proposition at first was considered favorably, but later was declined under legal advice.[3] A good deal of interest was aroused by the rumor that a certain Eastern capitalist expected to send $1,500,000 to Saint Louis to be loaned in the state at 8%. However, nothing came of it and the people turned again to the idea of a state bank. A demand for a special session arose on the ground that opinion was changing. The Cooper County representatives were quoted in the *Boonville Herald* as saying that they voted against the bank believing the people wanted them to do so, but that they would gladly reverse their votes if given the opportunity.[4] It is impossible to tell how far sentiment had really changed at this time, but all the forces of business depression, currency shortage, and political uncertainty were combining to make Missouri citizens wish to find some stable basis for business. *The Intelligencer* declared it was labor lost to try to collect debts.[5]

[1] *Mo. Intelligencer*, Feb. 21, 1835.

[2] *Ibid.*, April 11, 1835.

[3] *Ibid.*, Nov. 7, 1835.

[4] Copied from *Boonville Herald* in *Mo. Intelligencer*, May 9, 1835.

[5] *Ibid.*, May 9, 1835.

The coming of the Cincinnati Commercial Agency to Saint Louis somewhat stilled the demand for a special session. It promised that at least some facilities would exist for the transaction of business. It was evident, however, that the next legislature would have to meet very strong pressure from the advocates of the state bank.

CHAPTER VI

The Passage of the Bank Bill

Saint Louis business interests were becoming more and more insistent in their demands for banking legislation. The Cincinnati Agency was taking care of immediate needs, but it was regarded as a foreign organization to be tolerated only until better arrangements could be made. Benton's "hard money" ideas gained wide acceptance, and the *City Directory* of 1834 announced with joy that gold and silver generally were used for local payments. However, the city grew steadily from 1834 to 1837 and the "hard money" became more and more inadequate. The efficiency of the Branch Bank had made many converts to banking and, in spite of the opposition of Benton, the Chamber of Commerce had petitioned Congress to establish another national bank.[1] Illinois institutions had been asked to open Saint Louis offices. Persistent lobbying had been carried on in both the Seventh and Eighth Legislatures. Illinois notes were appearing in the city and were being accorded a welcome. The Branch Bank had received them on deposit, and the policy was continued by the Agency. They were also received at the land offices.[2] By 1836 the Illinois notes had become so numerous as largely to displace the specie circulation and to cause much concern as to the stability of business. It was evident to all observers that the failure of

[1] *Mo. Argus*, Aug. 5, 1836.

[2] See *Mo. Intelligencer*, Aug. 1 and Oct. 21, 1835.

the Eighth Legislature to pass a banking law had only served to intensify the demand, and that a strong fight for a bank would be made again at the next session.

Lilburn W. Boggs, in announcing his candidacy for governor, came out strongly for a state bank. His political card in *The Argus* said: [1]

> I am aware that objections numerous and weighty have been urged, but nothing better has been presented to my mind. Banking is unrepublican, but so interwoven with our business that it can't be interrupted without great inconvenience. It is an impetus to trade. Missouri is the only state without a bank, so we are at the mercy of the money of other states. We get all the evils of a state bank and none of the benefits.

The Argus supported the bank campaign, but *The Republican* was hostile. In a short time a lively newspaper fight had developed. *The Argus* professed to be opposed to all banks in principle but thought the peculiar business needs of Saint Louis demanded increased facilities and that a well planned state bank would be the surest way to avoid business derangement.[2] It attacked *The Republican* for allowing anti-bank propaganda to appear in its columns and appealed to the business men of the city to withdraw advertising from it. The fight between the two papers did not end with the organization of the bank. *The Argus* accused *The Republican* of attempting to hinder the sale of the state bonds and questioned its loyalty as a Saint Louis citizen.[3] Mention is made of this newspaper contest in order to suggest the difficulty of arriving at a clear conception of statewide public opinion. The country papers of the period, for the most part, have not been preserved. However,

[1] Announcement in *The Argus*, May 20, 1836.

[2] June 17, 1836.

[3] Aug. 25, 1837.

in the course of the campaign, the Saint Louis papers found occasion to quote quite liberally from them. *The Argus* maintained that every Democratic paper in the state, with the exception of the *Jeffersonian Republican* (Jefferson City), agreed that a state bank was the only solution, and that the new legislature could be depended upon to meet the issue.[1] By December the bank question was the chief topic of street talk in the city and the pro-bank party seemed to be largely in the majority. *Wetmore's Gazetteer* (written in 1836, but not published until the next year) was jubilant over the impending prosperity due to the state bank which would surely be organized by the coming legislature.[2] The conservative element, representing the friends of Governor Dunklin, had suggested that stockholders must be made individually liable for the circulation. *The Argus* had replied that such a procedure would ruin the bank, for no man of intelligence would have anything to do with it.[3] In this statement it unquestionably reflected the prevailing public sentiment.

Election day had demonstrated that Saint Louis at least knew what it wanted. All the new members elected from the city, eight in all, had pledged themselves to support a state bank.[4] A pro-bank governor had been elected. The bank had been the chief election issue. *The Argus* had said editorially that only the presence of the Cincinnati Commercial Agency had kept the grass out of the streets of the city.[5] More banking power was needed if Saint Louis was to enjoy a healthy growth.

[1] Sept. 16, 1836.

[2] Wetmore, *Gazetteer of Mo.*, 1837, p. 20.

[3] *The Argus*, July 1, 1836.

[4] *Ibid.*, July 22, 1836.

[5] *Ibid.*, Aug. 26, 1836.

As the returns came in it became evident that the bank plan also had friends in the country districts. A safe majority in both houses was assured if only agreement could be reached regarding the kind of a bank wanted. *The Jeffersonian Republican* was still hostile, but even it admitted that some sort of a state bank would likely be organized at this session. It accordingly turned its attention to a campaign for the exclusive ownership of the stock by the state.[1] This was the rock upon which the legislation of the previous Assembly had been wrecked, and it thus presented a possible line of attack.

So far as Saint Louis was concerned the suggestion of *The Jeffersonian Republican* caused little comment. She was ready to accept any sort of a state institution and risk the chance of improvement over present conditions. However, when the question was raised of expelling the Agency even though no state bank were organized, there was much alarm. St. Louis did not relish the idea of being left once more without banking connections. However, before the excitement had gone far, assurance was given that some kind of a state bank bill would be passed.

Before attempting to trace the legislation of 1836 and 1837 attention should be called to certain developments favorable to the state bank idea.

The case of Craig v. Missouri had regarded the Loan Office certificates as bills of credit and so had cast doubt on the constitutional right of a state to establish a bank of issue.[2] Kentucky, however, in Brisco v. The Commonwealth of Kentucky (1837), had maintained that bills when issued by a chartered bank are not bills of credit even though the state owns all the stock. The U. S. Supreme Court had upheld the decision, Justice Story, however, dissent-

[1] *The Argus*, Dec. 23, 1836. Letter from its Jefferson City Correspondent.

[2] 4 *Peters* U. S. 410.

ing.[1] This decision swept away the argument of unconstitutionality and thus made legislation much easier.

Another factor of importance was the increasing business of the Saint Louis land office. The receipts for 1836 amounted to $1,971,985.29.[2] The Palmyra land office was also active, having sold as much as $230,000 of land in three months.[3] All of this business could undoubtedly be obtained if a respectable specie-paying bank were established. It was a prize worth trying for.

One other motive remains to be considered: namely, the federal distribution of the surplus revenue. The operation of the high tariff and the withdrawal of credit on public land sales had greatly increased the income of the federal government. Between 1824 and 1833 the annual income from the public lands averaged over $2,300,000. As the Bank of the United States was no longer the federal depository, local banks were being created in great numbers to secure a share of the coveted funds. Between 1820 and 1836 the banking capital of the United States had increased from $102,000,000 to $281,000,000.[4] The national debt was being reduced, thus leaving foreign capital without investment. It naturally turned to the state banks and gave momentum to the process. The banks loaned to those who wanted to buy public lands, using the federal deposits as a basis for their operations. Land sales amounted to $24,800,000 in the year 1836. In that year the federal surplus was $41,468,859.97.[5] This great fund was being used by

[1] 11 *Peters* U. S. 257 discussed in Conant, C. A. (N. Y., 1896), *History Modern Banks of Issue*, p. 377.

[2] *Financial Register* (Philadelphia), Nov. 8, 1837, p. 146.

[3] *Mo. Intelligencer*, Oct. 24, 1835.

[4] 51 *Niles* 162.

[5] Bourne, E. G., *History of the Surplus Revenue of 1837*, (N. Y., 1885), p. 16.

Jackson for loans to his friends. He had founded a great political machine. To stop his activities the opposition party demanded distribution of the money among the states. Jackson threatened to veto the bill and was only persuaded not to do so by making the distribution in the form of a loan, a sort of temporary deposit with the states.[1] The amount actually transferred to the various state governments was $37,468,859.97.[2] Each state had to make a decision on the proper use of its share. In many cases special sessions of the legislatures were called for this purpose. Alabama, Arkansas, Delaware, Georgia, Illinois, Indiana, Kentucky, Tennessee, and Missouri used at least a part of their shares in banking projects. It is commonly stated that the state banks were organized to afford a means of using the Surplus Revenue. It may, however, be said with confidence that such was not true of Missouri. Her state banking project had been under discusssion for years and would have been passed irrespective of the federal fund. In fact the newspapers of the state had little to say about the distribution, and it played a part of little importance in the Assembly debates prior to the enactment of the bank bill. However, once the bank was organized, the question of investing the state's share was taken up.

When the Ninth General Assembly met it was with a determination to put through some sort of banking legislation. There was much diversity of opinion regarding the form this should take, but at least this much was favorable —the governor had given definite assurance that he would not oppose a state bank. His opening message, November 23, 1836 was largely taken up with a discussion of state finances. He could not bring himself to sanction fully a theory of moneyed monopoly, yet under present conditions

[1] Bourne, *op. cit.*, p. 17 for the interpretation given.

[2] *Ibid.*, p. 29.

he saw no other way. Accordingly he recommended a specie-paying bank, whose profits should be used for state expenses in order to defray taxation. He wrote in part as follows:

The subject of the bank is of engrossing importance. Moneyed monopolies are anti-republican in spirit, yet they are so interwoven with the business and interests of the people as to render their immediate abandonment productive of great inconvenience. No one can be more deeply impressed than myself with the necessity of enlarging the basis of our specie currency. Much more can be effected to promote this desirable end by action of the general government than by any policy which the states may see fit to adopt. But to insure the entire success of the plan, it is necessary for the states to cooperate. Might we not be better enabled to guard our currency against depreciation by the establishment of a sound, well restricted, specie-paying bank? The bank must possess the confidence of the people; that there is a great prejudice among many well informed citizens against any and every means of paper money is also true. I would therefore recommend the establishment of a state bank, the net profit to be used for state expenses in order to relieve taxation. The state should issue script to pay her part, redeemable at her option in twenty to fifty years at 5 per cent interest or less to be taken by the bank or sold for the benefit of the state as the bank wishes. No small bills should be issued, for it is wise to let the day-laborer get hard money, thus insuring a just reward for his labor. In order to assist redemption, the circulation should be limited to twice the paid-up capital or three times the cash on hand. In case of need the bank should lend funds to the state at 5 per cent interest. The state constitution provides for only one bank, and only one branch to be established at any one session of the legislature; but this will not prevent the opening of necessary agencies.[1]

[1] *Senate Journal, Ninth General Assembly of Missouri*, "Message of Governor L. W. Boggs," p. 19 *et seq.* Requirements of space have made some condensation seem desirable, but so far as possible the language of the governor has been preserved.

This message indicated that the governor felt the time for action had arrived, but it also made it clear that he could not be expected to approve a bank unless it was organized on sound and conservative lines. He did not recommend that gold and silver alone be accepted in payment for stock, because he saw clearly that the state was in no position to finance such a plan. He was, however, in favor of securing redemption of the circulation by any other reasonable method. Also it should be noted that he made no reference to the use of the Surplus Revenue Fund.

The Senate took no immediate action, but a House Bill to charter the Union Bank of Missouri was introduced early in the session and referred to a select committee. This committee proved to be a storm center. It seemed impossible to come to any agreement, even though a daily call was made for a report. On December 7th a resolution was passed that the Bank Bill should be the standing order of business in the afternoons until disposed of. Finally on January 7, 1837 the committee reported that it could reach no agreement, and asked to be relieved. This was done and the matter was placed in the hands of a new select committee of five members.[1] At this juncture William McCausland, representative from Howard County, created much excitement by offering his resignation. He said he had been instructed by his constituents to vote for the bank, but he could not do so on account of doubts as to its constitutionality. This action seemed to arouse all the enemies of the Bank Bill and numerous amendments began to be offered. One proposed to limit the salary of the president to $1,000 a year for the first four years.[2] This, of course, would have greatly impaired the efficiency of the bank by making it difficult to secure strong leadership through the critical organization period. Fortunately it was re-

[1] *House Journal, 9th General Assembly Mo.*, 1836-37, p. 162 *et seq.*

[2] *Ibid.*, p. 304.

jected. Another amendment required three-fourths of the capital of the bank to be invested in Missouri real-estate mortgages.[1] This was evidently a blow at Saint Louis. She wanted the bank left free to make commercial loans without restriction. Moreover, Missouri real estate was not the soundest type of security for the circulation. Fortunately this amendment also failed. The governor had asked that the note issue be limited to three times the specie reserve, but his suggestion had not been embodied in the proposed charter. Accordingly he saw to it that an amendment was introduced limiting the circulation to three times the gold and silver in the vault; but, like the others, it failed of passage.[2] A double liability bill completed the list of defeated amendments.[3] The original bill, without amendment, finally passed the House by a vote of 46 to 25 on January 18, 1837, and was immediately sent to the Senate.[3] A bill was then introduced providing that the main office be located in Jefferson City instead of in Saint Louis. This was rejected 51 to 17, and the feeling became so intense that the capital city was not even given a branch office.[4]

The Senate, after considering the House Bill, substituted for it an "Act to Charter the State Bank of Missouri". A rider was then added providing that at the time of opening, the main office must furnish the Fayette Branch with $500,000 capital provided the whole $3,000,000 of authorized capital were subscribed, otherwise with a proportionate amount. Ten per cent of the total paid-up capital was to be paid over to each new branch when established, but after sixty days any unused portion might be recalled.[5] An

[1] *House Journal, 9th General Assembly Mo.*, 1836-37, p. 304.

[2] *Ibid.*, p. 312.

[3] *Ibid.*, p. 314.

[4] *Mo. Argus*, Jan. 27, 1837.

[5] *Senate Journal, 9th General Assembly Mo.*, p. 281.

amendment, limiting the amount of bills of exchange that could be held to one-half the capital, failed to pass.[1] The original bill and rider were rushed through the next day (January 30, 1837) by a vote of 15 to 7. The House accepted the action of the Senate, apparently without much discussion.[2] In the meantime a House Bill to exclude all foreign agencies from the state had reached the Senate and was passed the following day. The new bank was to have monopoly privileges. The Cincinnati Agency had received its warning to leave the state. The governor signed both bills February 2, 1837.

Four days later (February 6, 1837) a bill was approved setting aside all moneys that might be received under the federal distribution act of June 23, 1836 for investment by the governor in the stock of the bank, all interest and profits to go to the School Fund, interest to be added to principal until such fund should reach $500,000. In the event of a recall of the money by the federal authorities, the bank stock represented by it was to be taken over by a state bond issue. The history of the bank may be anticipated by saying that a fairly adequate income was earned on this fund and that later it was invested in 6 per cent state bonds. Missouri was one of the few states that did not waste its share.[3]

This ended the fight for a state bank. The struggle had been in progress since statehood and had occupied a large part of the time of the last three sessions of the legislature. For the next twenty years it was to be the great financial power of the West.

[1] *Senate Journal, 9th General Assembly Mo.*, p. 281.

[2] *Ibid.*, p. 426.

[3] Bourne, *op. cit.*, pp. 80-81.

CHAPTER VII

The Charter

Thus far the discussion has had to do chiefly with the formation of pro-bank opinion and the struggle in the legislature leading up to the actual establishment of the Bank of Missouri. It is the purpose of this chapter to explain the working plan of the bank as shown by its charter.

The legislature had shown a disposition to give a maximum amount of specific guidance. The failures of the earlier chartered banks had left a wholesome spirit of caution. If such disasters could be avoided by a carefully worded and detailed statement of powers, duties, and limitations, the legislature was going to see that it was done. Accordingly the charter is a long and detailed instrument which shows great care in preparation. It comprises fifty-six articles covering thirteen closely printed pages. The obvious reason for so much detail was, of course, the lack of any general corporation law. The charter is given in full in the *Laws of Missouri,* 1837 (official state publication, pp. 15-28.) There is almost no other reliable source. The *Journals of the General Assembly* give very fragmentary accounts and the newspapers were too much involved in the political campaign for careful editorial comment. There are no records in the office of the Secretary of State.[1]

The charter is too long for quotation in full but its chief features are here given.

[1] The original records of the incorporation of the State Bank together with other records of the Secretary of State were lost in the State House fire of Nov. 17, 1837. See Shepard, *op. cit.*, p. 144.

The authorized capital was $5,000,000, divided into 50,000 shares of $100 each. One-half of this was reserved for the state, the rest to be sold to private individuals. There was no provision for building up a surplus. All accumulated profits were to be paid out in dividends twice a year.

On February 3, 1837 books were to be opened at various towns in the state for the subscription of $3,000,000 of the capital stock, and were to be kept open twenty days unless the desired total was sooner reached. Private stock was to be paid for in gold, silver, or certificates of deposit in government-depository, specie-paying banks in certain designated cities; but this latter type of payment was not to be considered final until such certificates had been honored in specie.[1] Ten per cent was to be paid to the commissioners at the time of subscription and the rest in three equal installments a few months apart. In case any purchaser failed to keep up his payments, the president and directors were authorized to cancel his certificates and to retain as a forfeit such payments as had been made. Such shares could then be resold.[2] For all practical purposes this meant that private stock was to be paid for in specie.

A different arrangement was made in respect to the share of the state. The governor was authorized to subscribe for one-half of the $3,000,000 issue just described, and to pay for it by placing the Seminary, Saline, and Three Per Cent funds in the treasury of the bank before the opening and to issue bonds for the rest. As these funds amounted to only about $150,000 a large bond issue would of course be necessary.[3] The bonds were to be in denominations of not

[1] *Charter State Bank of Missouri*, section 2.

[2] *Ibid.*

[3] Later the governor was authorized to invest the state's share of the federal Surplus Revenue in the stock of the bank.

less than $1,000 due in twenty-five years at 5½ or 6 per cent interest. They were not to be used in banking operations until sold, but the state did not become liable for interest until that time. An agent was to be appointed at once by the bank to sell the first $500,000 of the bonds.[1] This practically meant that the state was to buy stock not to exceed $1,500,000 in amount, but was not to get title to the shares until payment was made in specie or the equivalent. Considering the financial situation of the state this was about the best available plan.

In case the private stock were not subscribed in twenty days, the books were to remain open one hundred days longer, unless the necessary amount were sooner subscribed. After the expiration of this period the bank was authorized to sell stock in New York City, but any premium accruing was to go to the state. Whenever a branch office was opened the state was to purchase $500,000 additional stock, paying for same by means of an additional bond issue, after which an equal amount might be sold to the public.[2] This plan took for granted that the full $3,000,000 would be sold. Provision was made for the same proportional subscriptions in case a lesser amount of capital was used. Fayette was given the first branch and was to have ten per cent of whatever capital had been subscribed, provided, however, that any unused part might be withdrawn after sixty days at the option of the main office.[3] Subagencies could be opened in each judicial district as rapidly as warranted by business conditions. Not less than nine or more than fifteen were to be opened at once.[4] These had no power to lend money but might collect and transmit in-

[1] *Charter State Bank of Mo.*, section 3.

[2] *Ibid.*, sec. 11.

[3] *Ibid.*, sec. 33.

[4] *Ibid.*, sec. 34.

formation, examine titles, buy and sell bills of exchange, collect debts, and transfer money.[1]

The management was placed in the hands of a president and twelve directors. In case one-half the stock were taken by the private shareholders they were allowed six directors, otherwise a proportionately small number. The term was one year. Election was to be held by ballot at Saint Louis after notice in four newspapers.[2] Proxy voting was allowed, provided no director acted as proxy. Each share carried one vote.[3] The president and the public directors were to be elected by joint session of the General Assembly for a term of two years, and the governor was empowered to fill vacancies occurring between sessions.[4] No officer of the state or of the United States could be an officer or director of the bank.[5] Neither could any officer or director hold a similar position in any other banking institution, nor could business partners serve together on the board.[6] Each director was required to be a citizen of both Missouri and of the United States and private members had to be bona-fide holders of stock, the amount not being specified.[7] Although there were to be twelve directors, the president and any five constituted a quorum for the transaction of business; and, in case of illness or necessary absence of the president, any director could be named by those present to act in his place.[8] No salary attached to the office of director, but the president and all other employees were to

[1] *Mo. Republican*, Feb. 21, 1837.

[2] *Charter State Bank of Mo.*, sec. 14.

[3] *Ibid.*, sec. 20.

[4] *Ibid.*, sec. 1.

[5] *Ibid.*, sec. 17.

[6] *Ibid.*, sec. 21.

[7] *Ibid.*

[8] *Ibid.*, sec. 23.

receive a reasonable compensation, the amount to be fixed in each case by the board.[1] Within ten days after the election of the directors a meeting was to be held to organize the bank and to select employees including the cashier.[2] The cashier was to be placed under heavy bond and other employees could be bonded if the board so desired.[3] Each branch was to have a president and four state directors elected by the legislature, and a proportional number of private members. The branch cashier was to be elected by the branch board.[4]

In addition to the right of election of private directors, the private shareholders could protect their interests by calling a special stockholders meeting on petition of ten shareholders representing 5,000 shares. A majority of the board of directors could also call a special meeting. For all special meetings six weeks notice was required.[5]

As soon as the state had complied with all formalities in paying for its stock and cash had been received for seventy per cent of the private shares, paper currency could be issued. As a necessary preliminary, the governor was required to have the bank examined, to certify that the required cash was in the possession of the bank, and to publish the report in four newspapers in the state.[6] The currency was to bear the signature of both the president and cashier, and to be assignable by delivery or endorsement according to the tenor of the individual note. Unless signed by both officers no liability attached to the bank.[7] In case specie

[1] *Charter State Bank of Mo.*, sec. 22.

[2] *Ibid.*, sec. 15.

[3] *Ibid.*, sec. 25.

[4] *Ibid.*, secs. 33 and 41.

[5] *Ibid.*, sec. 24.

[6] *Ibid.*, sec. 18.

[7] *Ibid.*, secs. 28 and 29.

payments were suspended, the bank was subject to a twenty per cent penalty.[1] Notes were payable on demand in gold or silver; and, in order to facilitate redemption, the bank was required to immediately open an agency in New Orleans and one in New York, Baltimore, or Philadelphia where specie would be paid for all notes on presentation.[2] So long as specie payments were maintained, state funds were to be kept on deposit, and the notes were to be receivable for all dues to the state. For the first five years the circulation was not to exceed the capital stock, after which time the amount could be doubled at the option of the directorate.[3] The smallest denomination approved was $10.00, but with this restriction the particular denominations were left to the judgment of the board.[4]

The general banking powers included the right to deal in bills of exchange, checks and drafts, and to receive public and private deposits.[5] The bank was to act as fiscal agent for the state, negotiate all state loans without charge, and transfer funds about the state as required wherever it had a branch or agency.[6] Six per cent interest was to be paid for all state funds left to exceed one year, except funds for transfer over the state. The bank was not required by charter to make loans to the state. No real estate could be held except for a banking house unless acquired as security in the ordinary course of business.[7] If so taken, however, it could be retained—at least the charter made no provision for its resale.

[1] *Charter State Bank of Mo.*, sec. 35.

[2] *Ibid.*, secs. 36 and 42.

[3] *Ibid.*, sec. 46.

[4] *Ibid.*, sec. 39.

[5] *Ibid.*, sec. 19.

[6] *Ibid.*, sec. 42.

[7] *Ibid.*, sec. 26.

Maximum interest rates, which the officers were without power to change, were fixed as follows: one-hundred-twenty day paper, 6 per cent; four to six months, 7 per cent; and, over 6 months, 8 per cent. One year was the maximum time for commercial loans although renewal was permitted[1] In addition to regular interest rates, exchange could be charged on foreign bills, the rate not being fixed.[1] This latter provision was much abused as will be shown later. Loans were not permitted on the pledge of the bank's own shares, nor were stockholders to be given any preference in regard to loans provided other parties offered security of equal value.[2] If any director, officer, or agent loaned private money at rates higher than those established by law for the bank, he was to be immediately dismissed from service.[3]

Real-estate loans were not forbidden, but were provided for in a special manner. The bank was authorized to receive on deposit or to borrow not to exceed $5,000,000, and to lend it on approved real estate up to three-fourths of the market value, appraisal to be made by an agent of the bank. The interest rate was fixed at 8 per cent payable semi-annually. Such funds were required to be kept separate from the rest of the business.[4] This provision failed to satisfy the farmers, for the so-called real-estate loans were only short-terms advances, as 20 per cent of the principal had to be repaid each year. The average Missouri farmer was unable to meet such conditions, so as a farm-loan bank there was nothing but failure in sight. However, the service of the bank was not supposed to take that direction. It was to be preeminently a commercial bank.

[1] *Charter State Bank of Mo.*, sec. 30. The word foreign means payable outside the state.

[2] *Ibid.*, secs. 31 and 44.

[3] *Ibid.*, sec. 31.

[4] *Ibid.*, sec. 37.

Semi-annual dividends were to be paid from net profits, the state's share to be placed on deposit. No dividend declaration was to be made if it impaired the capital.[1] An annual bonus of twenty-five cents on each share of private stock was made payable to the state each year in lieu of all taxes.[2]

Careful provision was made for examination and audit. Twice each year a detailed expense account was to be submitted to the governor, and all accounts other than those of private individuals were to be published in two Missouri newspapers. Either house of the legislature might requisition a statement or, at its pleasure, demand a full examination of the bank. Before the opening of each session of the legislature the governor was to appoint a committee to make an internal audit and submit a report. No member of the committee could be a stockholder.[3] The parent bank was authorized to audit the books of all branches and agencies whenever it saw fit, its president and directors being given free access to the books. Branch officers and directors were given the same rights with respect to branch books.[4] In addition to all these examinations and reports, condensed statements were required to be submitted to the State Auditor four times a year. The directors were instructed to keep minutes of all meetings, recording yeas and nays on all votes. This book was to be exhibited to examining authorities.[5]

If at any time the legislature believed that the charter was being violated, revocation proceedings could be instituted in the circuit court of the county where the main

[1] *Charter State Bank of Mo.*, sec. 32.

[2] *Ibid.*, sec. 43.

[3] *Ibid.*, sec. 38.

[4] *Ibid.*, sec. 45.

[5] *Ibid.*, sec. 40.

office was located.[1] If the violation consisted of excesssive issue of currency or lending on the pledge of its own stock, the directors authorizing the same were to be held for the ultimate responsibility, *i. e.* if the bank failed and was unable to pay, suit might be brought against such directors. If the violation consisted of fraud on the part of any officer or employee, a penalty of imprisonment of from two to twenty years in the penitentiary was provided.[2] Copies of the bonds of the cashier and other officers were to be filed with the Secretary of State and suits could be maintained on them.[3] Each officer was required to take oath to perform his duties honestly, faithfully, and impartially.[4] In the event of the suspension of specie payments, the governor, in addition to collecting the twenty per cent penalty, might at his option declare the charter forfeited and place the institution in the hands of trustees appointed by himself.[5] If not revoked or otherwise surrendered the charter was to be effective until 1857.

The president and directors were instructed to enter into immediate negotiations for the purchase of the Cincinnati Commercial Agency, and, if possible, to make a deal with the federal government to act as its fiscal agent for Missouri.[6]

At the time the charter bill was passed, a law was also enacted requiring all foreign agencies to leave the state. It provided that no banking business could be carried on within the state except under state charter. There was a penalty assessed of $1,000 for each offense, and every day

[1] *Charter State Bank of Mo.*, sec. 48.

[2] *Ibid.*, sec. 47.

[3] *Ibid.*, sec. 50.

[4] *Ibid.*, sec. 53.

[5] *Ibid.*, sec. 55.

[6] *Ibid.*, sec. 59.

operation was continued constituted a separate offense. One-half the penalty was to go to the informer. Any note executed to such agencies after the passage of this act was declared void, and any money sent into the state by outside corporations to be used by private parties in banking with intent to evade the law was to be confiscated. This law was passed February 6, 1837 and was declared effective at once except for the Cincinnati Commercial Agency which was given until June 1st to close its accounts.[1]

This is the equipment which was furnished to the new State Bank. It started with a charter, which, judged by those of contemporary institutions, was unusually well balanced and conservative. It was not a paper bank. Real capital was behind it and the penalties for suspension were so drastic as to make "wild cat" methods unprofitable. Restrictions on loans were such as to furnish a reasonable guarantee of liquidity of assets, in so far as such a thing was possible in a pioneer state. The note issue was not protected by specific reserves, although it was secured by the general assets of the bank, and restrictions were placed on its expansion. In case these were violated the assenting directors became individually liable. There was no requirement concerning reserves against deposits, and no special protection for depositors beyond a pledge of the general assets. Of course it should be said that the issue function was expected to be much more important than that of deposit. This was true of most banks of the time and was likely to be especially so in such a state as Missouri. The restrictions all lay in the direction of safeguarding the assets. The flexibility of these provisions added much to the power of the bank to serve the state and there is no re-

[1] *Banking Laws of Mo.*, 1837, p. 261, "Act to Expel All Foreign Agencies from the State."

cord of any difficulties caused by a lack of fixed reserves. The provisions for examination were unusual at the time. Of course there was no specialized state banking department with its corps of trained accountants, but that belongs to a later period in the history of bank supervision. The history of the State Bank of Missouri adds one more example to the list of efficient banks founded on the principle of asset currency. A study of its progress during the first twenty years of its history will show how well it served the people of Missouri.

CHAPTER VIII

How the Charter was Made

In Chapter II some account was given of the condition of national and state banks of the United States prior to 1837 and of their bearing on events in Missouri. No attempt, however, was made to show specifically and in detail how Missouri banking was influenced by these factors from the outside. The problem of determining where the ideas embodied in the State Bank charter of 1837 originated is not an easy one. It is not possible to say who really wrote the document or to assign relative weights to local influences and to those from without the state. Missouri's previous banking experiences had provided a fund of information sufficient for the formulation of satisfactory banking regulations. It is certain, however, that the legislature was by no means so provincial. The official journals are so greatly condensed as to be of little help, but fortunately one of the Saint Louis papers published somewhat more than fragments of the debates.[1] These show an acquaintance with the views of Alexander Hamilton, Albert Gallatin, and Nicholas Biddle. Gouge's books were often cited and references were made to the experiences of South Carolina, Kentucky, and Tennessee. It will at least add something of local color to look into these debates. Hamilton's plan of reducing the voting power of stockholders as the number of shares held increased was brought up and strenuously opposed. The charters of

[1] *Mo. Republican*, Jan. 2, 3, 6 and 12, 1837.

South Carolina and Tennessee banks were cited in proof of the wisdom of paying directors. One member felt that farmers owning stock would never attend meetings unless they were paid for riding to town. The prohibition of loans to directors was bitterly opposed on the ground that only inferior men could be induced to serve under such conditions. The Commonwealth Bank of Kentucky was given as an example of the evil effects of such a plan. The country members protested against restrictions on real-estate loans and maintained that former Missouri banks had been monopolized by the commercial interests of St. Louis. There was discussion of the case of a wealthy farmer who was forced to mortgage his farm to secure a loan of $1,000 because the Saint Louis bank did not care to make loans outside the city. They argued that a certain part of the capital should be set aside for farm loans and that currency should be issued on mortgage security. Gallatin and Gouge were cited by the opposition to show the necessity for liquid assets. The debate on this point was very vigorous. One member cited the example of a Connecticut bank that had loaned its whole capital on real estate for thirty years without suspension or the loss of a dollar. He admitted that such a policy had been a failure in Maryland, but argued that land there was worth but three cents an acre and that everybody was on the verge of starvation. He then quoted from the statement of the Bank of New York showing an investment of $744,000 in real estate out of a total capital of only $2,000,000.[1] A member from Marion County protested against any division of the loans as to real estate or otherwise on the ground that applicants would not tell the truth about the uses to which loans were to be put, and that anyhow the bank's only right of inquiry

[1] *Mo. Republican*, Jan. 6, 1837.

was as to the solvency and punctuality of the debtor. Contrary to most country members he questioned the advisability of real-estate loans on account of their slow turnover, and supported his argument with liberal quotations from Adam Smith and Alexander Hamilton.[1] There was evidently a considerable element desirous of investing a large part of the assets of the bank in real-estate. The real estate boom in St. Louis made them overconfident of values. These brief notes on the bank-bill debate are too fragmentary to show in any systematic way the sources of the state of Missouri banking opinion of the time; but they at least indicate that the legislature was trying to make use of such help as could be found.

Senator Benton no doubt had a great deal of influence on the charter, but just how much cannot be stated with any assurance. The *House and Senate Journals* have little or nothing to say about it. He did not favor the bank plan; but, when it was decided to establish a bank, he was much interested in seeing that it be made safe. An editorial in *The Argus* suggests his attitude:

> Colonel Benton was and ever will be opposed to banks. In no shape or form, directly or indirectly, did he encourage the incorporation of the Bank of the State of Missouri. It was against his well known and publicly printed opinions and wishes. Yet when he found his people had chartered one, and that the soundest on the American continent, he was willing to use all his influence for it.[2]

Aside from Benton, Saint Louis contained a good deal of financial talent. The earlier chartered banks, the Branch United States Bank, and the Cincinnati Commercial Agency had at least developed a number of practical bankers. Gov-

[1] *Mo. Republican*, Jan. 12, 1837.

[2] *Mo. Argus*, July 11, 1837.

ernor Boggs himself was of this group. Their influence both in the legislature and in the formation of public opinion on the outside was no doubt considerable.

There is little evidence to show how far the Missouri legislature made use of the old charters which had been previously granted to the Bank of Saint Louis and to the Bank of Missouri. Certain provisions found in them also appear in the State Bank charter; but, as will be shown later, the different state banking enactments were copied and recopied until it is now all but impossible to trace immediate influence. With respect to the directorate, provisions regarding elections, notice of shareholders' meetings, requirements as to citizenship of directors, and proxy voting are sufficiently similar in all three charters to suggest direct influence. The same is true of the sliding scales of voting for directors and of regulations providing for the forfeiture of stock for non-payment. Some of the safeguards thrown about creditors of the State Bank are suggested in the earlier charters. These included fixation of maximum interest rates, limitations on the debts of the bank, penalties for suspension of specie payments, and declaration of unearned dividends. Too much weight, however, should not be assigned to these similarities. The legislature took a wider view, apparently trying to gather in the best of American experience. The influence exerted by the earlier chartered banks of Missouri seems rather to have been along the line of teaching St. Louis business men the utility of banks and of making the legislature extremely wary of permitting unsound practices.

Another method of approach is possible. The earlier settlers of the state came largely from Virginia, Kentucky, Tennessee, and the Carolinas. Many of them doubtless brought with them ideas on banking or at least memories of unhappy experiences with paper state banks. What is probably fully as important, they retained their interest in the places from whence they came and soon a good many newspapers from the outside were circulating in the state. It is difficult to evaluate this kind of influence, but no doubt it was considerable. It should, accordingly, be profitable to study the plans and experiences of those states from which the settlers chiefly came. With respect to Illinois and other nearby states the connection is more obvious. It may not usually be possible to show that Missouri is indebted to Kentucky, Illinois, or any other state for an idea merely because that state had it first; but at least the fact of precedence can be shown. With this in view the banking systems of various states will be discussed briefly; but their history will not be carried beyond 1837, the date of the passage of the Missouri charter.

As early as 1820 Alabama had organized a state bank and had invested her $1,800,000 school and university fund in it.[1] Three-fifths of the stock, however, was to have been privately owned, but as it found no purchasers the state furnished all. The president and directors were chosen by the legislature. It was expected that the profits of the bank would defray all expenses of the state government. Unfortunately, however, there were no profits and the bank lost over $4,000,000.

Arkansas had some very wild chapters in banking history but they came too late to influence the Missouri charter. Her first legislation was in 1836.

The case of Illinois is quite different. She had begun making experiments as early as Missouri and her close proximity to Saint Louis made her influence of extreme importance. Her problem, however, was complicated by elaborate plans for internal improvements, and often she

[1] Conant, *op. cit.*, p. 380.

regarded her banks as schemes to finance them. After the War of 1812 settlers from Kentucky and Ohio brought in money and they soon began to plan a bank investment. When the population of the territory was only 1,500, a bank was started at Shawneetown. This was in 1817. Although the authorized capital was $300,000, it was allowed to open with a $50,000 subscription and only $5,000 of this was paid in specie. The rest was paid in stock notes, payable on call of the directors. The circulation was limited to twice the paid-up capital, the interest rate was fixed at six per cent, and a twelve per cent penalty was provided for suspension. Some of these provisions appear in the Missouri charter. The next year three new banks were chartered at Edwardsville, Kaskaskia, and Cairo. The one at Edwardsville was like that at Shawneetown except that the territory was to take one-third of the stock. The Kaskaskia charter provided that all stock must be paid for in gold and silver, a requirement which could not be met and the bank was never organized. The Cairo project was a fantastic townsite and lot selling arrangement and never existed except on paper. The Edwardsville and Shawneetown banks were organized, and honest banking was attempted. They became depositories for the federal government and maintained specie payments until the depression following the panic of 1819. In 1819 they had combined deposits of $152,000 and a circulation of $52,000. The state at this time had a population of 30,000, but conditions of life were so simple that there was little need for banks. Land speculation, however, took hold on the people just as it did in Missouri, and soon a very ambitious state bank was planned. It was chartered in 1818 with an authorized capital of $4,000,000, one-half to be taken by the state. Ten per cent was to be paid in in specie or convertible notes, but only $15,000 specie was required at the start. No stock, however, was subscribed and, after the panic of 1819, the charter was revoked. In 1821, in order to relieve the depression, a new state bank was chartered, and owned wholly by the state. The nominal capital was $500,000, and $300,000 circulation was issued. These notes bore two per cent interest and were receivable for taxes. They were loaned at six per cent on real estate mortgages. The only real capital provided was $2,000 to pay for printing the notes. The state supreme court upheld the constitutionality of the Act, but the famous Craig v. Missouri case cast doubt on this decision.[1] The federal land offices refused to receive the notes, but the officials were undaunted. They merely said that, if nobody outside the state appreciated the notes, they would use them at home. The directors were political appointees and, after having borrowed over $50,000, they were no longer interested in keeping up the credit of the bank. No specie was kept on hand. One branch had two dollars and regarded them as curiosities. No one pretended to pay his loans. Moreover, the receiving of the notes for taxes bankrupted the treasury, although the statement showed an immense paper surplus. The legislature finally came to itself and redeemed the notes at par. One hundred thousand dollars of them in the state treasury were burned. The Bank of Edwardsville also had failed and its notes were likewise redeemed. The reaction from this banking orgy was so severe that a law was passed forbidding any corporation to exercise banking functions. This was the accepted policy for four years but, when Jackson commenced to select depositories for the federal funds, Illinois could not withstand the temptation to bid for a share, and Governor Duncan recommended another state bank. It was chartered in 1835 at just the time the Eighth Missouri Legis-

[1] 4 *Peters* U. S. 410.

lature rejected its bank bill. It provided for a bank with $1,500,000 state capital and such additions up to $1,000,000 as might be taken by private individuals. This was merely the authorization. It was to be allowed to start on $250,-000 specie, $100,000 of which was to be contributed by the state. Ten dollars was to be paid down on each share, the balance on call of the directors. To help make it a local institution, books were to be opened in the state sooner than elsewhere. No member of the legislature could hold office in the bank. The circulation was limited to two and one-half times and the loans to three times the paid-up capital. No notes under $5.00 were permitted. The bank was authorized to borrow $1,000,000 for real estate loans under conditions similar to the Missouri plan. The stock was quoted at 113 in 1835 and the governor on this showing asked the legislature to purchase $1,000,000 stock. The early years of the bank were unfortunate. Saint Louis and Alton were rivals for the lead trade and the bank tried to assist Alton. The bank lost $1,000,000 in the experiment. Saint Louis, due to this fight, naturally watched the bank with great interest. In fact all this banking activity so near to the Missouri border could not have failed to attract the attention of the whole state and particularly of the legislature. Unquestionably part of the answer to the query as to the sources of the Missouri charter is to be found here.[1]

Indiana legislation probably had some influence, for her state bank was early recognized as a model institution. It was modeled somewhat after the Bank of the United States

[1] For a very careful discussion of the early Illinois banking situation see Garnett, C. T., *State Banks of Issue in Illinois* (Univ. of Ill. Studies, H. H. Harris Prize Essay), 1898, pp. 1 to 30. Much of the material for this paragraph has been taken from this book. Other accounts are available in Ridgely, W. B., *Early Banking in the West*, p. 383 *et seq.* and Knox, *op. cit.*, pp. 712-720.

and in many ways was the most conspicuous success among American state banks of the time. However, it was not chartered until 1834 and most of its history was yet to be written when the Missouri bank bill was passed. Its charter provided that the state should own half of the stock, that all shares should be paid for in specie, and that notes should be limited to twice the paid-up capital. Each branch was to be assigned ten per cent of the capital and was to issue its own notes. These notes were redeemable in specie and receivable at par at any branch. The governing board was elected jointly by the legislature and the private stockholders. By 1835 the resources were $4,379,000; circulation, $1,290,000; specie holdings, $797,000.[1]

Iowa profited by the example of Illinois and refused to charter paper banks. For that matter none were chartered at all during this period. Beginning in 1836, however, one was operated in Dubuque under a Wisconsin charter, but there is no record that it influenced the Missouri legislature. However, "wild cat" banks were located just over the line in Nebraska and their circulation became almost the sole medium in the state. At least Iowa contributed no sound banking ideas to Missouri at this time.[2]

Kentucky exerted a much more pronounced influence. Large numbers of Missourians had come from Kentucky and correspondence between the two states was heavy. The first bank of issue west of the Alleghenies had begun business in Lexington in 1802 under an insurance company

[1] See Holdsworth, J. T., *Lessons of State Banking before the Civil War, Proc. Acad. Pol. Sci.*, vol. i, no. 2, Jan., 1911, p. 222 and *Doc. 65*, House Rep., 24th Cong., 2nd Sess., "Letter of Sec'y of Treas. relative to condition of State Banks," Nov. 21, 1835.

[2] See Ridgely, *op. cit.*, Conant, *op. cit.*, p. 68 and Palmer, P. G., "Banking in Louisiana Purchase," in *Bul. Amer. Inst. Bank Clerks*, Nov. 15, 1904.

charter. After a few years of success it was reorganized as the Bank of Kentucky (1807). The capital was $1,000,-000, one-half owned by the state. The state named the president and one-half the directors, but retained the right to add new state members when necessary to carry an important point of policy. This, of course, meant that the bank was constantly in politics. In 1818 it succumbed to the specie demands of the United States Bank and suspended along with the other Ohio Valley banks. It resumed, however, within a week. The legislature had large plans for debtor relief. The capital of the bank was increased to $3,000,000 using the school fund to finance it, and a state of semi-suspension was legalized. The bank was in good condition when this government meddling began. The president was a great conservative force. Fearing that he would not allow his bank to be used to champion cheap money, the Commonwealth Bank of Kentucky was chartered in 1820 with a paper capital. The power of the legislature to elect additional directors of the old Bank of Kentucky was used to provide a board pledged to accept the notes of the Commonwealth Bank. Of course this spelled ruin. The Bank of Kentucky suspended in 1820 and the Commonwealth notes went to a discount of from 30 to 50 per cent. It was this trouble that was reflected in the suspension of the Bank of Missouri and in the launching of the Loan Office experiment. Beginning as early as 1819 *The Missouri Intelligencer* and *The Missouri Republican* carried long articles about Kentucky distress. Governor Slaughter had been very fearful of the political effects of the banking power and had recommended that the state advise an amendment to the federal constitution prohibiting the exercise of any banking function by a corporation. This type of news was eagerly copied by the Missouri newspapers. In 1833 and 1834 it was decided to charter more banks to take over the business to be left by the retiring United States Bank. Three were organized with a combined authorized capital of $13,000,000, of which $9,000,000 was paid. The state's share was supplied by bonds in a way quite similar to the Missouri plan and a small surplus requirement was made. It is quite likely that this legislation was widely noticed in Missouri. At least *The Intelligencer* carried a good deal of Kentucky news. In the issue of December 22, 1832 the bank message of Governor Breathitt was published. It admitted the unhappy past of Kentucky banking history, but maintained that the new institutions were as good as gold and should not lead to currency depreciation.[1]

Louisiana has usually been presented as having had the model banking code of the South; but this was not enacted until 1842 so was too late to affect the Missouri charter.[2] Some of the earlier banks, like the Bank of Orleans (1818), were in the nature of partnerships with the territory, but there seem to have been no distinctive features. However, by 1835 the banking power of Louisiana was considerable and there must have been a good many business transactions with Saint Louis.[3]

Michigan did not pass a banking law until March, 1837 and her reputation as the great "wild cat bank country" was yet to be won. Beginning in 1818 a bank had operated in Detroit under federal charter, but it was not of a speculative nature.[4]

[1] For the Kentucky situation, see Gouge, Wm. M., *Short History of Paper Money and Banking in U. S.* (N. Y., 1833), pp. 99 and 127-132; art. by Root, *op. cit.*, in *Sound Currency* for Apr. 15, 1895; Knox, *op. cit.*, p. 629; and *Mo. Intelligencer*, especially June 25, 1819 and Dec. 22, 1832.

[2] See Holdsworth, *op. cit.*, p. 222.

[3] *Bul. 65*, House Rep. *op. cit.*, and Palmer, *op. cit.*, p. 641.

[4] Utley, H. M., "Wild Cat Banking System of Michigan" in *Mich. Pioneer Collections*, vol. v, 1882, p. 210.

Developments in Minnesota, Mississippi, and Nebraska came too late to affect conditions in Missouri. The same is almost true of Wisconsin, although a territorial bank with part public ownership, to be paid for in bonds, was chartered in 1836. It was, however, not approved by Congress.[1]

The experiences of two other states should be mentioned. Tennessee had three banks by 1819 and, although they suspended, their condition was better than those of Kentucky, and the suffering was less general. Against the wishes of Jackson a state bank for debtors was opened in 1820. There was no provision for the redemption of the notes and they were only made negotiable within the state. *The Missouri Intelligencer* expressed much interest in this proposition but did not favor it.[2] In 1834 the Union Bank was organized with a capital of $3,000,000 which was largely taken in the East. The state, however, purchased $500,000 stock, paying for it with bonds which were floated at a premium. The notes were receivable for taxes and a one-half of one per cent bonus on the capital stock was assessed in lieu of taxes.[3] Considering the number of Tennesseeans in Missouri this charter was probably not without influence. The other state experience was that of Virginia. She had chartered the Bank of Virginia in 1804 and its success had been remarkable. The central office at Richmond and each branch had its own president and board of directors. The branches were to a large degree independent. The circulation was not to exceed the deposits by more than $4,500,000; otherwise there were no restrictions on the issue right. The state owned a part of the

[1] Hadden, C. B., "History of State Banks and Early Banking Systems of Wisconsin" in *Wisconsin Acad. of Sciences*, vol. x, p. 164.

[2] *Mo. Intelligencer*, Sept. 9, 1820.

[3] Knox, *op. cit.*, p. 667.

stock. The circulation was well received all up and down the Atlantic seaboard and there had been no losses on it. As many of the earlier Missourians were of Virginia extraction it is quite likely that the good will of the system reached the state.[1]

So far account has been taken only of experiences in those states from which influence may reasonably be assumed to have come. What little evidence is available in the newspaper accounts and in the legislative debates seems to point to a larger use of the records of nearby states than of those of the Northeast states or of the federal government. Indirectly of course these Western and Southern state banks were greatly indebted for their form of organization to the First and Second United States Banks and to the institutions of Massachusetts, New York, and Pennsylvania. Without attempting to determine how far they were considered by the Missouri authorities, it may be profitable to note some of the features of the State Bank Charter of 1837 which had previously appeared in these banks. With respect to the United States Bank, however, it may be said that Senator Benton was thoroughly familiar with its form of organization and such influence as it had can likely be traced through him, except in so far as John O'Fallon and others connected with the branch at Saint Louis may have made suggestions. It seems impossible to trace the specific work of these men. It may be said, however, that in the large amount of discussion of the United States Bank which appeared in the Missouri newspapers little attention was given to its actual charter provisions. The political element always seemed to be uppermost in the minds of the editors.

The task of comparing the Missouri charter with those of

[1] Royall, W. G., *Hist. of Va. Banks Prior to Civil War* (N. Y., 1907), *passim.*

the other banks suggested is made easy by the researches of Dr. Davis R. Dewey.[1]

The method of paying for stock in part at least by bonds was common practice. Even Massachusetts had not been able to enforce a total specie payment. Hamilton had recognized the necessities of the case in his plan for the First United States Bank and had required a specie payment of only 25 per cent. In practice the bank never got more than $500,000 of its $10,000,000 capital in specie. The government took $2,000,000 stock but at once borrowed it back at six per cent. In New York the Safety Fund Act of 1829 required specie payment for capital, but it was usually borrowed back by shareholders on pledge of their stock. Pennsylvania required 20 per cent of the stock to be paid up, but notes of other banks were often accepted in payment. Even in Indiana private shareholders were allowed to borrow from the state to pay the second and third installments and the state floated a bond issue to care for this.

The Missouri attempt to sell stock locally and to restrict management to her own citizens was not unusual. *The Report of the Bank Commissioner of Massachusetts for* 1841 contains bitter criticism of non-resident control. New York, however, was silent on this point. The large foreign holdings in the Tennessee banks no doubt served to increase Missouri vigilance. Most of this agitation was an outgrowth of the war feelings of 1812 for the foreign holdings were chiefly British.

The principle of state partnership was everywhere recognized, due to shortage of private capital and the desire of the state governments for special privileges. Moreover, there

[1] Dewey, D. R., *State Banking Before the Civil War* (National Monetary Commission). The data for this section has been taken wholly from this book. Page citations have not been given.

was the example of the two national banks. By 1812 all of the older states except New Jersey and one or two New England states owned bank stock. Massachusetts and Pennsylvania had large blocks. All of the Southern states accepted the principle. The special motives were various, ranging from a desire to invest the Surplus Revenue to hopes of providing means for building internal improvements and conducting the state affairs without taxation. In some of the states, notably Missouri, there was an honest desire to get a reasonable and safe return from the funds set aside for the public schools.

Missouri's limitations on the note issue was less unusual than is commonly supposed. The national banks had set definite limits and most of the states to some degree followed their example. In the South $3.00 of notes to $1.00 of specie was a common requirement. The prejudice against small denominations in Missouri was unusual. By 1830 only Pennsylvania, Maryland, and Virginia prohibited the small notes. However, Illinois' unhappy experiences with them doubtless accounts for the Missouri restriction. Penalties for suspension were also common. Massachusetts, New York, and the Second United States Bank had drastic rates. In the South, except in Louisiana, penalties were either not assessed or were evaded, and even in Louisiana the restrictions came later than 1837. The Ohio Valley banks, including those of Indiana and Ohio, were much more liberal in this respect than those of Missouri.

The liability of directors for illegal acts was put into the charter of the First United States Bank and was very largely copied. The Missouri rules were, however, more drastic than those of most of the other states. Residence requirements, stock ownership, and prohibition of interlocking directorates were accepted practice in Massachusetts.

The arrangements for supervision of the State Bank of Missouri judged by present standards, were quite crude, but they were far in advance of the average of the time. The attitude of secrecy on the part of the First United States Bank had carried great weight. The branch system was too common to require comment and the semi-independence accorded to branches was the general rule.

In these days of specific reserve requirements against circulation and deposits, the lack of such provisions in the Missouri charter may seem strange, but in 1837 the principle of asset currency with minimum restrictions had scarcely been questioned. Missouri practice was fully in line with the best banking thought of the day.

Other details of the charter requirements need not be considered, for enough have been discussed to make it evident that the Missouri charter was not a particularly original document. It did, however, represent the best type of American organization. It was drawn up with considerable care and the analysis here given leaves a presumption of large reference to other charters. So much, of course, is evidenced by the bank debates.

The outstanding fact of American state bank administration is that many of the institutions were better than their charters while others were much worse. Unless the people really desired sound banks the ways of evasion were many. The State Bank of Missouri started with a good charter, but the causes of its success will for the most part be found elsewhere. The matter of administration is all-important.

CHAPTER IX

THE ORGANIZATION OF THE BANK

PURSUANT to charter provisions, the legislature immediately took steps to organize the new state bank. John Brady Smith was elected president with only two negative votes. He was a man of stern integrity, serious, dignified, and sturdy. He was born in Kentucky, but came to St. Louis when twelve years old. His father had been identified with local banking interests, having been a director of the old Bank of Saint Louis. At this same time six directors for the state were also elected: Hugh O'Neil, Edward Walsh, S. S. Rayburn, Edward Dobyns, W. L. Sublette, and John O'Fallon.[1] O'Fallon had earned the confidence of the business community by his masterful management of the Branch Bank of the United States, and all of the others seem to have been fully representative of the sound business interests of the city. *The Argus* said they were men of sterling integrity, and even the unfriendly *Republican* admitted that the legislature had shown rare judgment in its selections.

The story of the organization and reception of the bank can perhaps be obtained best by a study of the Saint Louis newspapers of the time. For this purpose *The Argus* and *The Republican* have been chosen. *The Argus* favored the bank while *The Republican* was as hostile as it could well be without sacrificing the support of the business men of the city. *The Argus* said the charter suited the city and that everyone was imbued with the prevailing spirit of compro-

[1] *Mo. Argus*, Feb. 10, 1837.

mise.[1] *The Republican* was less cordial, but admitted the bank might become a great power if well conducted and that, at any rate, the people wished it success now that it had been chartered.[2] *The Clarion,* another opposition sheet, objected to the large state representation on the board of directors on the ground that individuals do not like to invest money where they cannot control it. However, it found much consolation in the plan for real estate loans and said that the superior natural advantages of Saint Louis would likely overcome the defects of the charter. Like both the other papers quoted, it complimented the legislature for its choice of president and directors.[3]

Commissioners were appointed to open books for subscription of stock on February 20, 1837 in St. Louis, Jefferson City, Columbia, Ste. Genevieve, Palmyra, Fayette, Independence, Liberty, Potosi, Jackson, and Boonville.[4] The governor announced that he would take stock for the state as soon as $50,000 private shares had been sold.[5] St. Louis, of course, furnished the bulk of the buyers. Her citizens bought 108 shares the first day and 260 the second.[6] The largest single subscription was $10,000. By February 24th the St. Louis total had reached 1400 shares,[7] and, at the expiration of the twenty-day period, it was announced that 1973 shares had been sold in the city.[8] Some of the stock was sold to nearby farmers, one man taking 40 shares.[9] The country officers reported sales of 600

[1] *Mo. Argus*, Feb. 17, 1837.

[2] *Mo. Republican*, Feb. 8, 1837.

[3] *Ibid.*, Feb. 21, 1837—an editorial copied from *The Clarion.*

[4] Edwards, *op. cit.*, p. 358 and *Mo. Republican*, Feb. 16, 1837.

[5] *Mo. Republican*, Feb. 8, 1837.

[6] *Ibid.*, Feb. 21 and 22, 1837.

[7] *Mo. Argus*, Feb. 24, 1837.

[8] *Mo. Republican*, Mar. 15, 1837.

[9] *Ibid.*, Feb. 27, 1837.

shares.[1] However, the amount contemplated by the charter had not been reached, and it was announced that the books would remain open indefinitely.[2]

Payment was accepted in either specie or the notes of specie-paying banks. The officials claimed that only such notes had been taken as could be turned into specie without loss. *The Republican* asked for details of the process by which this was accomplished, as the notes were at least six per cent undercurrent.[3] The record is not clear, but at least the bank made no statement that these notes were received at par. They were mostly issues of banks in Ohio, Indiana, and Illinois. However, on July 7, 1837 the bank had $250,000 in specie in its vaults.[4]

On the 10th of March the following statement of resources was given out:

Available April 1,	
1. Two first installments of the Surplus Revenue allotted to Missouri by Act of the Legislature	$254,500
2. Seminary and Saline Funds	70,000
3. First and second installments on 1700 private shares	68,000
	$392,500
Available July 1,	
1. Third private installment	51,000
2. Third installment Surplus Revenue	117,250
	$560,750
Available October 1,	
1. Last two installments Surplus Revenue	178,500
	$739,250

[1] *Mo. Republican*, Mar. 15, 1837.

[2] *Ibid.*

[3] *Ibid.*, Dec. 19, 1837.

[4] *Ibid.*, July 7, 1837.

"Under the rule of $2.00 of discounts to $1.00 of paid-up capital by October 1, the bank will be able to lend $1,478,500".[1]

On July 1 it was to have its resources increased by becoming depository for the United States Government.[2] *The Republican* by this time was ready to admit that the bank would be able to do enough business to avoid public inconvenience and stated that its opposition had only been for the purpose of satisfying itself as to its soundness.[3]

Late in February the directors had held their first meeting, elected Henry Shurlds cashier, and appointed an agent to go East to sell the state bonds as provided for by the charter. The selection of Mr. Shurlds was most fortunate. His service was to extend over fifteen years and to be the greatest single factor in the success of the bank. He was the choice of the state directors, for no private members were elected until several months later. He was a lawyer by profession but had been Secretary of State and Auditor of Public Accounts, resigning the latter office to become cashier of the bank.[4] His manner was genial but back of that was extreme caution in business dealings. Probably Missouri has produced few abler financiers.

The bank opened for business May 10, 1837 in temporary quarters in the Chouteau House.[5] Besides the president and cashier the force consisted of two tellers, two bookkeepers, a note clerk, and a messenger.[6] The opening had been announced for April 15 but had been delayed. The offerings were large and beyond the power of the bank to discount; but an effort was made to accommodate everyone to some extent. The bank was not yet in a position to is-

[1] *Mo. Republican*, Mar. 10, 1837.

[2] *Ibid.*, Apr. 14, 1837.

[3] *Ibid.*, Mar. 14, 1837 and *Argus*, May 5, 1837.

[4] Bay, W. V. M., *Bench and Bar of Mo.*, article on "Henry Shurlds."

[5] *Mo. Republican*, May 11, 1837.

[6] *Mo. Argus*, May 5, 1837.

sue currency but it offered to lend a part of the Surplus Revenue allotment on short time terms.[1] The first two installments of this had been placed on deposit in Ohio and Indiana banks, and a part of it had been transferred to St. Louis by draft.[2]

On July 1st the private stockholders elected as their two representatives on the board of directors, G. K. McGunnegle and F. L. McGill,[3] and on July 28th the governor issued a proclamation stating that the private stock had been paid for according to the requirements of Section 18 of the charter and that notes might now be issued.[4] There had been much speculation about the affairs of the Cincinnati Commercial Agency, but its purchase by the State Bank was not announced until the end of July. The Agency's banking house and equipment was included in the purchase, so abandonment of the temporary quarters was now possible. The taking over of the business of the Agency gave the new bank a large volume of business from the start. A statement of September 16, 1837 showed loans of $1,109,250, deposits of $819,855, and specie holdings of $466,715. It had been declared to be the settled policy to retire the circulation of the Agency as rapidly as possible and to substitute for it the notes of its own issue. However, the change was made very slowly. The statement first mentioned showed a circulation of only $28,000.[5] No notes were issued under $20, although the charter allowed denominations as low as $10. *The Republican* charged that this concession was made to secure the good will of Senator Benton.[6]

[1] *Mo. Argus*, May 5, 1837.

[2] *Ibid.*, Apr. 17, 1837.

[3] Shepard, *op. cit.*, p. 142.

[4] *Mo. Argus*, Aug. 1, 1837.

[5] *Financial Register* (Philadelphia), May 23, 1838.

[6] *Mo. Republican*, Dec. 20, 1837.

The slowness of the expansion of the circulation was in large part due to the failure to market the state bonds. It had been reported that $900,000 of the bonds were sold at a premium before the bank opened, but this was untrue.[1] The directors had wisely refused to issue post notes pending the floating of the loan, although there was much demand for such action.[2] A letter from President Smith to Governor Boggs, dated November 28, 1837, explains the situation:

Just before the death of the Agency its debt was purchased on terms of advantage to the bank. We expanded our business enough to save the city. Moreover, one-fifth of the business of the Saint Louis office has been done in the country. The bank has done what it could with its capital and has done its best to sell the state bonds. Special agents have been twice sent East. We are trying again and think we will succeed by the end of the year. However, in spite of all this the bank will probably declare a January dividend that will be surprising. Overgrown dividends, however, indicate overissue. Issues should be made only against specie, not against notes. We have issued no small notes.[3]

Criticism of the bank was not confined to the restriction of the circulation. The country districts were impatient for the establishment of agencies as provided by the charter. None had been established. The bank promised action as soon as possible, but said it must wait on the marketing of the bonds. A vigorous denial was made to the charge that the city was getting all of the benefits of the bank. One hundred thousand dollars had been loaned to farmers during the first five months of business. *The Argus* vigor-

[1] *Mo. Argus*, Apr. 14, 1837.

[2] *Mo. Republican*, Aug. 31, 1837.

[3] *Ibid.*, Dec. 16, 1837.

ously defended the policy of the bank, maintaining that every country customer who had offered a note with good security had been accommodated, that the bank had paid specie on demand, that it had refused to issue more notes than it could be certain to redeem, and that it had protected the farmers by refusing to make collections for customers who made unreasonable demands for specie.[1] It argued, that the fact that State Bank notes commanded a premium of 7½ per cent over those of Illinois was evidence enough of the soundness of the bank.[2] *The Argus,* however, had been liberal in its praise from the beginning. When the bank was selected as a government depository, it had characterized the action as a recognition of management by its able directorate which had given the bank unlimited confidence at home and abroad.[3] It might be mentioned that the government contract was made when the bank had been in operation less than thirty days, although no deposits were made until after July 1st.

On October 11, the Bank announced that all stock had been paid up, that the superintendents of the subscription offices had turned the proceeds over to the bank, and that no loans had been made to assist payment.[4]

A public statement was made for November 21, 1837, showing the following condition:[5]

[1] *Mo. Argus,* Oct. 11, 1837.

[2] *Ibid.,* Sept. 5, 1837.

[3] *Ibid.,* Aug. 29, 1837.

[4] *Mo. Republican,* Oct. 11, 1837.

[5] *Ibid.,* Nov. 21, 1837.

Resources

Branch at Fayette for Capital		$60,000.00
Discounts		738,846.58
Domestic Bills of Exchange		118,201.60
Real Estate		49,906.75
Personal Property		840.50
Expense Account		10,018.48
Due from Banks and Public Officers		60,394.84
Interest on Cincinnati Commercial Agency Debt		17,966.65
Cash and Notes of Other Banks		212,100.00
Specie		628,468.12
Other Resources		21,234.89
		$1,917,978.41

Liabilities

Capital		
State	$415,864.59	
Private	163,056.00	$578,914.59
Treasurer U. S.		167,382.79
Bills Payable		
Debt Cincinnati Commercial Agency payable in four semi-annual installments beginning Jan. 4, 1838		342,251.29
Capital for Real Estate Loans		4,229.99
Individual Deposits		508,696.40
Interest		33,609.16
Circulation		33,940.00
Due to Banks		210,884.19
Other Liabilities		38,070.00
		$1,917,978.41

Of course a large part of this business represents the accounts taken over from the Commercial Agency. *The Republican* deducted the interest on the Agency debt and the expenses from the interest account, and suggested that the remainder ($5,624.03) was not a satisfactory return on the capital. Considering the circumstances under which the bank started, it was, however, something of an achievement to avoid a deficit. What these circumstances were, and how the bank weathered the panic days of 1837, will be taken up in the next chapter.

CHAPTER X

THE STATE BANK AND THE PANIC OF 1837

THE failure to recharter the Bank of the United States and the consequent unwise multiplication of state banks, speculation in public lands, and improvements for which the country was not yet ready all led to a very unstable financial situation in the United States. Morever, the effects of the European crisis of 1836 were soon to be felt.

The state banks apparently were prosperous, but they had managed their loan accounts with great laxity and had issued more currency than they could hope to redeem. Often too the issues were wholly out of proportion to business needs. In July, 1836 President Jackson determined to slow down the inflation which had been going on at such an uncontrolled rate since 1834. He issued his famous Specie Circular, making only gold and silver receivable at the land offices in payment for public lands.[1] This precipitated the crash. Heavy demands were made on the banks, but they could not furnish the necessary specie. To save themselves the New York City and Philadelphia banks suspended specie payments and their action was generally copied by the banks of other sections as fast as the news reached them. The western banks were accused of hoarding specie received from the land offices after the Specie Circular went into effect, but the truth was their holdings were very modest. At the time of the general suspension the banks of Ken-

[1] See Spaulding, *op. cit.*, p. 43.

tucky, Indiana, and twenty-three in Ohio had deposits of $19,442,224 and specie to the amount of only $4,710,416.[1]

It is not the intention here to discuss the causes and general aspects of the panic of 1837, but rather to inquire into its local manifestations in Missouri. The important point to be noted is that the State Bank began operations at a time of great national financial stress. However, speculation in Missouri had been controlled more than in many other places, and so her difficulties were correspondingly less. A large proportion of the people believed in "hard money", and the Internal Improvement craze had scarcely reached the state. The simple agricultural life of the country districts had made it possible to get along without banks and to restrain somewhat the demands of Saint Louis for legislation. The Branch Bank and the Cincinnati Agency had cared for the more urgent needs of the city throughout the inflation period, and their officers, particularly John O'Fallon, had constantly counseled care in business dealings. At any rate Saint Louis escaped having many banks organized between 1830 and 1836 and had only begun to borrow from the new state bank when the panic came. She still had many conservative French business men and they were slow to contract debts. There was, however, an unhealthy expansion of business in the city. The legislature of 1836-37 had considered requests for charters for railroads, insurance companies, gas plants, and hotels. Saw mills, foundries, theatres, and wholesale dry-goods houses had been built. The streets were paved 600 yards back from the river. Pittsburg was manufacturing $350,000 to $400,000 of steamboats a year for St. Louis traders.[2]

As panic conditions became more pronounced specie became very scarce in St. Louis. Illinois and Indiana notes

[1] *Financial Register Philadelphia*, Aug. 16, 1837, p. 58.

[2] See Wetmore, *Gazetteer of Mo.*, 1837, p. 188.

were present to some degree and those of Mississippi, Alabama, Wisconsin, and Michigan were abundant but nearly worthless. Boatmen refused them for freight and passage money. Eastern exchange became very scarce and commanded a premium of 5-9 per cent. New York drafts were practically unobtainable. The merchants had not been caught with large stocks and they preferred to hold what they had rather than to sell for suspended notes. Estimates in May, 1838 stated that business had declined 90 per cent over that of the previous year. Few failures, however, were recorded.[1]

On May 22, 1837 the Cincinnati Commercial Agency suspended specie payments. This was twelve days after the news of the suspension of the New York banks reached Saint Louis.[2] There was comparatively little excitement. The State Bank paid specie as usual and on June 1 announced the purchase of the accounts of the suspended Agency. The federal government was still paying specie to soldiers and through the Indian agency, so the pressure was lessened. Before the end of 1837, however, the State Bank voted to suspend as a measure of protection to its reserves. Advantage was taken of this protection to make an added profit. Specie to the amount of $100,000 was sold to the United States Bank at Philadelphia at a premium of 2 per cent.[3] There was much local criticism of this act. Missouri was represented in the New York City Conference on resumption in 1838 and voted for resumption. Illinois stood with her. The motion passed 10 to 7. Martin Thomas, a Missouri representative, was on the committee which drew up this resolution. A second resolution to resume by January 1, 1839 was passed by a vote of 11 to 4, but here

[1] *Financial Register Philadelphia*, May 23, 1838, p. 377.

[2] Shepherd, *op. cit.*, p. 140.

[3] *Financial Register Philadelphia*, Jan. 3, 1838.

Missouri dissented.[1] One hundred and forty-three Western delegates were present, chiefly from Illinois, Indiana, and Missouri, but the vote was by states. The State Bank of Missouri did not wait for the expiration of the period named by the convention but resumed in 1838.[2] On September 6, 1838 it declared a three per cent dividend, announced a fifty-percent reduction in the New York exchange premium, and a policy of discounting up to the limit of its ability, which it said was quite small at that time.[3]

Not everybody was friendly to the bank. Charges of mismanagement were frequent, but they seem to have grown chiefly out of the campaign of hostility waged by the *Missouri Republican.* A letter published in its columns in 1837 shows the character of the charges:

Can the bank give a safe and available currency and send money east of the mountains without its being shaved? If not it is not doing what it was created for. If it can and does not the directors should be discharged. It would not be heard of fifty miles from Saint Louis except for the wrangling of its managers. Nobody sees the notes of the bank. It is an insult to print Benton's portrait on them. Starting during the suspension it was to be expected that it would not redeem its currency, but it could have issued post notes. As for discounts it does little. It gives punctuality but no facility. As for exchange it is 3 to 5 per cent instead of our old rate of ½ of 1 per cent. In published controversy it had been asked who stole its funds. It is clear they were stolen. The great fundamental requirement was disregarded when paper money was accepted for stock. This cut off the specie supply. Moreover, $100,000 of its scanty stock was sold to the United

[1] Minutes of an Adjourned Meeting of Delegates from Various States, City Hall, N. Y., Apr. 11, 1838.

[2] *City Directory of St. Louis*, 1838.

[3] *Mo. Argus*, Sept. 6, 1838.

States Bank for its notes. The governor asks the officers of the bank if they are honest men and they answer "yes".[1]

The query of the governor mentioned in this letter refers to an investigation instituted by him to find the basis of the stories being circulated about the bank. He addressed a communication to the president of the bank asking very pointed, but not quite diplomatic questions about the conduct of the business. *The Republican* made a great deal of sport of this questionnaire, indicating that no man, when asked pointblank if he were honest, would deny it.[2]

The reply of the president was to appoint a committee of three directors to examine the bank and report their findings to the governor. The members of the committee were John O'Fallon, S. S. Rayburn, and F. L. McGill. They reported that no favoritism had been shown in making loans and that they had been scattered as much as possible in order to accommodate the maximum number of people. One or two large loans for short periods, to be paid at maturity, had been made in the East, but these were regarded as exchange transactions. The total loan account stood at $737,037.07 but $324,000 of this had been purchased from the Commercial Agency. Of the rest $119,472.47 had been loaned in the state outside of Saint Louis. Replying to the charge that city customers had been favored, the committee stated that barely one-half of the city applications had been granted while nine-tenths of those from the country had been approved. The five largest loans purchased from the Agency were to city merchants and were respectively for $17,000, $14,000, $14,000, $13,000, and $9,000. These had been reduced at the rate of ten per cent each four months. Loans of from $6,000 to $10,000 had been made to other city merchants since the opening. The banking house of

[1] *Mo. Republican*, Dec. 28, 1837. Adapted from a long letter.

[2] *Mo. Republican*, Dec. 16, 1837.

the Agency had been purchased for $37,500 to be paid for one-half in two years, one-fourth in three, and the balance in four years, with 6 per cent semi-annual interest. It was being carried on the statement at $49,906.75, the increase representing expenses of remodeling and interest as paid. In answer to the governor's question about overdrafts it was stated that none had been allowed intentionally. Of the outstanding stock $163,050 was owned by individuals. Fifteen-hundred-and-twenty dollars had been forfeited for non-payment of installments. The specie in the vaults was given at $628,000 or $50,000 more than the paid-up capital stock. With regard to the questions of the governor about the character of the officers, the committee said their character was good and they believed them to be efficient and economical. *The Republican* published the report in full without comment, but *The Argus* called it a vindication of the bank and a proof that the officers had regarded their oaths.[1]

Much difficulty had been experienced in marketing the state bonds. An attempt had been made to sell them to John Jacob Astor, but negotiations had been broken off.[2] In August, 1838 the sale of $400,000 of them in New York was announced. The name of the purchaser was not given.[3] The Tenth General Assembly convened on November 19, 1838 and Governor Boggs in his opening message took up the question of the bond difficulties. He said in part:

The bank was incorporated last session and started up but a short time before the general suspension throughout the Union, so it was unable to render much aid to the country.

[1] *Mo. Republican*, Dec. 21, 1837 and *Mo. Argus*, Dec. 23, 1837. Copied from *Jeffersonian Republican* (Jefferson City, Mo.).

[2] *Financial Register Philadelphia*, Feb. 28, 1838.

[3] *Ibid.*, Aug. 8, 1838.

But the Bank has done its best to relieve the pressure. It has been managed so as to maintain its credit unimpaired and now stands in successful operation. According to the charter I took $624,000 stock for the State School Fund The residue, $875,000, is held for the use of the state. State bonds are to be used to pay for this but they have not been sold, although the bank has tried. The trouble is a technical mistake in the bonds. Moreover, the charter is not right for there is no provision for a surplus. If in some year there were no profits, the state interest would not be paid. This irregularity in dividends may make the stock unpopular. The charter doesn't closely define the relation of the bank and its branches. The amount of branch capital and the number of branches should be limited by law.[1]

A House committee was appointed to study the recommendations of the governor. It reported that $401,856.18 of the bonds were still unsold, but that the failure was not due to lack of state credit or negligence of the bank, but rather to technical defects in the bonds themselves. It made four recommendations as follows:

1. Change the interest rate on the unsold bonds from 5½ to 6 per cent and make both interest and principal payable in London in pounds, francs, or guilders. This should increase the quotation from 5 to 7 per cent.

2. Change the charter provision requiring the net profits to be paid out in dividends semi-annually so that 1 per cent can be set aside each year as a surplus to cover bad debts.

3. Reopen subscription books for private stock as the authorized amount has not all been sold. After twenty days let the state take all that is unsold.

4. Allow the bank to sell its holdings of state bonds at its option in order to get funds in time of sudden pressure.[2]

[1] *Jour. Senate of Mo.*, 10th General Assembly, 1838-39, pp. 19-21. Adapted.

[2] *House Journal*, 10th General Assembly Mo., p. 119, Report of the Committee to which was referred the Matter of the Sale of the State Bonds.

Most of these suggestions were embodied in the following amendments to the charter made during this session:

Section 1. All unsold state bonds were to be withdrawn.

Section 2. New bonds bearing 6 per cent interest payable semi-annually were to be substituted for them.

Section 3. Principal and interest were made payable in London.

Section 4. The faith and credit of the state was pledged under Section 37 of the original charter to guarantee deposits and all bills payable.

Section 5. Under Section 37 the limit on loans to one person was made $5,000 but smaller borrowers were to have the preference.

Section 6. One per cent of the capital stock was to be set aside from each year's earnings for surplus.

Section 7. Interest on state bonds already sold may be paid by the bank and taken from the state's share in the dividend.

Section 8. Inland exchange may be charged by the bank and its branches.

Section 11. Subscription books to be reopened for 20 days, after which the state shall take the unsold balance.

Approved, Feb. 8, 1839.[1]

A bill was also approved establishing a branch at Palmyra under much the same conditions as that at Fayette. The president and four state directors were to be elected by the General Assembly and four private directors were to be appointed by the private directors of the mother bank. In case not all the private stock should be taken the number of private directors could be reduced proportionately to not less than two. Their terms of office were the same as for the mother bank. Ten per cent of the paid-up capital of the bank was assigned to Palmyra but any unused part could be recalled after sixty days.[2]

[1] *Laws of Mo.*, 1st Session, 10th General Assembly Mo., p. 10 *et seq.*

[2] *Ibid.*, p. 10.

The legislature took occasion to offer some advice about the conduct of the business. A resolution was passed asking that loans be renewed unless funds were in demand by other customers. It was also suggested that measures be taken to prevent depositors of public funds from checking them out for private purposes.[1] An attempt was made to aid manufacturers by forcing the bank to make loans to them at low rates. This was referred to the Judiciary Committee which reported that such action would be in violation of the bank's charter, that the charter was a contract to which the state was one party and those who purchase stock were the other. Being a contract a change could not be made without the consent of both parties. Such a bill as this, the committee said, imposes a duty on the bank to lend money in a manner not mentioned in the charter, to a particular class not mentioned in the charter, and at a rate unreasonably low. If it could force the bank to lend money for five years, why not for twenty? If to a manufacturer at 5 per cent, why not to a farmer at 1 per cent? It suggested that rumors of tamperinng with the bank by the legislature would impair its credit and that the lending of its funds was the business of the president and directors. The logic of this report was accepted by the legislature and, instead of the proposed law, a resolution was passed saying that in the judgment of the General Assembly it would be expedient for the bank to make liberal loans to manufacturers.[2]

The condition of the bank at this time is shown by the following comparative statements:

[1] *House Journal*, 10th General Assembly Mo., 1838-39, p. 357.

[2] *Senate Journal*, 10th General Assembly Mo., p. 282, 1838-39.

	Jan. 14, 1837 [1]	*May 15, 1837* [2]	*Dec. 30, 1837* [3]
Loans	$1,298,811	$879,384	$1,034,852
Real Estate			50,101
Other Investments ...	3,241	3,241	67,335
Due from Banks	508,204	56,684	45,271
Notes of Other Banks	449,064	719,977	223,930
Specie	222,924	409,553	628,167
Capital			607,398
Circulation			94,000
Deposits	2,262,900	1,188,137	748,655
Due to Banks	299,749	835,128	348,995
Other Liabilities			188,836

This gives something of a picture of the effect of the panic. Loans were contracted. Deposits sharply decreased and specie holdings increased. The bank had evidently withdrawn all possible funds from other banks and turned their notes into specie wherever it could. The panic had been weathered without serious injury, but grave problems were ahead in the depression period.

[1] *Financial Register Philadelphia*, Apr. 25, 1838, p. 346.

[2] *Ibid.*, May 9, 1838, p. 364.

[3] *Ibid.*, July 25, 1838.

CHAPTER XI

THE FIGHT AGAINST UNSOUND MONEY

AFTER the panic of 1837 the State Bank steadily refused to expand its circulation or take any unusual risks. Accordingly it furnished a very small part of the currency needed for the transaction of business in Saint Louis. The deficit was made up by notes of the banks of surrounding states. Illinois currency became especially plentiful.

The officials of the bank became fearful for the safety of these notes. They were not then redeemable in specie, and conditions seemed to be growing worse rather than better. Accordingly on November 12, 1839 the board of directors passed a resolution that in the future the bank would receive on deposit only its own notes and specie or the notes of specie-paying banks. In case exception was made to the rule of refusing suspended notes offered for deposit, repayment was to be made in the same sort of funds as paid in.[1] This drastic action greatly excited the merchants. Many of their customers, particularly those in Illinois, had no means of payment except these notes of suspended banks. And now without warning the bank had shaken their standing as media for the settlement of debts and contracts, thereby increasing their depreciation. The merchants felt the bank had not played fair, for in 1837 it had borrowed funds from the State Bank of Illinois and had issued a circular containing a list of approved currency including the issues of the Illinois bank. Relying on this,

[1] Edwards, *op. cit.*, p. 367 and *City Directory St. Louis*, 1839.

the merchants accepted these notes in business transactions and claimed the policy should not have been changed without reasonable warning.[1] A committee of business men asked President Smith to allow them to protect their business honor by paying all collection paper already discounted at the bank in paper of the kind hitherto considered bankable. They also asked that other loans already contracted be considered as accommodation paper and made payable under rules applying to such paper, i. e. interest and any curtailment of the loan to be paid in specie. President Smith was not inclined to favor the proposal but finally agreed to lay it before the directors. The board, however, decided to adhere to its original plan on the ground that the refused notes were sure to grow worse and that, as trustees, they were bound to protect the bank. At this juncture eleven well-known business men of the city came forward and offered to indorse the currency, thus indemnifying the bank for any loss it might suffer. These men were George Collier, Pierre Chouteau, E. Tracy, John Walsh, William Glasgow, Henry Van Phul, John Kerr, G. K. McGunnegle, John O'Fallon, and J. C. Leville.[2] It is to be noted that several of these men were also directors of the bank. However, they evidently represented minority opinion, for the board declined the offer.

It was not expected that the bank would refuse a citizens' bond. Nothing seemed ahead but ruin and there was no way to avert it. A mass meeting of business men was held at the court house to discuss the action of the bank, and the following resolution was passed:

That it be the sense of this meeting that it will be no discredit to any individual having paper maturing this day at

[1] *Mo. Argus*, Nov. 20, 1839.

[2] Edwards, *op. cit.*, p. 367.

the Bank of Missouri, to allow said paper to go to protest, if a tender is made at the bank or to a notary of currency hitherto bankable, and is refused.[1]

It was also decided to remove deposits. A copy of the minutes of this meeting, signed by Wayman Crow, Secretary, was sent to President Smith. In a public reply Smith said:

It would set all law and order at defiance to let your paper go to protest. Reason will resume her sway. The tone of defiance makes it impossible to give reasons.

John Smith, President[2]

The Republican condemned the bank in no uncertain terms, charging that the weakness which made such action seem advisable was due to excessive loans to directors and to mismanagement. The statement was made that one director had borrowed more than any business man in town. *The Argus* entered a general denial.[3] The state of popular excitement is shown by the following editorial:

The bank excitement continued very high during yesterday. In fact it is the only subject matter of conversation or consideration. The merchants, it might literally be said, have forsaken their counting rooms, and the mechanics their shops. Wherever two or three met, the action of the bank was the theme of conversation; and in every circle which we have fallen in with, the resolution of the directors was condemned without measure or reserve. In truth there has never been, in this community so universal and unanimous a condemnation of any measure as this.[4]

[1] *Mo. Republican*, Nov. 13, 1839.

[2] *Mo. Argus*, Nov. 22, 1839.

[3] *Ibid.*, Jan. 31, 1839.

[4] *Mo. Republican, Nov.* 13, 1839.

The Argus attempted to defend the bank. It characterized the indignation meeting as a bluff and commended the directors as men worthy of the trust committed to them. The withdrawal of deposits was called, "a run created by politicians with results too pitiful to notice". An attempt was made to give the reasons which actuated the directors. It was claimed that the circular of 1837 in no way bound the bank when conditions changed, especially since the bank had expressly reserved the right to vary the list of approved notes from time to time as deemed expedient. Everyone knows, it continued, that the Illinois Bank will probably be unable to resume specie payment and may fail. It called attention to the fact that its paper was depreciating daily and that it was quoted 8 per cent to 10 per cent under current the day before the Bank of Missouri resolution was made public. Moreover, no statement of the State Bank of Illinois had been published for some months. A vigorous denial was made to the charge that the Illinois State Bank had received unfair treatment. On the contrary the Bank of Missouri had tried to protect it by demanding specie only in case of necessity. It concluded that for the Bank of Missouri to attempt to hold up $3,000,000 to $5,000,000 of bad Illinois paper would be suicidal and would render no help.[1]

Public opinion, however, was with the merchants. The stand of *The Argus* ruined it. Subscribers rapidly dropped off and it was soon sold at a forced sale.

Now just why did the State Bank of Missouri consider it necessary to take such a stand? In the first place its own condition was rapidly becoming unsatisfactory. It held large amounts of the notes of suspended banks ($593,550 in 1838),[2] and their value was daily becoming more uncertain. Large loans had been made to St. Louis merchants

[1] See *Mo. Argus*, Nov. 20 and 22, 1839.

[2] See Pope, *op. cit.*, p. 91. Statement is published in *Mo. Argus*, Dec. 31, 1838.

and their payment seemed remote. Banks all around were suspending specie payments or had done so. If the Bank of Missouri was to be anything better than a "rag bank" it was evidently time to take drastic means to protect its credit. At this time, however, it held specie to the amount of $691,000.[1] This general condition with a slight change for the worse continued all through 1839. The second main reason for the action of the bank had to do with the situation of Illinois. A large part of the notes of other banks held represented those of the State Bank of Illinois. That institution was rapidly on the down grade. It had resumed specie payment on October 3, 1838 but had soon been forced to suspend again. Its statement for February 28, 1838 showed specie holdings of only $524,992 or less than those of the Bank of Missouri, while its circulation was $1,838,325 and individual deposits $177,085. The trouble, however, was not here but in its loan accounts. Nearly $3,000,000 had been loaned on speculative real estate and state canal and road projects. Everybody was expecting a crash and its notes were regularly quoted at least 10 per cent under current. The complete statement is here given:

Assets	*Jan. 8, 1838*	*Liabilities*	
Discounts	$2,929,325	Capital	$3,515,000
Real Estate Loans	484,740	Real Estate Fund	500,000
Bills of Exchange	593,154	Circulation	1,838,325
Ill. Improvement Stock	1,765,000	State Banks & Branches	2,847,601
Ill. and Mich. Canal	525,000	Other Banks	347,077
Real Estate	25,806	Unclaimed Dividends	1,350
Personal Property	4,944	Retained Dividends	81,130
Expense Account	5,099	Canal Fund	420,000
State of Illinois	23,200	Fund Commission	4,473
State Banks & Branches	2,740,983	Individual Deposits	177,085
Other banks	144,529	Interest	51,601
Ill. and Mich. Canal	43,631	Surplus	54,556
Notes of Other Banks	46,433	Profit and Loss	17,652
Specie	524,992		
	$9,856,836		$9,861,850[2]

[1] *Ibid.*

[2] *Financial Register*, Philadelphia, Feb. 28, 1838, p. 283. Cents are omitted but there is another slight error as statement does not balance.

The fears of the Bank of Missouri directors were soon realized. By 1842 Illinois bank paper had fallen to 66 and state warrants were quoted at 50.[1] In 1842 Governor Carlin had called attention to the suspension of the bank and had recommended legislative action. He laid the trouble to railway and canal loans.[2] His successor, Governor Ford, recommended liquidation and cancellation of $2,050,000 of state bonds on the surrender of that amount of bank stock held by the state. The legislature in 1843, acting on his suggestion, repealed the charter and gave four years time for liquidation. In order to protect its interests the Bank of Missouri brought suit in the United States Courts and secured the appointment of three receivers to wind up the bank and apply the assets to payment of its debts.[3]

The effect of the refusal of the Bank of Missouri to receive notes of suspended banks was unquestionably far reaching, but it is almost impossible of estimation. Other factors were involved in the condition of the bank. At any rate between January 1, 1840 and January 1, 1841 deposits decreased from $1,174,532 to $322,909, and notes of other banks held decreased from $212,465 to $42,345.[4] Much of this can be explained by the general business depression of the time and the consequent falling-off of government land sales. The Saint Louis land office was still furnishing by far the largest part of the deposits.

The immediate result was, however, a substantial withdrawal of deposits from the State Bank. During one day withdrawals exceeded deposits by $20,000.[5] The govern-

[1] Garnett, *op. cit.*, p. 38.

[2] *Hazard's Register*, vol. iii, p. 428.

[3] Garnet, *op. cit.*, pp. 40 and 42.

[4] For discussion on this point see Pope, *op. cit.*, p. 91.

[5] *Mo. Argus*, Nov. 22, 1839.

ment was depositing heavily at just this time, so specie holdings and deposits both held up well. In a very short period $162,000 in specie was deposited by the land office and after the run the bank reported specie holding of $570,-000.[1] Government funds, however, were rapidly withdrawn after this date. It is evident that the bank had saved itself at a heavy cost of local esteem, but it, at least, had the satisfaction of being the only bank in the West that did not suspend. It could not, however, drive out the depreciated Illinois notes. Its own circulation was too small to do more than set standards, but it did do that much, even though the effort was not appreciated. The Illinois notes continued to pass current in small transactions and were received at a discount in larger deals.[2] It was soon necessary for every business house to have a counterfeit detector.

The funds withdrawn from the State Bank were deposited with insurance agencies, private bankers, and particularly with the Saint Louis Gas Light Co. The latter institution was incorporated by the Missouri legislature in 1839 with a minimum capital of $100,000 with permission to increase it to $600,000. It was in fact started with a fully paid capital of $200,000. Its business was to provide lights for the city, but, although $40,000 was spent on the works, its early business was mostly of another sort. It received money on deposit and made loans, but issued no currency. The banking business was, however, transitory and was wholly given up in 1842.[3] Likely most of its depositors eventually went back to the State Bank.

As the period of depression continued the State Bank found itself more and more unable to withstand the forces of suspension. The business community had to use such

[1] *Mo. Argus*, Nov. 22, 1839.

[2] Carr, *op. cit.*, p. 165.

[3] See *Report of Directors St. Louis Gas Light Co.*, 1848 (Harvard Library).

money as was available and the refusal of the bank to receive it on deposit was a constant inconvenience. Accordingly, on March 12, 1841 the resolution was rescinded and deposits of the notes of paper banks were again accepted.[1] This action caused much criticism in the bank journals. *The Philadelphia Journal of Banking* accused it of acting as agent for the suspended banks of Illinois and of carrying on its business under cover of a mere technical maintenance of specie payments.[2] By receiving such notes on deposit and paying them out again it facilitated their use as currency in Missouri. Moreover, it ceased redeeming the notes of its branches at the Saint Louis office.[3] This caused them to be rejected at the land office as transportation was too poor to give much value to redemption at the branch counters. However, they were always redeemed when presented. In spite of the method used it remained true that the notes of the home office were always redeemed at par on presentation. This was possible because of the lessened burden on account of throwing the branches on their own resources and because the issues were carefully restricted. The circulation was only $257,430 on July 1, 1841.[4] Eastern quotations were not par, however. Part of this was due to difficulties of distance and transportation and part to the fear that redemption might not be maintained. The branch policy gave some grounds for this fear. Five to seven per cent was the usual discount.[5] Small dividends were declared throughout the period of depression as follows:

[1] Pope, *op. cit.*, p. 91.

[2] *Jour. Banking Philadelphia*, Nov. 24, 1841.

[3] *Ibid.*, July 21, 1841, p. 26.

[4] *Ibid.*, July 21, 1841.

[5] Quotations were regularly given in the *Jour. of Banking Philadelphia* each week. The Mo. figure was usually not far different from those of other Western banks.

January 1, 1839	$17,515.81
July 1, 1839	19,710.38
January 1, 1840	10,146.17
July 1, 1840	8,167.91 etc. until 1843 [1]

Owing to the fact that many of the notes of the banks held were never redeemed, these dividends were likely, in part at least, paid out of capital. Dividend payment was suspended after January, 1843 and was not resumed until 1845. On June 1, 1840 the suspended debt was given as $65,-191.59.[2] The statement for July 1, 1841 shows a considerable decline in business from the days of 1838. The suspended debt had increased to $148,932. Other figures were: notes of other banks, $156,510; specie, $273,290; circulation, $257,430; and individual deposits, $258,233. The state owed the bank $275,000 and there was a bills payable account of $183,000.[3]

About the best that can be said is that the bank was able to maintain its organization and pay specie on its notes until national conditions began to improve in 1843. It was forced to lower its ideals somewhat, but a more or less constant struggle against cheap money forces was carried on and, judged by other Western banks of the time, it achieved no small measure of success. At least the organization remained intact and the bank was in a position to expand as opportunity offered. Its officers had become familiar with the problems pressing for solution. The next twenty-five years were to be years of great service to the state. It was largely to take the form of the setting of standards—and that work had already been begun.

[1] "Report Mo. Auditor," 1840, p. 504 in appendix *Senate Jour.*, 11th General Assembly Mo.

[2] *Hazard's Register*, June 30, 1840, p. 94.

[3] *Jour. Banking Philadelphia*, July 21, 1841.

CHAPTER XII

THE CAREER OF THE BANK 1843 TO 1857

FOR a few years after 1839 the State Bank had been engaged in a not altogether successful fight against the forces of unsound money; but by 1845 it was in a sound condition and had begun its decade of greatest prosperity. It was during this period that it earned the title of the " Gibraltar of the West ". From this time until the panic of 1857 it dominated the financial affairs of the state and managed its business with a skill and safety rarely equaled in the history of early American banking. The story of its progress and service to the state can perhaps best be set forth by a chronological treatment

The fight against cheap money had aroused great bitterness. The legislature had shown its confidence in Smith by reelecting him to the presidency of the bank, but his position became to unpleasant that he resigned in 1842, ostensibly because of inadequate salary. The Hard-Money Democrats attempted to secure the election of Dr. Penn of Howard County to succeed him, but St. Louis feared his policy would be too drastic and threw her weight for F. Kennett, a director who had been in favor of depreciated currency.[1] Kennett, however, did not prove to be a satisfactory political tool. He at once instituted a more aggressive policy and refused to accept any notes on deposit except those of his own bank. This completely discredited

[1] McClure, C. H., "Early Opposition to T. H. Benton in Mo.," in *Mo. Historical Review* (Columbia, Mo.), April, 1916, p. 168.

the Illinois currency and caused so much disturbance of business that Congress made it the subject of an investigation.[1]

The Thirteenth General Assembly passed a considerable amount of legislation relating to the bank. It made provision for new branches at Jackson and Springfield under the usual charter terms, and then proceeded to the question of the proper attitude to be taken on depreciated currency. It indorsed the action of the bank, but criticised it for ever having receded from the position taken in 1839. A committee was appointed to make an examination of the suspended debt and to find the names of all state officers holding stock in the bank, together with the amount owned by each. An act was passed providing that it should be unlawful for the mother bank or any of its branches to receive notes under $5.00 after July 1, 1843 or under $10.00 after January 1, 1844. It was to deal in no notes not redeemable in specie on demand. All contracts in depreciated paper made after this date (February 28, 1843) were declared void and a fine of $500 was to be assessed on all violators. Brokers were to be fined $1,000, and any guilty corporation was to lose its charter. An exception was made in the case of the State Bank which was allowed to sell its Illinois notes, provided they were sent out of the state.[2] All foreign banking agencies were notified to leave the state and were denied the protection of the courts.[3]

The bank now seemed to have the full confidence of the legislature. At this time the state stock amounted to $954,-205.22 but was not being increased. The dividends were being paid to the University and to the county common

[1] Shepard, *op. cit.*, pp. 162 and 163.

[2] It had $225,000 of such paper. See Sumner, W. G., *History of Banking in All Leading Nations*, vol. i, p. 412.

[3] *Laws of Mo.*, 13th General Assembly, 1st Session, 1843.

school funds.[1] Branches were being operated in Fayette, Palmyra, Jackson, and Springfield. These were as yet little more than one-man banks, but the home office had nine employees.[2]

The next legislature established a branch at Lexington and passed a resolution suggesting reduction of salaries of officers to a maximum of $1200 a year. The bank was also instructed to return all unsold state bonds in its possession. A few years before the state had borrowed a large sum for the capitol building at Jefferson City. The new president did not think this a satisfactory loan and had requested its payment. Accordingly a bill was passed authorizing the issue of $175,000 bonds for this purpose. The bank endorsed them without recourse to aid in their marketing.[3]

The bank was rapidly getting into better condition. On December 31, 1845 it had a circulation of $2,195,540 and deposits of $1,295,508. Loans were $1,433,000; bills of exchange, $1,277,000; and cash and sight exchange, $1,685,000. This last item did not include about $207,000 Illinois paper still held.[4] F. Kennett was still president and Henry Shurlds, cashier. Other members of the board were E. C. Angelrodt, W. T. Christy, John O'Fallon, W. L. Sublette, R. A. Barnes, George Collier, J. B. Sarpy, Ed. Walsh, R. Campbell, O D. Filley, T. M. Horne, and W. C. Hardin.[5]

Comparative statements for the next year or so show a steady growth but a continuance of the policy of extreme caution.

[1] "Report Mo. Auditor," 1844, in Appendix *Jour. 13th General Assembly Mo.*, p. 134.

[2] *City Directory St. Louis*, 1844.

[3] *Laws of Mo. 1845*.

[4] *Bankers Magazine* (Boston), Feb., 1848, p. 547.

[5] Skillman, W. D., *The Western Metropolis* (St. Louis, 1846), p. 93.

(000 omitted)	Dec. 31, 1847[1]	Dec. 30, 1848[2]	June 30, 1849[3]
Capital	$1,204	$1,208	$1,208
Surplus	98		135
Undivided Profits	196	186	182
Circulation	2,404	2,569	2,336
Deposits	1,363	1,735	1,785
Discounts	1,726	1,816	1,877
Bills of Exchange	647	1,064	953
Specie	2,314	2,427	2,226

Regular five-percent dividends were paid after setting aside the regular state bonus and required additions to the surplus account. President Kennett had been succeeded by Robert Campbell and, upon his resignation in 1849, J. M. Hughes had been elected to the presidency.[4]

A considerable local sensation was caused during 1849 by the refusal of the bank to redeem $5,000 of its own notes in the legal currency of the United States. It had given these notes in return for deposits of foreign coins and insisted on the right to repay such coins at the rates at which they were received. There is no record, however, that the case was taken to the courts.[5]

The year 1850 brought heavy declines in deposits and specie and an increase in loans.[6] It was also a year of exciting incidents. It was discovered that large quantities of the notes of the bank had been counterfeited in California.[7] They finally reached St. Louis and were discovered by a teller of E. W. Clarke and Brother. Page and Bacon had a large amount of them in their vaults and had had them for

[1] *Bankers Magazine*, Feb. 1848, p. 547.

[2] *Ibid.*, Mar., 1849, p. 585.

[3] *Ibid.*, Sept., 1849.

[4] *Ibid.*, March, 1849, p. 585.

[5] *Ibid.*, Oct., 1849, p. 359 copied from *St. Louis New Era*, Oct. 6, 1849.

[6] *Ibid.*, May, 1850, p. 933.

[7] *Ibid.*, Dec., 1850, p. 508.

some time. The signatures were excellent. Cashier Shurlds called his a perfect copy. A robbery inside the bank was also causing great difficulty. On August 11, 1849 it was discovered that a large amount of gold had been stolen.[1] Page and Bacon had presented a draft on the bank and demanded gold. The specie teller was absent and had taken the key to the money vault with him. Officials of the bank went to a reserve compartment to get the required gold and discovered that one bag of gold had been removed from each of sixteen boxes ($120,700 in all). The boxes had been resealed with counterfeit seals. Nathan Childs, Jr., who had been specie teller almost from the organization of the bank but who had recently resigned, was placed under arrest. He was released under heavy bail. At the preliminary hearing the case was transferred to the grand jury which found a true bill, and Judge Cox of the criminal court fixed the trial for September. When the case was called the bank asked for more time in which to secure evidence and was given until December. At the trial only circumstantial evidence was offered and the jury found a verdict of not guilty. An appeal was taken, but on account of the death of the chief witness the attorney for the bank took a non-suit. The trial had caused great excitement. The state had six lawyers, the defendant seven. The bank had attached Childs' property, giving bond for $250,000. This and injury to his character caused Childs to bring suit against the officers of the bank for $50,000. Judge Treat, however, sustained a demurrer entered by the defence on the ground that the officials were acting in a corporate capacity. The excitement produced by the case

[1] *Bankers Magazine*, Oct., 1849, pp. 330 and 358; Dec., 1849, p. 492; Feb., 1850, p. 674; Apr., 1850, p. 865; Mar., 1851, p. 776. See also *City Directory of St. Louis* for 1850. Further details of this case as they appear in the official state examinations will be given in the next chapter.

caused the bank to publish a special statement of condition as of August 15, 1849. It is given here:

Resources

Branches for Capital	$600,294.20
Discounts	960,450.11
Exchange on East and South (sight)	322,412.72
Exchanges Maturing	200,716.31
Banking house	50,000.00
Due from State for Interest	100,842.25
Loan to State	4,276.93
Bills Receivable Sale of Real Estate	31,310.78
Suspended Debt	88,241.48
Suspense Account	1,208.17
Expenses since June 30	1,536.33
Protest Account	90.31
Due from Banks	38,785.17
Certificates Bank of Illinois	191,533.33
Warrants Mo. Treas.	14,742.93
Gold and Silver	1,577,734.53
Foreign Coin Deficit	120,921.62
	$4,305,097.17

Liabilities

Capital	$1,208,751.83
Due Depositors	1,447,858.29
Due on Dividends	6,635.62
Surplus	252,139.54
Circulation	1,264,480.00
Due to banks	125,231.89
	$4,305,097.17

In 1851 efforts were made to secure settlement of claims against the state. Short term advances had been made in considerable amounts but, due to disagreements about the interest charge, these had not been paid and had been carried on current acount for some years. The legislature appointed a commission with power to make full settlement and the bank agreed to accept its award. Ninety-seven thousand dollars were paid in satisfaction of the bank's claim for one-hundred and ten thousand dollars.[1]

During 1852, 1853, and 1854 the bank statement remained fairly constant. The specie holdings rarely exceeded $1,500,000 and the circulation remained somewhere near the $2,500,000 mark. The number of branches was not increased although there was one change. The Jackson office was closed and transferred to Cape Girardeau. This took place in 1853. The reason for the transfer is not altogether clear. The Jackson Branch had been highly prosperous, having shown total net earnings of $79,628.[2]

The impending expiration of the bank charter in 1857 was already causing a good deal of discussion. This will be taken up in a later chapter, but here an incident may be mentioned which reacted somewhat unfavorably on the bank's political standing. There had been much criticism of the management of the state bond sales by the bank. Charges of inefficiency had been made more than once. In 1852 the president of the bank made a trip to New York and found at the Bank of America $215,000 of state bonds duly executed and indorsed by the bank. They had been placed there for sale in 1838. The bank had no record of their existence. President Hughes took possession of them and sent them to Jefferson City for cancellation. When they reached Jefferson City, however, it was found that all records relating to them had been burned in the capitol fire of 1838. The bank, of course, was unable to make satis-

[1] *Bankers Magazine*, Aug., 1851, p. 167.

[2] Douglas, *History of Southeast Mo.* (Chicago, 1912), vol. i, pp. 256, 262 and 318. R. Sturdivant was made cashier at Cape Girardeau. He remained in this position until the closing of the branch at the time of the sale of the state stock. He purchased the business and converted it into a private bank which was incorporated in 1882 as the Sturdivant Bank. It is still in existence and highly prosperous.

factory excuse for such gross negligence and the facts were used against it during the debates on the recharter bill.[1]

The year 1852 also marks the death of Henry Shurlds. He had been elected cashier when the bank was organized in 1837 and had retained his position until 1850. He had since acted in an advisory capacity. His sound business judgment and conservative tendencies had perhaps been the greatest single factor in the success of the bank. He had worked in a quiet way but had exerted more influence than any of its presidents. His policies had been so stamped upon the bank that they continued to dominate it until the purchase of the state interest by Mr. Eads. Shurlds deserves to be considered as one of the greatest bankers the Middle West has ever produced.[2]

The statement published in February, 1854 as of January 1st preceding caused wide and favorable comment. In round numbers its essential features were as follows:[3]

Resources		*Liabilities*	
Discounts	$1,963	Capital	$1,215
Bills of Exchange	1,994	Deposits	1,313
Suspended Debt	77	Circulation	2,487
Cash and Bank Deposits subject to check	1,413	Surplus and Profits	321

After making the usual additions to surplus and charging off some doubtful paper, a ten per cent semi-annual dividend was declared. For the preceding six months a seven per cent dividend had been paid. This 17 per cent net distribution for the year was a remarkable showing compared with other banks of the time. *The Bankers Magazine* commended the management and especially its spirit of helpfulness to the community. It expressed doubt whether any other bank in

[1] *Bankers Magazine*, Oct., 1852, p. 334.

[2] *Ibid.*, *Sept.*, 1852, p. 252.

[3] *Ibid.*, Feb., 1854, p. 636 (000 omitted).

the United States had made so good a showing during the past year. Even the antagonistic *Missouri Republican* was unsparing in its praise.[1]

During 1855 and 1856 the State Bank continued prosperous and refused in large measure to enter into the growing craze for internal improvements. Its influence remained distinctly conservative. Its statement for June 30, 1855 showed the following condition:[2]

Resources		*Liabilities*	
Discounts	$2,327	Capital	$1,215
Bills of Exchange	1,208	Deposits	1,640
Specie and Sight Exchange	1,721	Surplus and Profits	344
Suspended Debt and Bills receivable	242	Circulation	2,234

The business of the branches was given, viz:

Office	*Discounts*	*Bills of Exchange*	*Suspended Debt*	*Specie*	*Deposits*	*Circulation*
Fayette	202	70	1	101	63	224
Palmyra	58	125	24	87	24	106
Cape Girardeau	144	55	11	66	17	168
Springfield	133	16	16	66	23	99
Lexington	167	93	16	93	47	220

The outstanding features of this statement are increased discounts, decreased bills of exchange, transfer of part of the suspended debt to bills receivable, increasing deposits and circulation, and disappearance of all Illinois paper. The first two of these came about largely from public criticism. It was felt that the limited capital of the bank should not be used for distant investments. Eight per cent dividends were declared.

Local economic conditions were somewhat peculiar. Seemingly the wave of business expansion which was soon

[1] Annual Review *Mo. Republican*, 1854, p. 23.

[2] *St. Louis Democrat*, July 10, 1855 (000 omitted).

to culminate in the crash of 1857 had aroused only mild interest within the State. During most of 1855 and 1856 it was reported that money was easier than for some years and offerings were relatively light. In spite of newspaper demands for additional banking capital both the Boatmen's and the State Bank repeatedly stated that they were in a position to more than satisfy the existing demands of their customers.[1] However, at crop-moving times the shortage of banking capital always became evident and the usual newspaper demands for more banks appeared. At such times President Joseph Charless made use of his characteristic good humor and persuaded his customers to curtail their business where possible. This personal trait was of untold value to the State Bank.[2] *The Democrat* suggested that one could always get a smile at the State Bank even though loan applications might be turned down.[3] As a whole the city was much less prosperous than one might guess from the condition of the State Bank. Sheriffs sales were unusually numerous. Advertisements of such sales appeared in almost every issue of *The Democrat* during the spring and summer of 1855. The single issue of May 15th contained 112 and this was not an unusual list. It gives the impression that part of the reason for light offerings at the banks might be found in the inability of customers to give satisfactory security. Accordingly they made no requests. It was known that the State Bank considered it no part of its business to be an agent of philanthropy. The continued insistence of the St. Louis merchants that Illinois notes be received by the banks, and the increasing use of counterfeit detectors give additional evidence of local hard times. The

[1] *St. Louis Democrat*, July 16, 1855. Notes on economic and banking conditions in St. Louis appeared in almost every issue.

[2] Charless succeeded J. M. Hughes.

[3] *St. Louis Democrat*, Oct. 24, 1855.

merchants felt they could not afford to give up the Illinois trade, even though it involved very risky credits. The State Bank remained hostile to the Illinois notes. It had disposed of its supply and wanted no more. The other banks, however, voted to receive these notes at some sort of a rate and to use their influence to sustain them. The State Bank was later induced to render some assistance.

Its statement for June 1, 1857 showed no great change except a considerable decline in deposits and further increases of discounts. It went into the panic with a specie reserve amounting to 30 per cent of combined deposits and circulation.[1] Moreover, it was now better able to control its business by a variation in the discount rate. The old charter restrictions had been removed. Ten per cent interest was now legal by contract. This law applied not only to the bank, but to the state in general. It had been enacted in the hope that it would attract capital for investment in proposed railroad lines.[2]

After 1857 the State Bank was to lose its commanding position, but at this time it stood far above all competitors. It had enjoyed the exclusive right to issue currency since 1837 and during all that time had been fiscal agent for the state. Its limited capital and cautious management had restricted its business, but this had given Missouri a national reputation for banking integrity. So long as the bank functioned in such a way as to give general satisfaction, little was said about it. Most of the current newspaper criticism turned on the question of the need for additional banking capital, rather than on the management of the State Bank. The panic of 1857, however, demonstrated so clearly the inadequacy of the existing facilities

[1] *St. Louis Democrat*, June 13, 1857.

[2] See *Bankers Magazine*, April, 1855, p. 816, and *ibid.*, May, 1856, p. 848.

that the state never again attempted monopoly control.[1] After 1857 the State Bank was allowed to go its own way with no further attempts by the government to offer constructive aid.

[1] It must not be thought that the panic of 1857 was the cause of the revocation of the exclusive issue privileges of the State Bank. The law providing for the charter of the independent banks of issue was enacted before the panic came, and the result of a reasoned decision that more adequate organization was required. This point is discussed further in later chapters.

CHAPTER XIII

An Economic and Statistical Study of the Accounts of the Bank

Considerable notice has already been taken of the accounts of the State Bank, but chiefly in a manner incidental to questions of policy and historical development. It is difficult, however, to get a clear conception of the working of the bank without making a detailed study of its condition from time to time. Fortunately first-hand materials are available for this work. The General Assembly made frequent examinations and published the reports in the legislative journals. All of these have been preserved.

The life history of the bank covers the period from 1837 to 1877; but after 1857 it was little more than one of several chartered banks, and, from 1866 to the failure in 1877, the business was carried on under a federal charter. Accordingly, a study of its first twenty years will bring to light the distinctive features of the business and give a picture of its time of greatest power. For this purpose a somewhat detailed analysis of the published reports prior to 1858 will be attempted. A more general survey of later statements will be found in subsequent chapters.

The charter had this to say about public supervision:

Section 43. Twice each year the bank must submit a detailed expense account to the governor and at such times all accounts except private accounts of individuals must be published in two newspapers in the state. Either house of the legislature may demand a statement and examine the bank by means of a committee. Before each General Assembly convenes, the governor must appoint an examining committee none of whose members may be stockholders of the bank.

Section 52. Statements must be given for November 1 preceding each regular meeting of the General Assembly.

In accordance with this authority regular examinations were made and, although they would scarcely be called adequate audits to-day, they were evidently honest efforts to get at the true condition of the bank.

The first regular examination was made in 1838.[1] The committee stated that its instructions had been very vague, so it had tried to make a general examination and had met with the greatest possible co-operation from the officials of the bank. The cash was found in boxes, bags, and packages, each carefully labeled showing the amount inside. In every case these counts were verified by the committee, but as for the rest the method of examination seemed to be to ask the president and cashier questions and take their sworn answers. Many of these went into considerable detail. In round numbers the condition of the home office was found to be as follows: loans, $1,718,000, of which $326,000 represented bills of exchange purchased; cash on hand including specie and notes of other banks, $1,116,000; circulation, $556,000; and individual deposits, $723,000. The complete statement is here given:

[1] *Senate Jour.*, 1838-39, General Assembly Mo., p. 64 *et seq.*

NOVEMBER 1, 1838

Resources

Capital Fayette Branch		$238,060.00
Bills discounted		1,084,411.08
State Bond Loan		70,000.00
Domestic Bills of Exchange		326,406.40
Suspended Debt		4,410.19
Real Estate		43,220.09
Furniture and Fixtures		138.00
Expense Account		5,454.85
Due from Banks		373,081.45
Due from State		6,361.01
Exchange		930.00
Premium on Exchange		2,215.54
Protest Account		119.84
Notes of Other Banks		435,090.00
Specie		681,778.77
		$3,271,677.22

Liabilities

Paid-up capital		
State	$840,980.78	
Individuals	178,770.00	
		$1,019,750.78
Treas. of U. S.		237,301.92
Treas. of U. S. Postoffice Fund		204,498.85
Deposits		723,350.38
Unclaimed Dividends		9,389.49
Interest and Exchange		47,615.67
Circulation		556,070.00
Due to Banks		468,700.13
		$3,271,677.22

It was further stated that the total loans made since the opening amounted to $4,058,934.75, and discounts on the local and exchange line to $650,640.08. The total operating expenses had reached $29,237.02 all of which had been taken care of before dividends were declared except $5,454.85 incurred since July 1st last. The furniture ($1,427.68) had all been paid for except an item of $138.00.

The banking house cost $50,980.10 but $7,760.01 had been charged off from this amount. The suspended debt account was given in some detail. This may cause some difficulty to one not familiar with banking practice of the time. Instead of charging off doubtful paper by deducting it from undivided profits, it was customary merely to transfer it to a suspended debt account and to continue to carry it on the statement. At this time there was only one branch. It was located at Fayette and reflected frontier conditions. Its customers had not yet become familiar with deposit currency, as is evidenced by the fact that its circulation exceeded $141,000 and deposits were under $20,000. Its notes were chiefly of the denomination of $20. The complete satement follows:

Resources		*Liabilities*	
Expense Account	$751.25	Deposits	$19,174.80
Discounts	198,992.89	Due Bank of Mo. for capital	109,000.00
Domestic Bills of Exchange	15,482.17	Due Bank of Mo. Current Account	26,888.53
Real Estate	3,191.08	Premiums	19.87
Protest Account	2.00	Interest	5,338.64
Cash	83,061.94	Circulation	141,060.00
	$301,481.34		$301,481.34

The committee noted that the main office charged Fayette with $238,060 for capital while the Fayette Branch listed only $109,000. It was explained that this was due to the fact that the main office had added in notes furnished to Fayette for circulation and which were carried in a separate account by the branch. The committee made no attempt to criticize the statement or to offer suggestions for its improvement. Later in the year (December 31, 1838) the regular semi-annual dividend declaration was made. The state received $50,498.13 as its share.[1]

[1] *Senate Journal*, 1838-39, General Assembly Mo., p. 233.

The Examination of 1840 was much more complete.[1] In brief it showed that the effects of the depression were begining to be felt. The total resources were down to $3,-040,000, a loss of $231,000 in two years. The circulation had increased, but the main office had deposits of only $197,000. The Fayette branch was constructing a $16,000 building and a new branch was in operation at Palmyra.

The general method of the former examination was continued. The money was counted and found to agree with the books. The expense account was examined and found correct except there were no vouchers for certain items of protest. The books of the Saint Louis office were declared correct so far as the committee was able to see. They then went to Fayette and Palmyra and conducted the same sort of examination as at the main office. The cash was found correct at both places. The Fayette officials explained their new building by the statement that the old one was wholly unsuited for the purpose of a bank office. The committee commented that the new one was suitable for nothing else and could never be sold if the branch were ever liquidated.

The report itself was short, but a large number of exhibits, mostly under oath, were appended. Most of them are included here.

The statement of the main office for October 26, 1840 was as follows:

[1] Pamphlet, "Examination of Bank 1840" from *Senate Jour.*, 11th General Assembly Mo., 1840-41.

Resources

Branch Fayette for Capital		$109,000.00
Branch Palmyra for Capital		101,616.18
Bills Discounted		882,111.95
Loans to State		
To pay volunteers	$100,000	
Board of Internal Improvements	20,000	
Building State Capitol	155,000	
		275,000.00
Domestic Bills of Exchange		184,469.34
Suspended Debt		82,825.46
Real Estate		54,137.07
Personal Property		40.00
Expense Account		5,657.27
Due from Banks		240,981.41
Protest Account		63.16
State of Missouri		12,984.92
Bank Notes on Hand		
Parent bank	$621,071.00	
Fayette	24,000.00	
Palmyra	710.00	
Other banks	51,480.00	
		697,290.00
Specie		394,366.60
		$3,040,543.36

Liabilities

Capital Paid Up		
State	$272,263.60	
School Fund	558,132.91	
Seminary Fund	97,768.89	
Sinking Fund	6,061.51	
Private	244,640.00	
		$1,178,866.91
Treas. of U. S.		727,210.81
Deposits		197,600.45
Bills Payable		9,871.87
Unclaimed Dividends		1,370.62
Interest and Exchange		20,903.59
Contingent		16,524.84
Circulation		792,500.00
Due to Banks		95,694.27
		$3,040,543.36

An exhibit was included purporting to show the amount of the state stock in detail including the sources from which payment was made. It is incomplete, however, showing a total of only $829,271.87, whereas the state stock as shown by the statement amounted to $934,226.91. It is, however, included here as showing the method by which the state made payment. It also explains in part the fact that the capital is not in even figures. The state was merely given credit on the books of the bank for such funds as it invested and dividends often went to increase the capital. The following schedules of state stock were printed in this report:

STOCK OWNED BY STATE WITH DIVIDENDS THAT HAVE ACCRUED TO THE DIFFERENT FUNDS

Seminary Fund	$75,059.65
Missouri Bond returned from Prime, Ward and King	1,000.00
Surplus Revenue Fund invested in stock for use of School Fund	435,154.92
Saline Fund in stock of State School Fund	45,793.70
To balance	272,263.60
	$829,271.87

The state payments were made as follows:

June, 1837	Cash, account of Seminary Fund	$8,333.18
	Cash, account of Saline Fund	17,030.24
	Cash, account of Surplus Revenue	254,890.20
July, 1837	Cash, account of Surplus Revenue	77,445.10
	Cash, account of Surplus Revenue	50,000.00
Oct., 1837	Cash, sale of bonds to War Department	3,165.87
	Cash, sale of bonds to War Department	5,000.00
Dec., 1837	Cash, sale of bonds to War Department	26,834.13
Feb., 1838	Cash, sale of bonds to War Department	27,894.37
Apr., 1838	Cash, Dividend on Surplus Revenue	11,470.06
	Dividend on Saline Fund	510.91
	State Treas. Saline Fund	996.32
June, 1838	100 6% Mo. Bonds to J. J. Astor	100,000.00
	100 6% Mo. Bonds to De Lizards Co.	100,000.00
July, 1838	Treas. check for dividend	17,400.90
Aug., 1838	100 6% Mo. Bonds Prime, Ward, and King	100,000.00
Feb., 1839	Cash dividend Saline Fund	2,693.74
	Cash dividend Surplus Revenue	25,597.35
		$829,271.87

The expense account received careful analysis. The salary schedule was quite liberal:

President	$3,000	Individual Book-keeper	$1,250
Cashier	3,000	Discount Clerk	1,250
First Teller	1,400	Attorney	1,000
Specie Teller	1,350	Porter	600
General Book-keeper	1,300	Watchman	540

The absence of adequate machinery of transportation and communication made many expensive trips necessary. In this connection one page of the expense account is of particular interest.

Paid to Agents November 1, 1839 to October 31, 1840

N. Childs	Expenses in remittance of Eastern paper funds	$145.00
John Lynch	Trip to Jefferson City relative to amendment of charter	75.00
J. Smith	Agent for sale of state bonds in East and in Europe	1,944.67
H. O'Neil	Expenses to Cincinnati to pay debt Cincinnati Commercial Agency	112.00
H. O'Neil	Expenses to Cincinnati to adjust exchange bought by bank	70.00
A. R. Corbin	Expenses to Jefferson City relative to state bonds	65.00
G. K. McGunnegle	Expenses and service to Fayette to get specie	79.00
A. R. Corbin	Expenses and service to Palmyra to get specie	47.50
A. R. Corbin	Expenses and service to Burlington to get specie	72.00
E. Dobyns	Expenses to Cincinnati to pay Cincinnati Commercial Agency Debt	70.00
J. Smith	Expenses to Jefferson City to arrange for specie	31.50
H. Boggs	Expenses to Cincinnati and Ohio River points to get specie	115.50
J. Smith	Expenses to Fayette to visit branch	30.50
G. W. Dent	Expenses to Jefferson City for specie	23.37
J. Smith	Agent for state bonds	6,000.00
N. Childs	Expenses to New Orleans relative to lost gold	84.00
F. H. Martin	Conveying coupons to New York	30.00
J. Smith	Expenses East to negotiate loan	350.50

J. Smith	Expenses East to negotiate loan	241.00
A. R. Corbin	Expenses East relative to government deposits	253.90
G. W. Dent	Expenses to Bellville relative to government deposits	4.50
A. S. Robinson	Expenses to Springfield for specie	31.00
G. W. Dent	Expenses to Jefferson City for state bonds	27.00

McGill and Mullanphy who took a quantity of gold, say $100,000, East for purpose of paying transfer drafts of U. S. Government, and expenses of cashier East to look after interests of bank, and having $150,000 sent from Philadelphia to New York are not included in above, but are listed as expense in transporting specie.

Considerable information was included regarding the financial operations of the bank. Since November 1, 1838 specie had been purchased to the amount of $330,725.08. It was paid for with the notes of suspended banks to the amount of $353,077.07. The bank insisted, however, that it was not responsible for the loss as the banks suspended after the deposits were received. However, they had been held instead of sent in for redemption. It was denied that any specie had been sold except $6,000 in mixed silver coins. However, in September, 1839 $200,000 in coin had been sent to a Philadelphia bank for deposit. The Philadelphia bank paid the transportation charges. No state bonds had been sold since November, 1838, although the bank had borrowed $500,000 on the security of $1,000,000 of state bonds and had paid 10 per cent interest. Individual deposits had shown a steady decline:

January 1, 1839	$549,225.42
January 1, 1840	346,715.38
October 26, 1840	197,600.45

On November 12, 1839 a statement of deposits was shown distinguishing between specie and bankable funds: $418,185.66, currency or notes of suspended banks; and $218,572.14, specie and Bank of Missouri notes. The suspended debt account was defined as paper actually in suit, *i. e.*

placed in the hands of an attorney for collection. It was admitted that the bank held $11,645.00 of protested paper which had not yet been charged to the suspended debt account. Since 1838 $2,000,000 had been borrowed from the United States Bank of Pennsylvania and $80,000 from the Bank of America. The interest charge for part of this was paid by the federal government, the funds having been obtained for government convenience. The United States government deposits had been regularly received, but recently $720,000 federal money had been transferred to New York City. Arrangements were made to pay all but $122,000 of this without shipment of specie and the bank was now attempting to get this balance transferred back to it. In regard to the management of loans it was stated that no individual or firm was allowed to borrow more than $15,000 or to have liabilities, including indorsements, of more than $40,000. Officers and directors had at times been allowed to overdraw their accounts but had always made such overdrafts good on notification. No loans were ever made to any officer or director whose account was overdrawn; and no officer or director, with slight exception immediately fixed, had ever let his paper go to protest. The directors were, however, accustomed to borrow quite heavily from the bank. Their liabilities on October 20, 1840 may be taken as typical:

	Notes		*Bills of Exchange*	
Director	*Payer*	*Indorser*	*Discounter*	*Indorser*
G. K. McGunnegle	$5,133	$1,646		
McGunnegle and Way ...	14,903	1,843	$11,560	$1,410
Hugh O'Neil	14,742	26,712	500	3,051
T. L. O'Neil	1,540			
Von Phul and McGill ...	100	8,612	2,000	2,900
John Smith			700	325
W. and D. Smith and Co.	7,624	8,345	2,900	
W. L. Sublette	2,074			
Sublette and Campbell ...	12,020	7,128		

Bryan Mullanphy	6,755			
Ed. Dobyns	5,055	6,132	1,513	2,028
Dobyns and Wimer	5,736	15,519	1,187	
A. R. Corbin	4,550	5,870	1,885	1,050
S. S. Rayburn	3,641	2,183	900	
Bridge, Rayburn and Co.	3,012			
E. Walsh		2,899		
Ed. Walsh and Co.				
R. Cathart and Co.	3,480	5,703	34,100	
C. Detchmandy	1,055			
D. C. M. Parsons	270			
J. B. Bryant		13,608		

In every case it was stated whether any of them had ever had any past due paper, and the record was remarkably clean. Remembering that these directors were the substantial business men of the city, their credits were not too extensive. A quarterly statement of notes discounted and bills of exchange purchased was included. It showed a total of $7,090,313.89 for the eight quarters, November 1, 1838 to October 31, 1840.

The report contains an account of a mysterious gold robbery.[1] On January 17, 1840 N. Childs Jr., the specie teller, was instructed by Mr. Shurlds, the cashier, to pack $100,000 in gold for shipment to New York. He went to the vault and carried upstairs all the gold on hand except one keg and placed it on a table behind the discount clerk's desk. He assorted all the foreign gold, placing each kind in a separate tray. Then he put it into small bags, as far as possible in even amounts, and placed a slip in each bag stating the number of coins and gross value. The bags were left unsealed and set on the end of the table until copies of the slips were made. Then the bags were tied with red tape and compared with the specie book to prove the count. Next a common specie keg was brought by the porter and all twenty-three of the bags were put into it. It

[1] Pamphlet "Examination of Bank 1840" from *Senate Jour.*, 11th General Assembly Mo., 1840-41, p. 25 *et seq.*

was not quite full, so a gunny sack was added to fill it. At three p. m. a dray was called and the keg sent to the steamer, *George Collier,* then at the St. Louis landing. This was in substance the affidavit sworn to by Mr. Childs. G. W. Dent, another employee, supported him. He said Mr. Shurlds sent him to find Mr. Childs and that he helped make the count and seal up the keg. The gold was never heard of again. The list prepared by Childs was as follows:

12 bags	$5,000 each	$60,000.00
1 bag	old coins 474 pieces	2,529.30
1 bag	1,000 sovereigns	4,830.00
1 bag	1,000 sovereigns	4,830.00
1 bag	1,000 sovereigns	4,830.00
1 bag	500 sovereigns	2,415.00
1 bag	mixed sovereigns	1,212.47
1 bag	Ten thalers 1,000	7,500.00
1 bag	(172 doubloons (861 20 francs (138 40 francs	6,929.75
1 bag	Southern gold	5,000.00
1 bag	(87 ten guilders (147 sovereigns	700.35
1 bag	Southern Mixed	1,582.50
		$102,359.37

The branches were also examined by this same committee. Palmyra submitted the following statement as of October 31, 1840:

Resources		*Liabilities*	
Discounts	$80,262.65	Bank of Mo. Capital Stock	$101,616.18
Real Estate	6,437.07	Circulation	160,000.00
Protest Account	97.98	Interest and Exchange	1,927.46
Expense Account	813.37	Due to Banks	780.40
Suspended Debt	9,741.26	Bank of Mo. Special Account	2,982.75
Due from Banks	447.37	Deposits	5,715.88
Specie and Currency	175,223.27		
	$273,022.97		$273,022.97

Three people were employed at salaries ranging from $800 to $2,000. Liabilities of officers and directors were given as in statement of parent bank. Most of them were borrowers but usually in comparatively small amounts.

At Fayette more details were gotten. The statement follows:

Resources		*Liabilities*	
Discounts	$152,779.34	Bank of Mo. Capital	$109,000.00
Domestic Bills Discounted	5,290.00	Deposits	3,234.26
Suspended Debt	10,597.75	Interest and Exchange	4,068.30
Banking House	13,032.44	Protest Account	19.00
Due from Bank of Mo.	1,003.19	Circulation	104,870.00
Expense Account	761.67		
Currency and Specie	37,727.17		
	$222,191.56		$222,191.56

This showed heavy declines from the previous statement. Quarterly figures for discounts usually ran between $175,000 and $200,000, but no new discounts had been made since August, 1839. During 1838 the bills of exchange owned averaged well over $35,000, but had now dwindled to a fraction of that amount. Directors' liabilities ran considerably heavier than at Palmyra, and salaries of officers were less. C. F. Jackson, afterwards governor of Missouri, was local cashier. The branch extended its business over a great deal of territory as shown by the table of distribution of liabilities by counties:

Howard	$58,324.00	Linn	$1,012.00
Boone	7,858.00	Chariton	11,707.00
Calloway	815.00	Carroll	525.00
Monroe	11,877.33	Ray	3,072.25
Randolph	21,710.00	Clay	2,400.89
Cole	7,981.00	La Fayette	1,165.00
Cooper	13,215.00	Marion	697.00
Morgan	375.00	Newton	480.00
Saline	14,271.00	Macon	415.00
Pettis	2,246.00	Lewis	272.00
Greene	2,040.00	Jackson	591.75
Livingston	3,230.00	Benton	180.00

The year 1844 saw an increase in both deposits and circulation of the State Bank, but the suspended debt had increased to $147,000, and $328,000 of Illinois notes and certificates had been acquired.[1] These latter were a very uncertain investment.

By 1848 deposits had increased to $1,359,000 (they were only $980,000 in 1846), and the cash reserve was nearly as great. The circulation to be covered by this same reserve was $633,000 (a decrease of $214,000 from the 1844 level).[2]

For some little time there had been a tendency to render superficial reports, but the examination of 1848 was unusually well done. It inquired into the question of net profits and found them to range from 8½ per cent for the Springfield branch to 13⅘ per cent for the home office. By this time there were five branches, located at Springfield, Jackson, Palmyra, Fayette, and Lexington. The bank owned no real estate except for office requirements and this in general was considered modestly taken care of. Although the legal limit for note issue was now three to one, the actual circulation was far below that and a two-to-one policy had been publicly announced.[3] Whatever may have been the effect of this action on the popularity of the bank, it caused recognition of its innate conservative tendencies and the stock was now selling at or above par. There were eleven employees at the Saint Louis office with salaries ranging from $2500 for the cashier to $1,000 for book-keepers. The liabilities of the directors were published in the usual form, and a detailed expense account was given. This latter fur-

[1] *Legislative Journal*, Mo., 1844.

[2] *House Jour.*, General Assembly Mo., 1844-46, "Report of Bank Commissioner."

[3] This refers to the required proportion between capital stock and circulation.

nishes many interesting side lights on the conduct of the bank. There was a liberal appropriation for advertising. Bank publications such as the *Bankers Magazine* were received at both the main and branch offices. The expense account of the home office for the year was a little less than $15,000, which was not excessive considering the volume of business done. The St. Louis office had loans of $1,978,000; exchange, $504,000; deposits, $1,141,000; and circulation, $1,450,000. All of the branches were examined. In general they showed heavy loans, light deposits, and a large circulation. The comparative statement here given indicates their condition:[1]

Branch	*Loans*	*Deposits*	*Circulation*
Palmyra	$183	$38	$200
Fayette	150	21	232
Lexington	186	59	239
Jackson	200	6	195
Springfield	135	19	157

000 omitted.

The examining committee of 1850 determined to do something more than ask for stereotyped reports. It planned to find what the assets were really worth. The recent theft of $120,061 of the bank's funds had aroused the people to the realization that even the old State Bank might need watching. The gold and silver was counted with great care and the silver was weighed. Efforts were made to test every investment and the bank officials, it must be said, afforded every possible aid. The suspended debt of $195,407.663 (for the whole institution) was first taken up. $64,048 of this was adjudged worthless. The Jackson branch refused to admit any loss on its suspended debt. The $120,061 which had disappeared in connection with the Childs' case was still carried as an asset, the defence being

[1] *House Jour.*, General Assembly Mo., 1848-49, p. 105 *et seq.*

that the case was still in the courts. The committee deemed this a weak argument and ordered the entire amount charged off. It was also recommended that the depreciation in the Illinois paper be taken out of the statement. These notes were not considered worth 75 per cent. All in all, the committee recommended the charging off of $296,823.89. It was found, however, that the net profits for the year were $93,000 and that the entire recommendation could be charged off and still show a surplus of $62,000. So the bank was not insolvent. The losses had been heavy, but the fundamental defect was bad accounting. The deposits were still $814,000 and circulation, $1,585,218. Against this was a cash reserve of $1,490,000.[1]

In 1852 the total assets of the bank were given as $5,770,000 distributed among the various offices as follows: St. Louis, $3,983,000; Jackson, $349,000; Palmyra, $358,000, Fayette, $384,000; Lexington, $402,000; and Springfield, $291,000.[2] Deposits and circulation had both increased somewhat and the cash reserve was nearly $1,000,000. Illinois paper again appeared on the statement to the extent of $32,000 and the $120,000 Childs' abstraction had not been charged off. The committee found that $70,000 had been lost in the dealings in Illinois paper and that about $193,000 doubtful assets (including Childs' abstraction) were shown on the statement. It recommended that these be immediately charged off. The report was largely taken up with a discussion of the earning power of the bank. The state now had an investment of $947,000. The committee estimated that it had failed to earn interest at the market rate by something like $183,000. It was recog-

[1] *House Jour.*, General Assembly Mo., 1850-51, p. 26 *et seq.*

[2] The figures are given only in round numbers. Accordingly the totals for the branches do not quite check with that given for the entire assets of the bank.

nized, however, that the bank had never charged the state for fiscal services. As the stock was now at par it was suggested that it might be sold in order to avoid further loss, but the committee did not take a stand as to the advisability of such action. It may be said, however, that the agitation for the sale of the state stock received its first great impetus here.[1]

The committee of 1854 was extremely critical, although it seems to have made a less careful examination than some of its predecessors. The notes were counted but, when the members came to the coin, a few boxes selected at random were counted and the rest weighed. The bank was accused of neglecting local business for the larger profits to be made in exchange dealings. Indeed the statement strongly supported the views of the committee. The discounts were only $600,000, while the bills of exchange on hand amounted to over $2,000,000. The Palmyra branch was the most conspicuous offender. It had purchased so much foreign paper that it was able to render little local service. The cash, deposits, and circulation had, however, all shown substantial increases. The suspended debt was given as $47,690 and the committee classed much of it as doubtful. The question of state profits was now much to the fore and detailed exhibits of profits and losses were demanded. It was shown that between 1838 and 1854 dividends amounting to $1,519,367 had been paid and that of this amount the state had received $1,212,431. The lowest rate declared was 3 per cent, the highest 10 per cent. An exhibit was also made of total losses since the date of organization:

[1] *House Jour.*, General Assembly Mo., 1852, p. 50 *et seq.*

on Discounts	$82,504
Bills of Exchange	84,120
Overdrafts	17,243
Bad Checks	4,513
Forgeries	4,515
Gold Lost on Way to N. Y., May, 1840	21,469[1]
Stolen by book-keeper, 1839	6,000
Illinois notes	208,000
Abstraction, August 15, 1849	120,061
	$448,425
Miscellaneous	11,233
Total Losses in 17 years	$459,658 or $27,038 a year.

This of course looks heavy even for frontier conditions but it included the depression losses after 1837 while the bank was still weak as well as the extremely heavy losses due to robbery and depreciation in Illinois paper. The average loss on the latter amounted to 35 per cent.[2]

An especially careful audit was made by the legislative committee of 1856-1857, for the impending legislation made it desirable to know as much as possible of the condition of the bank and how far it was really failing to take care of necessary business. There was even talk of refusing to extend its charter. In order to show as clearly as possible the sort of an institution which had been built up after twenty years of effort, the findings of this committee are here presented in full detail.[3] Briefly it may be said

[1] Given as $102,359.37 in examination of 1840. See p. 211.

[2] *House Jour.*, 18th General Assembly Mo., 1854-1855, p. 83 *et seq.*

[3] *Ibid.*, 19th General Assembly Mo., 1857, p. 115 *et seq.* Also published as a separate pamphlet under the title of "Report of Committee to Examine Bank of Mo., 1857" (Harvard Library). Page references are those of the Harvard Pamphlet. See also *St. Louis Democrat*, Jan. 27, 1857. The answers are given essentially in the order presented by the committee, and with little attempt at organization, the purpose being to show the method of a complete examination as carried on by the committee.

the net profits for the past two years had shown a decrease, due largely to the pressure brought to bear on the bank to cease buying foreign bills of exchange. It was in fact buying less than one-half as much as had been purchased the year before. In view of the coming fight for the sale of the state stock, this decline in earning power assumes great importance.

The committee met on July 20, 1856 at St. Louis and proceeded to count all the paper money and part of the coin. The rest of the coin was weighed and approved. All notes and bills were then examined and compared with the statement. The expense account was then checked with the vouchers. Just what else was done is hard to say, but the committee reported that it made a general examination of the business of the last two years, and then left with the president interrogations "calculated to elicit a full statement of the affairs of the bank." They then went to each branch office and conducted the same sort of an examination. At Palmyra and Springfield the notes submitted fell short of the records by $600 and $9,000 respectively, otherwise the accounts were all found to be in good order.[1] The criticism was offered that branch officials renewed paper falling due between discount days and so gave undue favors to many customers. In every case the officers were commended for making the examination work as easy as possible. All of the interrogations left with the offiicals were filled out and sent to Jefferson City in time for consideration by the legislature. Probably there is no better way of getting at the condition of the bank than by reviewing these answers. The data contained in them is given below.

[1] "Report Committee to Examine Bank of Mo.," 1856 (Harvard Library), p. 1.

Parent Bank

Stock Owned by State in its Own Right	$272,263.60
Stock Owned by State School Fund	575,667.96
Stock Owned by Seminary Fund	100,000.00
Stock Owned by Sinking Fund	6,273.66
	$954,205.22 [1]

Present value $107.00 per share.

The Illinois notes had all been sold. Twelve hundred acres of Illinois land had been accepted in part payment and was regarded as a profitable investment.

The officers were all under bond, the amounts ranging from $2,000 to $75,000. There were fourteen employees including the president, cashier, two tellers, discount clerk, three book-keepers, two clerks, attorney, messenger, porter, and watchman. Salaries ranged from $600 for the watchman to $3,600 for the cashier.[2]

Real-estate holdings amounted to $81,500 and included the banking house, two city lots, and the Illinois land referred to above. The latter was carried at $3,000.[3]

On October 25, 1856 the total circulation was $2,846,550 of which $1,016,260 had been issued by the branches. The branch notes were redeemable both at the office of issue and at the main office. Such redemption, it was claimed, had been maintained since June, 1841.[4]

The home office held $1,126,765.34 specie, and this was to secure $924,601.35 of deposits and the circulation mentioned above. However, $145,570 of the home office notes and $234,000 of the branch notes were in the hands of the main office.

With respect to distribution of loans the bank had a rule,

[1] "Report Committee to Examine Bank of Mo.," 1856 (Harvard Library), p. 7.

[2] *Ibid.*

[3] *Ibid.*, p. 8.

[4] *Ibid.*

rigidly enforced, requiring that no individual or firm might owe the bank more than $100,000 as drawer, indorser, and discounter; and that exchange payable outside Missouri should not be owned to an amount greater than $800,000.[1]

The rate of interest on time bills was 6 per cent, but, in addition, an exchange rate was charged on time bills proportional to the maturity of said bills and to the condition of the market. On October 25, 1856, for example, this rate ranged from ½ of 1 per cent on thirty-day Eastern bills to 1½ per cent on ninety day Southern bills.

Some coin had been sold during the preceding two years and a profit of $489 had been made on it. In order to meet interest on the state bonds due in New York, July, 1856, $100,000 coin had been purchased at a premium of ¼ of 1 per cent.[2]

The Childs' case had been settled .In consequence of the death of the chief state witness the suits instituted by the bank against Childs were dismissed on June 26, 1855. In consideration of this Childs dropped his damage suit against the bank. Each side paid its own costs.[3]

In response to an inquiry about the status of a loan made to the Belcher and Brother Sugar Refinery, it was stated that at the time of the Belcher failure, the refinery owed the bank $97,500. Forty thousand dollars of this was paid by indorsers. The rest was extended four years, all original indorsers signing the new notes; and 575 shares of the refinery stock were put up as collateral. The loan was now deemed safe.[4]

Between July 6, 1854 and July 7, 1856 five dividends were paid as follows:

[1] "Report Committee to Examine Bank of Mo.," 1856 (Harvard Library), p. 8.

[2] *Ibid.*, p. 9.

[3] *Ibid.*, p. 10.

[4] *Ibid.*

July 6, 1854	.........7%	$85,078.36
Feb. 26, 1855	.........5¼%	63,155.77
July 9, 1855	.........8½%	103,309.44
Jan. 10, 1856	.........8¼%	99,617.93
July 7, 1856	.........8%	97,232.41
		$448,393.91
State's Share		353,055.91 [1]

The suspended debt account was given as follows:[2]

Payers	*Indorsers*	*Date Due*	*Amount*	*Remarks*
G. Arnes	R.M. McDonald	Nov. 15, 1855	$150.00	Loss
G. Brockman	Keys & Pignett.	Aug. 15, 1855	487.72	Doubtful
G. Brockman	Keys & Pignett.	Sept. 14, 1855	556.00	Doubtful
G. Brockman	Keys & Pignett.	Oct. 5, 1855	379.75	Doubtful
Check E. P. Tesson	Forged	....	2,200.00	Doubtful
J. Dent	G. I. Barnet	Aug. 8, 1856	2,500.00	Good
J. Dent	J. Dent, Treas.	Aug. 8, 1856	3,000.00	Good
J. Foley	Thos. Foley	Apr. 16, 1856	700.00	Good
Langford and Stevenson	J. Dent, Treas.	Aug. 16, 1856	585.25	Good
J. Largue	J. Snyder	Apr. 12, 1855	576.52	Paid
Bill of Exchange on Largue	M. White & Co.	Sept. 11, 1854	2,000.00	Loss
W. Taylor.	A. Jones.	Dec. 5, 1849	400.00	Loss
L. Pickering.	W. P. Pen.	June 30, 1849	1,020.50	Good
J. Sparks	W. H. Sparks	Dec. 8, 1854	55.35	Good
J. Sparks	W. H. Sparks.	July 8, 1854	55.35	Good
W. K. Willson	Thos. Keys	Sept. 17, 1855	550.00	Doubtful
Total	....	......	$15,210.44	

The liabilities of the president and directors were stated in full. The total amount was under $25,000 and was largely due to indorsements.[3]

The expense account printed in the report was an exact copy of the expense record book. The net total for the six months ending January 30, 1855 for example was $13,-

[1] "Report Committee to Examine Bank of Mo.," 1856 (Harvard Library), p. 11.

[2] *Ibid.*

[3] *Ibid.*, p. 13.

867.49. This was about an average list. One of the largest incidental items was for advertising and subscriptions to papers and magazines. It amounted to $156.00.[1]

The net profits for the two years amounted to $309,-793.02.[2]

A weekly statement of coin holdings and circulation was included. Essential items in the balance sheet, October 26, 1856 included (in round numbers) discounts, $941,000; bills of exchange, $942,000; specie, $544,000; capital, $1,-587,000; deposits, $459,000; and circulation, $601,000.[3]

The branch records were also given in detail. One or two of these will suffice for illustration.

Fayette Branch.

November 11, 1856.

No increase in capital or circulation during the past two years.

Salaries were as follows: President, $550; cashier, $1400; clerk, $850; night watch, $200.

Net profits for both 1855 and 1856 about 16 per cent.

Real-estate holdings, $6,000 including banking house and three lots in Fayette and some land in Benton County.

Proportion of coin to circulation and private deposits, one to three.

No loss in past two years on account of overdrafts or forgeries and only $300 such losses since the opening.

No rules on discount except the judgment of the board and a rule that coin reserves must not fall below $80,000. Rates the same as at Saint Louis office. Little demand for

[1] "Report Committee to Examine Bank of Mo.," 1856 (Harvard Library), p. 14.

[2] *Ibid.*, p. 26.

[3] "Report in Adjourned Session of 19th General Assembly Mo. *House Jour.*"

Eastern exchange. Deposits were usually very low, the proceeds of loans being taken in bills. The circulation was usually in the neighborhood of $240,000. Between meetings of the board, the cashier was authorized to renew loans.[1]

Palmyra Branch.

There were three employees, the president, cashier, and one clerk. Salaries were much like those of Fayette.

Profits for the two years ending October 31, 1856 were $30,778.57.

Real estate included only a banking house valued at $11,-575.30. Eight-hundred-eighty acres of land in Shelby County had been taken to secure a debt of $2,640, but it had been sold recently for $4,573.43.

No losses were reported on account of forgery or overdraft, but there were sixty names on the suspended debt account, representing a total of $22,625.64. Of this all but $5,580.68 was reported as either bad or doubtful.

Total expense account for the two years ending November 1, 1856, $6,666.70.

Total purchases of bills of exchange for the above period $738,282.07.

Statement October 31, 1856:

Resources

Discounts	$98,639.73
Real Estate	11,575.30
Suspended Debt	23,955.64
Domestic Bills	93,447.80
Expense Account	990.71
Gold and Silver	81,053.79
Bank of Missouri Notes and Branch Notes	78,660.00
	$388,322.97

[1] "Report in Adjourned Session of 19th General Assembly Mo. *House Jour.*," pp. 34 to 41.

Liabilities

Capital	$120,058.84
Circulation	204,850.00
Interest and Exchange	6,956.40
Due to Banks	13,098.17
Deposits	43,359.56
	$388,322.97

This in general was the condition of the bank at the time of the expiration of the charter in 1857. It was now far too small to care for the expanding commercial needs of Missouri; but, considered from the viewpoint of a private stockholder, it was in a satisfactory condition. The business was gradually increasing and was also becoming safer. The suspended debt account appeared to be well under control.

PART III

THE BREAK-DOWN OF BANKING MONOPOLY

CHAPTER XIV

PRIVATE BANKING AND BUSINESS DEVELOPMENT

It is useless to try to understand Missouri banking history if the private banking houses are left out of consideration. They have existed in every period of the history of the state and at times have actually furnished the bulk of the banking facilities. The State Bank was given a monopoly of the issue function, but it could not thereby monopolize the banking business. It could not care for the necessary business transactions of the people. Its capital was too small, even if full use had been made of what it had. As has already been shown, its conservative tendencies often kept it from expanding its business up to the limit of the charter regulations, and ordinary commercial risks of the time were frequently refused. Its limited capital made it necessary to decline much business or else fail to maintain any standards of banking honor. However, the business of the state had to be taken care of, and private enterprise found a way to do it. It was soon learned that note issue was not essential to the banking business. Men who had made fortunes in other lines began to receive deposits, sell exchange, and discount paper. The state government made no effort to prohibit this. The usefulness of the private banker was early recognized. Indeed, it is hard to see how the commercial development of the state could have been carried out except for these agencies. Often they carried more deposits than the State Bank.

Before there were any chartered banks, fur companies,

merchants, and brokers performed many banking functions. These were overshadowed by the Bank of Saint Louis, the Bank of Missouri, the Branch United States Bank, and the Cincinnati Commercial Agency; but they continued to exist and, in the intervals between the closing of one institution and the opening of the next, they cared for necessary business in some fashion. As early as 1819 William O'Hara and Co. maintained a banking house, and there were also several brokers who performed many banking functions.[1] In 1830 Keen and Page had an extensive forwarding business and made advances on shipments to New Orleans and other points.[2] L. A. Benoist and Co., a great French banking house of New Orleans, opened a St. Louis office in 1832, which was active in local business circles for ten years. One of their advertisements, taken from the *Missouri Republican*, indicates the scope of their business:[3]

L. A. Benoist and Co.

Exchange commission brokers. Notes of all solvent banks in United States discounted at lowest rates. Notes on broken banks purchased at highest market price. Drafts, notes, and bills collected on the most favorable terms; and funds transmitted to most of the principal towns and cities of the United States. Drafts on Philadelphia and Baltimore for sale. Sight and time bills will be purchased at a slight discount. Deposits will be received at the following rates: checking, 4 per cent; 30 days, 5 per cent; 90 days, 6 per cent. Checks and bank books furnished. English, French, Portugese, and German gold purchased.

The State Bank was chartered in 1837 and for a time St. Louis paid little attention to the private agencies. The

[1] Houck, *op. cit.*, p. 191.

[2] *Mo. Intelligencer*, Nov. 6, 1830.

[3] *Mo. Republican*, Jan. 14, 1837.

new bank was larger than any institution the city had had before and it was expected to care for all necessary business. However, its refusal in 1839 to accept the depreciated currency then so abundant in Saint Louis operated to bring the private banks back into public notice. The struggle of the business interests with the bank and the consequent growth of the banking department of the Saint Louis Gas Light Co. has been described in an earlier chapter. Soon insurance companies took on banking functions, at least to the extent of discounting short term paper, and many of them received deposits. Between 1838 and 1841 ten companies were so engaged.[1] In fact Saint Louis was so well supplied with banking facilities of her own that little interest was taken in President Tyler's proposed legislation in 1841. At least it was given scant space in the city papers.

It is difficult to secure data on the organization and growth of the private banking houses prior to 1855. They received little newspaper attention so long as they functioned properly. *The St. Louis Chamber of Commerce Report* for 1842 lists thirteen brokers and private banking houses but states that other names should be included.[2] These and the State Bank sold $9,548,601 exchange in 1841, but no attempt was made to separate the amount sold by the State Bank from that sold by the others.

In 1849 the private bankers came into prominence through their indictment by the Saint Louis County Grand Jury for violation of the small-note law. It was illegal to circulate notes of smaller denominations than ten dollars. The city was flooded with small notes of uncertain value, issued by the banks of neighboring states, especially Illinois; and the private bankers were accused of aiding their circulation by

[1] Edwards, *op. cit.*, p. 370.

[2] P. 21.

receiving them on deposit and paying them out again. It was admitted that they were received on deposit, but not that they were again paid out. However, in 1849, the *Bankers Magazine* published the following notice copied from a Saint Louis newspaper:[1]

> The undersigned private bankers of Saint Louis give notice that after this date we will only receive notes $10.00 and up. Have been indicted by the Grand Jury for violation of the small note law. Here we neither affirm nor deny the truth.[2]

The State Bank was forbidden by charter to issue notes of smaller denominations than ten dollars and it had, in fact, placed the minimum at twenty dollars. The private banks, notwithstanding the monopoly privileges of the State Bank, had thereupon issued small notes. The need for small change was so great that few people cared to question their legality. These notes circulated widely in Missouri and Illinois and were generally redeemed on presentation. The Grand Jury investigation, however, also took up this point and after much discussion it was agreed to abide by the law. Lucas and Simonds, Page Bacon and Co., and E. W. Clarke and Bro. advertised that they would pay all their issues in specie on demand and when redeemed such notes would not be reissued. They invited early presentation.[3]

It is difficult to determine how many private banks existed. They were mere partnerships or individual enterprises and so began and discontinued business without formality. Every list published contains different names. Some of these had little capital; others were houses of the

[1] *Bankers Magazine*, Mar. 1849, p. 642.

[2] This note was signed by eleven private bankers.

[3] *Bankers Magazine*, Mar., 1853, p. 750.

highest financial rating. *The Saint Louis City Directory* for 1853 published the following list:

J. J. Anderson and Co.
L. A. Benoist and Co.
Benoist and Sanguinet
E. W. Clarke and Bro.
Darby and Barksdale
Durkee and Bullock
Locker and Bro.
Lucas and Co.
Page and Bacon
Presbury and Co.
Renick and Peterson
Rokohl and Co.
Simonds and Taylor
Tesson and Dangin

The Chamber of Commerce Report for 1852 listed ten banking houses besides the State Bank and stated that the sales of exchange for the year had exceeded $22,000,000 and that of this amount the State Bank had supplied only $2,000,000. *The Annual Review of the Missouri Republican* for 1854 placed the sales at $38,000,000 but gave no figures for the State Bank.[1] It was quite evident that these banking houses were filling a large and growing place in the business life of the city.

There were other banking institutions. A number of savings banks had been opened under legislative charter and, although they had no issue privilege, they transacted much commercial banking business. The largest of these was the Boatmen's Savings Institution chartered in 1847. A. L. Mills was its first president. It was first organized without capital and the profits were to be divided among those

[1] *Annual Review Mo. Republican*, 1854, p. 22.

who deposited $100 during the first six months and maintained the balance for twenty years. Its beginnings were quite modest. When four years old it had deposits of only $47,000.[1] In 1854 it suffered a robbery of $19,000 in gold and Bank of Missouri notes. The directors at once announced that they would assume personal liability for all deposits, and no run occurred.[2] In this same year Sullivan Blood was elected president. He remained at its head for seventeen years and exercised a great influence in local banking circles. He at once secured a new charter, placing the bank on a profit-making basis with $400,000 capital. Ten per cent of the stock was to be paid down in specie and the balance within fifteen months. The first subscription was $100,000. The bank became popular at once. Mr. Blood adopted a liberal loan policy and catered to commercial accounts. *The Democrat* seemed particularly friendly to it and published items about it in almost every issue. By May 1855 its deposits were $560,000 and were increasing at the rate of $20,000 a week. Regular discount days were announced as Tuesday and Friday, answers to be given a day later. It was not uncommon for as much as $60,000 loans to be announced at the semi-weekly meeting. To carry on its expanding business it was necessary to secure more and more working capital and Blood did this by offering 5 per cent for call money deposited by other local bankers.[3]

The German Savings Institution was also started in 1854 with all banking privileges except note issue.[4] The next year the State Savings Institution was opened. The

[1] *St. Louis Democrat*, June 2, 1855.

[2] *Banker's Magazine*, May, 1854, p. 921.

[3] For notes on Boatmen's Bank see *St. Louis Democrat*, May 30, June 2, 6 and 20 and December 27, 1855.

[4] *Banker's Magazine*, Mar., 1854, p. 761.

Mutual Savings Institution was already in operation. By 1855 it had deposits of $135,207.25 to the credit of 1027 accounts.[1] There were a number of other such banks. As early as 1853 the *St. Louis City Directory* listed nine.

From 1845 to 1854 the private and savings banks seemed very prosperous. The Mexican War had meant large sales of supplies, and a consequent influx of Mexican silver coin. Sometimes as much as $50,000 would be received at once.[2] The California gold excitement of 1849 gave another big forward movement to St. Louis business. St. Louis became the outfitting point for the overland journey. Moreover, once the gold began to flow eastward, St. Louis became an important point of concentration. The two largest private banking houses, Page and Bacon, and Lucas, Turner and Co. had branches in San Francisco. No complete record of gold shipments to Saint Louis has been kept, but the Saint Louis papers were constantly printing accounts of the arrival of large amounts. For example:

June 11, 1855	$85,000 gold to Lucas & Simonds from San Francisco.
July 13, 1855	$169,000 gold to Lucas and Simonds from San Francisco.
July 24, 1855	$232,000 gold to Lucas and Simonds last Nicaragua steamer.[3]

By 1855 both these private banks and the savings institutions were local factors of the greatest commercial importance. Their combined deposits ran into the millions. The following is a typical advertisement:

[1] *St. Louis Democrat*, May 19, 1855.

[2] Stevens, *St. Louis the Fourth City*, p. 301.

[3] Files of *St. Louis Democrat* for dates given.

Darby and Barksdale.

Bankers and exchange dealers. Collections made on all the principal cities of the Union. Deal in bank notes, coin, etc. Interest allowed on deposits. Collections attended to and all proceeds remitted for on day of payment at current exchange, free of charge. Paper negotiated and stocks bought and sold on commision. Funds remitted to England and France. Currency bought, sold, and received on deposit.[1]

The largest of these private banking houses was Page, Bacon, and Co. The senior partner, D. D. Page, was a St. Louis merchant who had made a large private fortune. He was said to own $3,000,000 of city real estate. The junior partner, Henry D. Bacon, was a Massachusetts man who had come West in 1835 and married Page's daughter. They opened a banking house in 1848 and from the start pursued a liberal policy in regard to loans. Advances were made to the city for payments on its bonded debt. The Belleville and St. Louis Railroad was financed, thus enabling the city to get the cheap Illinois coal. Extensive loans were made to the Belcher Sugar Refining Co. Hundreds of houses were built for sale.[2] These were fairly representative of the kind of business done by the bank. Finally in 1853 it undertook to finance the Ohio and Mississippi Railway Co., a line from Cincinnati to Saint Louis. These projects all looked like benefits to St. Louis, but they were a part of the speculative tendencies of the early fifties. Affairs came to a crisis in New York in 1854 and soon spread to St. Louis. Real-estate values declined heavily. Duncan, Sherman, and Co., New York correspondents of Page, Bacon, and Co., declined to make further advances. Mr. Bacon made a trip to New York to see them and, after a three-day conference, secured the promise of a loan of $250,000 on real-estate security. Meanwhile Page,

[1] *St. Louis Democrat*, May 6, 1855.

[2] Stevens, *St. Louis the Fourth City*, p. 305.

Bacon and Co. had closed their doors. On the return trip Bacon was snowbound in Illinois and was forced to walk twenty miles through the snow to make connections. As soon as he reached St. Louis the bank reopened. This was on February 19, 1855. It had been closed seven days. A card was published thanking the people for their kindness during the suspension and announcing the reopening.[1] A few days later Duncan, Sherman and Co. wired cancellation of their loan.[2] Bacon appealed by telegraph but without avail, and the business was closed and assignment made on April 4, 1855. It was announced that the assets largely exceeded the liabilities but that they were not immediately available. All drafts were taken up and interest and protest fees paid.[3]

The assignment caused great local excitement. Runs were started on all the banks. Lucas and Simonds paid out $260,000 cash during the day; L. A. Benoist and Co., $100,000; Boatmens Savings Bank, $100,000; and there were heavy withdrawals from J. J. Anderson and Co. and E. W. Clarke and Bro. This was on Friday. The run continued all day. In all over $700,000 was paid out. Sunday gave time for thought. On Monday morning ten citizens representing private fortunes of over $8,000,000 pledged all their property to stop the run. The following notice was published:[4]

To the Public:

The undersigned knowing and relying on the ample ability of the following banking houses of the city of St. Louis, and

[1] *Banker's Magazine*, Mar., 1855, p. 742.

[2] Stevens, *St. Louis the Fourth City*, p. 306.

[3] *Banker's Magazine*, May, 1855.

[4] Stevens, *St. Louis the Fourth City*, p. 303 and Conrad, *op. cit.*, article on "St. Louis Banking."

with a view to quieting the public mind in regard to the safety of deposits made with them, hereby pledge themselves and offer as a guarantee their property to make good all deposits with either of said banking houses, to wit: Messrs. Lucas and Simonds, Bogy Millenberger and Co., Tesson and Dangin, L. A. Benoist and Co., J. J. Anderson and Co., Darby and Barksdale, and the Boatmens Savings Institution.

signed

John O'Fallon	J. H. Brandt	John How	C. H. Chouteau
Ed. Walsh	L. M. Kennett	James Harrison	
L. A. La Beaume	D. A. January	Andrew Christy	

This demonstration of financial honor was entirely effective. Page and Bacon made no further efforts to reopen but there were no other failures; and for two or three years the private banks seemed to prosper. Business, however, was quiet. The local panic had put a damper on speculation. During 1855 and 1856 the *St. Louis Democrat* continued to publish numerous items relating to monetary affairs. Offerings were usually light and far below the available supply. Insurance companies sought borrowers on the streets. One private bank in 1856 advertised $200,000 on call at 5 per cent. Numerous gold receipts from the West were recorded. Few offerings were rejected by either the State Bank or the Boatmens.[1] Early in 1857 the Boatmens published the following statement:[2]

[1] See especially the issues of July 13, 16, 18 and 24 and Oct. 3, 1855 and Jan. 26, 1856 of *St. Louis Democrat*.

[2] *St. Louis Democrat*, Jan. 13, 1857 (figures given in round numbers).

BOATMENS SAVINGS INSTITUTION

JANUARY 1, 1857

Resources		*Liabilities*	
Stock in Bank of Missouri	$6,500	Capital Paid Up	$317,500
Bills Receivable	663,000	Authorized .. $400,000	
Protested Bills none	000,000	Deposits	900,300
Exchange	351,000	Profits	43,000
Real Estate	18,000		
Bank Building	10,000		
Furniture	1,000		
Bonus to original six months depositors	14,000		
Cash	195,000		

Discounts for 6 months ending January 1, 1857	$1,946,000
Exchange sold for same period	1,148,000

It had grown very rapidly and was now the chief competitor of the State Bank.

The Panic of 1857 again tested the strength of the banks. On the morning of September 28th Darby and Barksdale failed, and almost immediately J. J. Anderson and Co. and Bogy Millenberger and Co. announced suspension.[1] This was followed on October 3rd by the failure of Chouteau, Harrison, and Vallé.[2] Next a run was started on the banks representing the Lucas interests. Lucas and Simonds, Lucas, Turner and Co. and J. H. Lucas and Co. were largely controlled by J. H. Lucas, the largest property owner of St. Louis and a director of the Boatmens Savings Institution.[3] The second of these three houses had a San Francisco branch of which General W. T. Sherman was manager.[4] The Lucas banks had enjoyed an extensive business, in fact they had competed with Page, Bacon and

[1] Stevens, *St. Louis the Fourth City*, p. 305.

[2] *Banker's Magazine*, Nov., 1857, p. 418.

[3] Knox, *op. cit.*, p. 788 and Reaves, L. O., *St. Louis the Future Great City* (Biographical Edition), p. 192.

[4] *Ibid.*

Co. on almost even terms. An attempt was made to stop the run by use of the method which had been so successful in 1855. Seventeen men pledged their personal fortunes for the deposits of the Lucas banks. They were J. E. Yeatman, James Harrison, John How, R. J. Lockwood, Ed. J. Gay, Ed. Walsh, John O'Fallon, J. H. Gay, W. Renshaw, Jr., J. S. McCune, D. A. January, D. H. Armstrong, C. K. Dickson, T. T. Gantt, William McPherson, J. B. Eads, and Chas. Tillman. This pledge quieted local excitement, but a few days later General Sherman announced the suspension of the Western branch. J. H. Lucas and Co. then went into liquidation on October 5, 1857. It had paid out over $1,000,000 to depositors.[1] J. H. Lucas assumed all its debts and gave personal notes bearing 10 per cent interest. He paid all of them in full although at the sacrifice of $500,000 of his private fortune. He brought no lawsuits to collect the debts due the bank.[2] On October 4th E. W. Clarke and Bro. had also suspended. The withdrawals continued. President Blood of the Boatmens announced that all the funds of his bank were in its own vaults, but this did not save it from suspension. It and the Mutual Savings Association closed on October 6th. Tesson and Dangin, Renick and Peterson, and the State Bank remained open until near the end of the month. A personal guarantee was arranged for the deposits of Renick and Peterson, but it proved useless. On October 24th the State Bank closed, but reopened after two days.[3] Through all the time of stress it had been the recognized conservative factor so it suffered less than most of its competitors. Late in 1857 and during the summer of 1858 J. J. Anderson and Co., Tesson and Dangin, and several other private

[1] Stevens, *St. Louis the Fourth City*, p. 307.

[2] Reaves, *op. cit.*, p. 192.

[3] Stevens, *St. Louis the Fourth City*, p. 309.

banking houses resumed specie payments.[1] The State Bank, however, was fearful of the situation and again suspended. The savings banks offered to lend it a large amount of coin but their aid was refused.[2] The Boatmens announced a continuation of specie payments but by the end of September it too had begun to receive and pay out bankable funds.[3]

Meanwhile a large number of new private banks had begun business. In 1859 St. Louis had twenty-one.[4]

Allen, Copp, and Nesbit
J. J. Anderson
L. A. Benoist and Co.
Barksdale and Co.
Clarke Brothers
E. S. Dame Co.
Darby and Poulterer
Durkee and Bullock
Haskell and Co.
Johnson, Phillips and Co.
Loker and Brothers
Millenberger and Co.
Nesbit and Co.
Page and Hartwell
Presbury and Co.
Rokohl Co.
Simonds and Taylor
Stout and Co.
J. M. Taylor
Tesson and Dangin
Thomson and Elliott

[1] *Banker's Magazine*, Jan., 1858, p. 585 and May, 1858, p. 843.

[2] *St. Louis Democrat*, Aug. 17, 1858.

[3] *Banker's Magazine*, Sept., 1858, p. 316 and *St. Louis Democrat*, Sept. 30, 1858.

[4] Sutherland and McEvoy, *Mo. State Gazetteer*, 1859-60.

There were twenty-eight other private banks in the state in the following towns:[1]

Alexandria	2	Hermann	1	Roanoke	1
Boonville	3	Independence	2	Saint Joseph	1
Brunswick	1	Kansas City	1	Shelbyville	1
Columbia	1	Kirksville	1	Syracuse	1
Deepwater	1	Lexington	1	Tipton	1
Flint Hill	1	Princeton	1	Weston	1
Hannibal	3	Renick's Mills	1	Washington	2

During the war their numbers largely decreased, but many new ones were organized after peace was declared. In September, 1867 the *Bankers Magazine* reported thirty-four in Saint Louis and forty-four in thirty-three other towns in the state. Twenty-one were started during the year 1867.[2] In 1871 there were ninety-nine all told.[3] They continued to play an important rôle in the financial affairs of the state though they were later overshadowed by the chartered banks under the law of 1857. However, as these banks were limited in number and extended their branch system slowly, the small towns were long dependent on private bankers. The old established houses of St. Louis gradually lost business to the newly chartered banks. L. A. Benoist and Co. may be taken as an example. It had been one of the great banks of the city, yet, when it failed in 1869 the assets were given as $74,000 and liabilities as $120,000.[4] At this time, however, Benoist was dead and his heirs had retained no interest in the business.

[1] Sutherland and McEvoy, *op. cit.*, 1859-60.

[2] *Banker's Magazine*, Jan., 1868, p. 583.

[3] *Merchants and Banker's Register*, New York, 1871, p. 22.

[4] *Banker's Magazine*, Oct., 1869, p. 311.

CHAPTER XV

The Demand for Additional Banking Capital

Between 1840 and 1857 the sentiment against banking monopoly steadily grew. The State Bank had expanded its business but had not kept pace with the commercial development of the state. It had always looked first to its own safety and had declined to assume what it considered abnormal risks. At times it had carried this policy to the extreme point of refusing to assist its own branches. If this policy throttled the growth of private business, the bank did not consider itself responsible. Only so much capital had been provided and accordingly only a limited amount of business could be done. By following this policy the bank could at least teach by example the principles of conservative business. If it was to be expected to do more, the state must provide more capital. Such was the creed of the bank.

However much its usefulness may have been recognized, its conservatism antagonized those business men who wanted large loans on risky security and who wished to carry on extensive dealings in depreciated Illinois currency. Beginning with the refusal of the bank in 1839 to accept Illinois notes, the opposition steadily increased. If the State Bank would not meet their needs, private individuals could be found who would do so. Out of this feeling there developed the extensive private banking described in the preceding chapter.

These private banking houses were always regarded as mere makeshifts. Many of them were strong financially and rendered excellent service, but it was also true that others of them operated with little capital. At any rate they were uncontrolled except for the example set by the State Bank. If they were to exist, it was felt that they should be chartered and placed under proper supervision.

Moreover, the private bankers themselves were not satisfied with their position. They could not issue notes and, considering the fact that people were not accustomed to check books and that pioneer conditions favored the use of currency, this was a serious disadvantage. It is certain that much of the agitation for banking reform was inspired by men who desired to invest their capital in chartered banks of issue, unhampered by partnership with the state. At least the opposition was voiced chiefly by the St. Louis Chamber of Commerce and by those newspapers which carried the most extensive advertising.

The demand was doubtless in part psychological. The private banks in large measure made up for the deficiencies in the State Bank. However, banking in the popular mind seemed to be inseparable from note issue, and in local statistics of banking capital it was usual to consider only the State Bank. So far as St. Louis was concerned this, of course, amounted to only $600,000, but the private banking capital ran into the millions. With this in view it seems impossible to escape the conclusion that much of the propaganda was to this extent deliberately dishonest. It is of course true that definite figures were hard to get regarding the business of the private banks. Accordingly, it was an easy matter to disregard them. Statistics published by the *Bankers Magazine* and by *The Merchants and Bankers Register of New York* took account only of the State Bank. If only chartered banks of issue are considered, the situation of St. Louis was of course ridiculous. The following table of comparative statistics shows the condition in 1857:[1]

[1] *Merchants and Banker's Register*, New York, p. 152.

City	*Population* (*000 omitted*)	*Banking Capital* (*in millions*)
New York	515	35.4
Philadelphia	409	10.5
Baltimore	169	7.1
Boston	138	24.5
New Orleans	119	12.2
Cincinnati	116	1.7
Brooklyn	96	1.3
Saint Louis	82	.6
Albany	50	2.0
Pittsburg	50	2.6
Louisville	43	2.9
Charleston	42	9.1
Providence	41	8.7
Buffalo	40	.9
Washington	40	.8
Newark	38	1.8
Rochester	36	.9
Lowell	33	1.1
Troy	28	1.7
Savannah	27	2.3
Richmond	27	2.1
Portland	26	1.1
New Haven	22	1.9
Syracuse	22	.8
Springfield, Mass.	21	1.1
Detroit	21	.7
Mobile	20	2.0
Milwaukee	20	.2
Manchester	19	2.0
Salem	18	1.7
Lawrence	18	.5
Hartford	18	4.6
Nashville	17	5.0
Columbus	17	.6
Utica	17	1.6
Cleveland	17	.4
Bangor	14	1.0

Of course such a table is nearly useless for accurate comparison. It only considers chartered banks of issue and does not indicate how much of the capital really represents specie. It is given here because it is a fair sample of the kind of statistics that were used to prove the desperate need of St. Louis for more banking capital. The same authority gives figures for various states as follows for 1858:

State	Population (000 omitted)	Capital	In millions Specie	Circulation
Massachusetts	994	43.3	3.0	17.0
New York	3070	58.4	7.0	27.2
Pennsylvania	2311	18.9	6.2	12.0
Virginia	1421	10.2	3.6	11.6
Indiana	989	2.0	1.3	3.6
Iowa	192	.2	.05	.1
Kentucky	982	10.1	3.3	7.4
Louisiana	500	12.2	4.3	3.5
Michigan	398	.7	.1	.6
Missouri	682	1.2	1.5	2.4
Ohio	1977	7.8	2.8	11.6
Tennessee	1003	8.4	1.9	5.3
Wisconsin	304	.2	.2	.2
Illinois	858			
Arkansas	210			

When all allowances are made for the shortcomings of the statistical method, it is evident that Missouri was handicapped to a much greater degree than most of her neighbors. John Jay Knox thought it remarkable that a state of such commercial importance as Missouri should have bank deposits of only $3.00 per capita.[1] His error was in not realizing the unusual development of private banking in Saint Louis. The local papers of 1855-1856 give evidence that business was being cared for in a reasonable fashion. In the summer of 1855 money was plentiful and the banks found it hard to keep their funds employed.[2] Some of the private banks had deposits in excess of a million dollars,

[1] Knox, *History of Banking*, p. 789.

[2] *St. Louis Democrat*, June 11, 1855.

and gold was constantly arriving from San Francisco.[1] At crop-moving time some scarcity of funds was reported, but by the beginning of the new year the stringency was over.[2] *The Democrat,* however, constantly carried on its campaign for the revision of the state constitution and the breaking up of the monopoly position of the State Bank. Evidently what was wanted was not more banks of discount and deposit so much as chartered banks with the privilege of note issue.

The St. Louis Republic also favored the proposals for banking expansion. It called attention to the fact that the failure of the Illinois banks had caused business stagnation, and that lack of adequate assistance from the banks had retarded recovery. The State Bank was given scant credit for its services. It was charged that most of the $38,-000,000 exchange sold in 1854 was furnished by the private banking houses and that, although six local wholesale houses had increased their sales by $2,955,000 between 1845 and 1853, the capital of the State Bank had remained station-ary.[3] These statements, however, were not quite fair to the State Bank. Its business had not remained stationary even if there had been no increase in capital, as is evidenced by the following table of comparative accounts:[4]

State Bank of Missouri (000 omitted)

Date	*Loans*	*Specie*	*Capital*	*Circulation*	*Deposits*
1839	1,570	691	1,027	671	1,101
1844	951	1,260	1,200	731	1,735
1849	3,152	2,427	1,208	2,569	1,313
1854	3,958	937	1,215	2,487	3,123

The reports of the St. Louis Chamber of Commerce should serve to indicate the viewpoint of the business men.

[1] *St. Louis Democrat,* June 20, 1855.

[2] *Ibid.,* Aug. 8, 1855 and Jan. 26, 1856.

[3] *Annual Review St. Louis Republic,* 1854, pp. 13 and 22.

[4] Knox, *op. cit.,* p. 792.

In 1842 the Chamber of Commerce accused the State Bank of failing to care for essential business and stated that the merchants were forced to rely on themselves.[1] Ten years later the report stated that the city was doing business on a foreign depreciated currency and that eastern exchange was obtainable only by paying a premium of 14-16 per cent. The amount purchased by the merchants during the year was estimated at $30,000,000, of which the State Bank furnished but $2,000,000. It also charged that State Bank of Missouri notes did not constitute one-third of the circulation of the city.[2]

It was quite evident by the end of 1856 that some sort of change in the banking laws of the state would have to be made. The State Bank was conducting its own business on a sound basis, but a great part of the banking business of the state had passed into other hands and they were totally uncontrolled except for the limitations set by public opinion. The State Bank never wholly lost its influence here.

Before attempting to discuss the legislation of 1857, it will be desirable to consider with some care the actual condition of the State Bank. Just how much and what was it doing to relieve business pressure? How extensive was its service at this time?

The statement for March 3, 1857 showed a total capital of $1,215,405, of whch the state owned $954,205. Specie holdings were $1,245,000; deposits, $1,186,000; circulation, $2,780,000; and discounts, $2,511,000. However, much of its business was done outside of St. Louis. Each of the five branches, at Fayette, Palmyra, Springfield, Lexington, and Cape Girardeau, had been assigned $120,058.84 of the

[1] *Proc. St. Louis Chamber of Commerce*, 1842, p. 24.

[2] Report of Committee Appointed by Chamber of Commerce of St. Louis on "Trade, Commerce and Manufacturing," 1852.

capital stock, or about one-half that of the whole institution. The division of the business between the various offices is shown in the following table:[1]

DECEMBER 31, 1856 (000 OMITTED)

Office	*Loans*	*Suspended Debts*	*Specie*	*Individual Deposits*	*Exchange*	*Circulation*
Fayette	164		67	49	160	229
Palmyra	80	22	100	56	190	200
Cape Girardeau	159	9	82	23	98	186
Springfield	148	14	87	54	52	155
Lexington	182	15	97	53	74	215
St. Louis	1,775	9	809	949	861	1,793

Commenting on this statement, *The St. Louis Democrat* noted a decrease in deposits due to higher interest rates offered by competitors and increasing discounts due to public opposition to the bank's policy of investing in the more lucrative out-of-town bills of exchange. The average earnings for the past four years including the bonus and additions to surplus, were given as 18½ per cent. The suspended debt came in for criticism, but it was noted that most of this was in the country offices. At first sight this large suspended debt seems to discredit somewhat the claims of the bank to conservative policies. However, it must be remembered that country loans in a pioneer state were necessarily slow of liquidation. Means of communication were undeveloped and it was customary to transfer to suspended debt all paper more than a few weeks past due. Much of it was later collected. The bank was constantly criticized for its failure to expand its circulation. It was always under the three-to-one legal limit. However, the officials of the bank felt it desirable to consider the reserve as against all demand liabilities. This was not a charter requirement but was certainly sound policy. When the state-

[1] 34th Congress, 3rd Session *Executive Document* 87, p. 202.

ment is viewed from this angle the charge that the bank was doing too little business loses force. In spite of all the criticism, there was much recognition of the service of the bank. *The St. Louis Democrat* of April 15, 1857 praised it for straining every nerve to ease the market and said it was discounting to the full measure of its ability. *The City Directory* for 1857, although deploring the great lack of local banking capital, gave the State Bank credit for extending all the facilities justified by its limited capital and praised the efficiency of its management. It said no other notes in the city were considered as good as gold, that State Bank notes were classed as coin while all others were currency. By receiving only its own notes and coin and paying out nothing else, it was conducting all its dealings on a specie basis. This, of course, was written prior to the outbreak of the panic and refers to conditions in 1856.[1] The legislation of the coming General Assembly was not to take the form of antagonism to the State Bank; it was rather to be directed to the larger end of providing more adequate banking facilities.

[1] *City Directory of St. Louis*, 1857, p. 8.

CHAPTER XVI

The Legislation of 1857 and Banking Progress Until the Outbreak of the Civil War

In the preceding chapter an attempt has been made to outline some of the conditions which made banking reform desirable or at least politically inevitable. From this time on the activities of the State Bank were to be merged in the larger banking organization of the state. The period of monopoly was at an end.

In 1854 the governor touched on banking problems in his message to the General Assembly. He called attention to the fact that the charter of the State Bank would expire on February 2, 1857 and that some action must be taken to "stabilize property, facilitate business, and keep out worthless paper". The problem was whether to recharter the State Bank or to establish free banking. He called attention to the constitutional provision allowing only one bank and five branch offices, and argued that the simplest solution would merely be to recharter the State Bank with an adequate capitalization.[1]

The legislature began consideration of his proposal early in the session, but the election of a United States Senator and bank directors consumed so much time that action was postponed until the next meeting. A resolution was passed asking the new legislature to make it the first order of business.[2] The plans discussed had been quite varied.

[1] *Banker's Magazine*, Dec., 1854, p. 721.

[2] *Ibid.*, April, 1855, p. 822.

Some members had been inclined to insist on individual liability for note issues, but this did not seem to be the prevailing sentiment. Another plan was to change the constitution and charter ten banks on a specie basis with a combined capital of $20,000,000. There seemed to be much sentiment to do away with investments in state bonds.[1]

When the General Assembly of 1856-1857 convened, banking problems were at once taken up. The retiring governor advised the recharter of the old bank with a capital of $5,000,000. The Saint Louis papers generally pronounced this inadequate.[2] *The St. Louis Republican* continued its fight on the State Bank. It argued for the constitutional amendment, and urged that the State Bank be given only a temporary extension of its charter in order to provide reasonable time for liquidation. For this, two years was thought sufficient. The liquidation of the State Bank, it said, would give bank management to those who were interested and would remove a source of corruption from the legislature.[3] *The Missouri Intelligencer* opposed the plan for a new $5,000,00 State Bank if other banks were also chartered under the plan for a $20,000,000 maximum aggregate capital. It felt that one-fourth of the possible capital concentrated in one institution would lead to unfair competition. Moreover, it could see no reason for state ownership at all if the principle of monopoly was to be given up.[4]

The first financial legislation passed was an act to permit brokers to buy up depreciated small notes for purposes of sending them out of the state.[5] As a temporary measure

[1] *Banker's Magazine*, July, 1855, p. 52.

[2] See *St. Louis Democrat*, Mar. 4, 1857.

[3] The attitude of the *Republican* is well stated in *Banker's Magazine*, July, 1855, p. 52.

[4] *St. Louis Democrat*, Jan. 26, 1857 copied from *Missouri Intelligencer*.

[5] *Laws of Mo.*, 1857, p. 57.

until something better could be formulated, the charter of the State Bank was extended until February 2, 1861.[1]

Work was then begun in earnest on the bank question. Two problems were pressing for solution, namely: (1) What should be done with the State Bank? and (2) How could more adequate banking facilities be secured?

The solution for the first of these problems was a recharter bill. It provided that the present stockholders of the State Bank might reincorporate and increase the capital to $3,500,000. The state was to increase its holdings to $1,000,000, paying for the stock by taking funds from its deposit account. A meeting of stockholders was called for the first Monday in April, 1857 to decide whether or not to accept the new charter. If rejected the bank must liquidate in 1861; if accepted its privileges were extended to December 31, 1887. Its circulation was made receivable for all debts due to the state, as long as specie redemption was maintained. Public funds were to be deposited in the bank; and in return the bank was to perform all the duties of public fiscal agent. The state agreed to pay actual costs of transferring funds, but was to receive 6 per cent interest on all deposits left for more than one year. The governor, on the advice of the newly created banking department, might remove state deposits at any time he deemed the bank unsafe. The old bank was to be liquidated and all branches closed; but the new organization was to re-establish the St. Louis main office and to open branches at Fayette, Palmyra, Springfield, Chillicothe, Jefferson City, Cape Girardeau, and Louisiana. In practice the only real change was the closing of the Lexington branch and the opening of a new one at Louisiana. The Lexington business was being turned over to a new independent bank at that place. The total branch capital was

[1] *Laws of Mo.*, 1857, p. 14.

not to exceed two-fifths of the aggregate capital of the bank.[1]

The way was now open for the consideration of the larger questions of banking and currency expansion. To do this it was of course necessary to amend the constitution. The proposed changes had been advertised according to law so the legislature had full power to make them effective. In general the proposal was to charter not more than ten independent banks, of which the State Bank might be one. The combined capital was not to exceed $20,000,000 and was to be on a specie basis. All the insitutions were to be allowed to operate branches.[2] A joint committee on banking was charged with the working-out of the details of the plan. Before an official report was made, the *Bankers Magazine* published the following forecast of its contents: issues to be limited to one and one-half times the specie reserve for the first three years, after which a three to one rule would be applied; no notes under $5.00; annual bonus to the state of one per cent of capital; two per cent of each year's earnings to surplus; 12½ per cent of circulation to be invested in state bonds; monthly statement to be published; and each bank organized under the law to have a minimum capital of $1,000,0000.[3] This forecast proved to be substantially correct. The report, however, recommended in addition that all the banks be placed under the supervision of the state banking department, which should take over all the work then done by the state auditor and in addition require very much more detailed reports.[4]

[1] *Laws of Mo.*, 1857, "Act to Regulate Banking and Currency," art. iv, chap. x, secs. 1, 2, 6 and 7.

[2] Carr, *op. cit.*, p. 165. Also printed in full in *Banker's Magazine*, Apr., 1857, p. 48 *et seq.*

[3] *Banker's Magazine*, Mar., 1857, p. 745.

[4] *Ibid.*, Feb., 1857, p. 662. This also was preliminary and non-official information.

The committee report was accepted with little opposition, and a new general banking law was immediately passed. This law made such far-reaching changes in bank policy and administration that it is essential here to discuss it in considerable detail. It is too long for quotation in full, but its essential features were as follows:

An Act to supply the state with an ample, sound, and safe currency, the Notes to be Payable on Demand in Specie and to circulate in the State at Par etc.[1]

Article I.

Section 4—No notes under $5.00 to be issued. No bank shall deal in the notes of banks outside the state or in those established by the law of any other state, but all banks chartered under this act may deal in the notes of any bank or its branches established by Missouri law.

Section 5—A quarterly statement of condition must be published in at least two newspapers.

Section 6—Adequate provision for state examination as hereinafter provided.

Section 9—Penalty for suspension 20 per cent interest on circulation, and forfeiture of charter if suspension lasts for more than ten days.

Section 10—All officers placed under bond.

Section 13—Ten per cent of the capital of each bank organized under this act to be paid in gold and silver before opening.

Section 14—Within one year ten per cent of the paid up capital must be invested in state or railroad bonds, such bonds not to be sold below par without the consent of the bank commissioner.

Section 15—Two per cent of the net annual earnings must be placed to surplus account and invested in state bonds.

Section 16—Any state bonds held may be sold at or above

[1] *Laws of Mo.*, 1857 quoted from *Merchants and Bankers' Register* for 1857, p. 115 *et seq.*

par by first securing the consent of the bank commissioner, but if sold an equal amount of similar bonds must be purchased to replace them.

Section 22—All directors must be stockholders.

Section 25—Ten per cent of each stock subscription must be paid down in cash and the balance on call of the directors provided all be paid within one year. Failure to do this might involve forfeiture of the stock.

Section 26—No real estate except for banking house and to secure debts previously contracted. The latter type was to be sold.

Section 28—No loans on the security of a bank's own stock.

Section 29—Each bank to have thirteen directors, any five, however, constituting a quorum.

Section 30—Not over five-eighths of the capital of any bank to be used in exchange transactions.

Section 31—Each branch office to have its own board of directors, four-ninths of whom were to be elected by parent bank, and the rest by the local stockholders.

Section 32—Bonus of one per cent of capital to be paid to the state each year in lieu of all taxes.

Section 33—Interest rates fixed at 6 per cent on 120 day paper or less, 7 per cent on longer time paper. Exchange charges might be added to this rate.

Section 34—Semi-annual dividends to be declared from net profits.

Section 36—The owners of twenty per cent of the stock might demand a special stockholders meeting at any time.

Section 37—Circulation for the first year limited to $2.00 for each $1.00 of paid-up capital, second year $2.50 to $1.00 and third and thereafter $3.00 to $1.00, provided, however, that the gold and silver reserve must always equal 33⅓ per cent of the circulation.

Section 38—If state buys stock in any bank, it must be given proportional representation on the board.

Section 42—Circulation redeemable only at the counter of the issuing bank.

Section 43—Only gold, silver, or notes of Missouri specie-paying banks to be received on deposit or in payment of debts due to the bank.

Section 45—No loans may be made to stockholders whose shares are not fully paid up. Stock may not be transferred if holder is in debt to the bank.

Section 46—Loans may be made only in those communities where the bank has offices.

Article II. On Branches.

Section 1. Each bank organized under this act must have at least two branches, each of which must have a minimum capital of $100,000, but total branch capital must not exceed two-fifths of the capital of the bank.

Section 4. The branch earnings to be considered a part of the general dividend fund of the parent bank.

Article III. Supervision.

Section 1. Provides for a bank commissioner and assistant with salaries of $5,000 and $2,500 respectively, to be appointed by governor, and placed under bonds of $100,000 and $50,000 respectively. Must examine each bank before opening. They were to have notes printed at the expense of the issuing bank and sign and deliver them to the bank. It was their duty to burn all mutilated notes. Each bank was to be examined by them every six months and quarterly reports were to be required. Notes issued by parent banks redeemable at main offices and branch notes at branch office issuing them. No loans to be made to the bank commissioners.

Article IV. Establishment of banks.

Charters were offered to the following banks:

Section 1. Exchange, St. Louis, $1,000,000 authorized capital. Branches at Glasgow and Neosho.

Section 2. Bank of St. Louis, St. Louis, $1,000,000 authorized capital. Branches at Kirksville and Boonville.

Section 3. Merchants, St. Louis, $2,000,000 authorized capital. Branches at Brunswick, Osceola, and Ste. Genevieve.

Section 4, City Bank, St. Louis, $2,000,000 authorized capital. Branches at Kansas City, Columbia, Hannibal, and Gallatin.

Section 5. Mechanics, St. Louis, $1,500,000 authorized capital. Branches at Warsaw, Weston, and Fredericktown.

Section 6. Southern, St. Louis, $1,000,000 authorized capital. Branches at St. Charles and Independence.

Section 7. Farmers, Lexington, $1,000,000 authorized capital. Branches at Liberty and Paris.

Section 8. Western, St. Joseph, $1,000,000 authorized capital. Branches at Fulton and Bloomington.

An amendment was later passed providing that weekly statements of coin, maturing bills, and circulation be published in the St. Louis newspapers.[1] A fight was made to have deposits included but this failed.[2]

Commenting on this legislation, William Barrett Ridgely, one time comptroller of the currency, has said that the Missouri banking law of 1857 was well drawn and better than that of any neighboring state, although its early administration was not all that could have been desired, chiefly on account of crude and imperfect methods of examination. He especially called attention to the fact that the general scheme of supervision by a commissioner which was adopted at this time has remained a permanent part of the banking machinery of the state.[3] *The Bankers Magazine* characterized the law as, on the whole, judicious and said it compared favorably with the systems of Indiana, Illinois, New York, and Ohio. The influence of Louisiana in the 33⅓ per cent specie requirement was particularly noted.[4]

[1] *St. Louis Democrat*, Mar. 4, 1857.

[2] *Ibid.*, May 28, 1857.

[3] Ridgely, *op. cit.*

[4] *Banker's Magazine*, Apr., 1857, p. 828.

It was at least quite evident that an honest attempt had been made to make a satisfactory law. It, however, had certain weaknesses. Attention was still centered on the issue function, no special provisions being made for the safety of deposits. The requirement that the surplus added each year must be invested in state bonds was of doubtful wisdom. Moreover, the machinery of note redemption was inadequate. By making branch notes payable only at the counter of the issuing branch they were inevitably placed at a disadvantage compared with the circulation of the main office. Still the new banks could not be paper institutions. The law, if enforced, would produce institutions that would meet their obligations. The State Bank was given no special privileges. It was to become merely one of a group of chartered banks. The state was not yet ready to give up its investment. However, the theory of one great banking house with a monopoly of the circulation and furnishing banking facilities for all the people had been abandoned.

The State Bank at once made plans to comply with the law. There was some delay about holding the meeting to consider acceptance of the new charter, but on May 23rd notice was given that it would be accepted. The existing stock was converted into stock of the new bank, ten per cent being paid down at once and the balance in sums of ten per cent at each of the following times: August, Septemper, October, November, December, 1857; April and May, 1858; and 20 per cent, June, 1858. Branch capital was assigned as follows:

Palmyra	$125,000
Fayette	125,000
Cape Girardeau	150,000
Jefferson City	200,000
Springfield	200,000
Louisiana	300,000

No provision was made at this time for the Chillicothe office.[1] The increase in the state stock was paid for out of deposits to the state's credit as required by the charter, but later this was repaid from the state's share of surplus and profits and from a small appropriation from the General Revenue Fund.[2] On August 3, 1858 *the New York Evening Post* reported that books for subscription to the new stock had been opened at the Bank of Commerce and that 20 per cent of the amount offered had been taken during the first few days. *The Post* called it a good investment due to the favorable commercial position of St. Louis and the consequent large business in bills of exchange drawn against products shipped down the Mississippi River. It predicted that the stock would soon rise to a premium.

The St. Louis Democrat expressed fear that the payment of the 10 per cent initial subscription to the stock of the proposed new banks would derange business. The State Bank, however, recognized that it would have to meet this situation and began to reduce loans and convert exchange into cash. It thus increased its cash holdings by more than $500,000 by the time their subscription books were opened.[3]

Claiborne F. Jackson was named as the first bank commissioner and immediately prepared to supervise the opening of the newly chartered banks. Most of them opened subscription books in both New York and Saint Louis. Stock was eagerly taken in spite of the fact that monetary stringency was beginning to appear. By four p. m. of the first day 68 people in St. Louis had purchased Bank of Saint Louis stock.[4] It had 150 stockholders on the opening

[1] *Banker's Magazine*, Aug., 1857, p. 151.

[2] *Report State Auditor*, 1859, p. 18.

[3] *St. Louis Democrat*, Mar. 11, 1857.

[4] *St. Louis Democrat*, Mar. 18, 1857.

day.[1] The first day's subscription to the Farmers Bank of Lexington exceeded $100,000.[2] Under the charter requirement $100,000 specie was necessary before any of the banks could be opened, but it soon became evident that most would meet the requirement. Local capital for the branches was assured by judiciously planning that no two banks would establish branches in the same town. This ideal, however, was later broken down. In Saint Louis the capital for the various banks came from rather distinct groups. The Bank of St. Louis represented the interests of steamboat men and manufacturers; The Merchants Bank, dry goods and grocery trade; The Southern, boats and shoes and mechanical trades; and The Exchange, the lumber interests.[3]

Before the autumn of 1857 the reorganized State Bank, the Bank of St. Louis, The Southern, The Mechanics, The Exchange, all of St. Louis, and the Farmers Bank of Lexington had opened for business. The year, 1857, however, was not a favorable time for the launching of new enterprises. The panic came and brought with it the necessity for suspension. Several of the new institutions wished to maintain specie payments, but were overruled by the State Bank. By the middle of September the banks of Philadelphia, Baltimore, and Washington had suspended, but the panic did not reach Saint Louis until September 28th. Then the runs on the private banks, described in chapter XIV, started. The newly chartered banks had as yet done comparatively little business and so did not suffer greatly. Finally on October 24th the State Bank closed for two days. The Mechanics alone of the banks of issue refused to sus-

[1] *St. Louis Democrat*, Mar. 24, 1857.

[2] *Ibid.*, May 7, 1857.

[3] *Ibid.*, Mar. 18, 1857.

pend.[1] One other bank, the State Savings Institution (later the Bank of Commerce), maintained specie payments.[2]

The banks continued to transact business but remained in a state of illegal suspension. Of the newly chartered banks only the City Bank failed to survive. It had been slow in getting started and was not yet open for business when the panic came on. Its board of directors voted to surrender the charter.[3] The charters of all the rest were legally subject to forfeiture, but no one pressed the case and in November the special session of the General Assembly passed an act to relieve them of the penalties set down in their charters. This act legalized suspension until November 1, 1858 unless the bank commissioner and the directors of the banks concerned agreed to resume sooner. While suspended the notes were to draw no interest and no more could be issued. A cash reserve of 33⅓ per cent, however, was required to be maintained. In return for this relief the banks were ordered to renew all loans, provided they were reduced 20 per cent (of which one-fifth was to be paid in cash) and provided good security were offered. Of these payments the one-fifth just mentioned was to be held in the vaults of the bank until the time of resumption.[4]

The new banks, however, took a minimum of advantage of this relief law and, by the end of 1857 or early in 1858, most of them had made arrangements to resume specie payments. Indeed the State Bank resumed sooner than any other bank in the Southwest.[5] This early resumption was due in part to the relatively strong position of the State

[1] *St. Louis Democrat*, July 2, 1858.

[2] *Banker's Magazine*, Feb., 1858, p. 682.

[3] *Ibid.*, Jan., 1858, p. 585.

[4] *Laws of Mo.*, 1857, p. 10.

[5] *Report of Indianapolis Monetary Commission*, p. 293.

Bank and in part to the fact that the other banks had started on a specie basis and had not yet done a great deal of business when the panic came. The private banks, however, did not fare so well, as has been shown in chapter XIV. A number of them remained closed and most of their business passed into the hands of the chartered banks. A consolidated statement of the chartered banks for the beginning of 1857 compared with a similar statement at the end of the year shows something of the effects of the panic:

	Beginning of Year	*End of Year*
Discounts	$2,925,000	$2,534,000
Specie	3,488,000	1,489,000
Circulation	3,655,000	1,812,000
Deposits	6,308,000	1,486,000
Ratio of Circulation and Deposits to Specie	1.80 to 1	2.28 to 1

On the whole, however, St. Louis suffered less from the panic than did many other cities. Her percentage of business failures was only one-half as great as those of Boston and New York, and only three-eighths that of Chicago.[1]

The resumption, however, was only partial. The St. Louis city banks paid specie on demand, but made informal agreements to accept one another's notes in settlement of balances. The notes of the country branches, being payable only at the office of issue, were discriminated against in St. Louis. The city bankers began to collect and send them home for redemption. This caused ill feeling and in some cases led to mob violence. There was no method of shipment except by stage coach and in more than one instance agents of St. Louis banks who had drawn cash from country offices redeposited it again for safe keeping. The worst case happened at Chillicothe. A St. Louis agent presented $11,000 of the local branch notes and demanded gold.

[1] Pope, *op. cit.*, p. 93.

Seventy-five men gathered at the bank and ordered him to leave town in five minutes. The bank, however, by resolution of the board, expressed itself as out of sympathy with the act and made arrangements to have its notes redeemed in Saint Louis.[1]

The name "bankable funds" came to be applied to the notes of the stronger St. Louis banks, although it soon came to be loosely used to describe all manner of bank notes in local circulation. The banks themselves, however, continued to draw a more careful distinction. By the end of September, 1858 the last of the St. Louis banks, The Boatmen's, had gone to a "bankable fund" basis.[2] The banks all tried to hoard their specie and to meet necessary obligations by expanding their circulation. However, there was, on the whole, a distinct tendency toward contraction of business all during 1858. The bank rates varied between six and ten per cent, but street loans at fifteen per cent were not uncommon.[3] "Bankable funds" passed for most transactions. Little gold circulated, and Ohio, Indiana, and Kentucky paper began to disappear.[4] *The Democrat* was inclined to be critical of the issue policies of the banks and called attention to the fact that they had issued less than one-half the notes permitted by their charters.[5] Outside of the state Missouri notes were not highly regarded. Cincinnati banks took them only at a considerable discount and threatened to refuse them altogether.[6] In spite of unsettled conditions most of the banks paid their usual dividends. The weekly statements were published as re-

[1] *Banker's Magazine*, Oct., 1859 and Mar., 1860, p. 744.

[2] *St. Louis Democrat*, Sept. 30, 1858.

[3] *Ibid.*, Aug. 16, 1858.

[4] *Ibid.*, Oct. 28, 1858.

[5] Oct. 21, 1858.

[6] *Ibid.*, Sept. 10, 1858.

quired by law. The one here given is for December 11, 1858:

Bank	*Circulation*	*Specie*	*Maturing Exchange*
Merchants	493	417	736
Bank of St. Louis	279	179	293
Southern	284	186	379
Mechanics	238	209	434
Exchange	264	202	263
State	426	552	1,015
Total	1,984	1,745	3,120

(Note 000 omitted)

Compared with statements for July 3, 1858 this shows declines in circulation and specie of $260,000 and $573,000 respectively and an increase in maturing exchange of $1,600,000.[1] The increase in this last item was largely due to the efforts of the banks to provide eastern balances for payment of the state debt.

The use of "Bankable Funds" continued in 1859 and bankers of other states discriminated more and more against Missouri paper. In July Cincinnati banks sent in $125,000 for redemption at one time. It was redeemed and this action did much to stop the rising tide of unrest. Cincinnati bankers had determined to refuse Missouri notes altogether, but after this they were usually taken at par.[2] Indiana, however, continued to refuse them and they passed at a discount in Kentucky and in Ohio outside of Cincinnati. New York City banks received them at a discount, regarding them as inconvertible but reasonably safe.[3] The banks did not seem to be in danger of failure.

[1] *St. Louis Democrat*, for dates given in statements.

[2] *Cincinnati Gazette*, June 10, 1858, quoted in *Banker's Magazine*, July, 1859, p. 76.

[3] *Banker's Magazine*, Aug., 1859, p. 152.

In spite of unfavorable conditions St. Louis financial interests showed an increasing tendency to invest in bank stock. The Mechanics Bank added $250,000 to its capital stock. Subscriptions to the amount of $757,000 had already been made and fully paid for.[1] No doubt its refusal to suspend in 1857 had added greatly to its prestige. Earlier in the year the Union Bank had opened its books and had started with $200,000, partly foreign capital, although there were ninety-five local stockholders. It planned to open branches in La Grange, Milan, Richmond, Warrensburg, Kansas City, and Charleston.[2] It was announced that the Western Bank of St. Joseph would soon open for business.[3]

Meanwhile a hard fight on the savings banks had developed. They had incurred the enmity of the branches of the chartered banks, and therefore also of their home offices by receiving branch notes on deposit and sending them home for redemption. The legislature took up the fight, sided with the chartered banks of issue, and passed the Richardson Bill, prohibiting any savings bank from receiving on deposit any notes quoted below par.[4] This caused one of the largest of them, The State Savings Institution, to surrender its charter.[5]

In May, 1859 the *Bankers Magazine* published a detailed consolidated statement for all the chartered banks of the state as of January 1, 1859. Summarized figures given below are taken from this source:[6]

[1] *Ibid.*, Nov., 1859, p. 399.

[2] *Ibid.*, April, 1859, p. 825.

[3] *Ibid.*

[4] *Ibid.*, Mar., 1859, p. 745.

[5] *Ibid.*, Apr., 1859, p. 829.

[6] *Ibid.*, May, 1859, p. 1887 *et seq.*

CONSOLIDATED STATEMENTS (000 OMITTED)

JANUARY 1, 1859

Assets

Banks	*Discounts*	*Bills of Exchange*	*Suspended Debt*	*Notes of Other Banks*	*Due from Banks*	*Specie*
State Bank	1,425	2,141	48	257	306	1,382
Southern	409	488	5	132	5	264
Farmers	537	753	34	146	185	712
Mechanics	468	676	5	48	13	363
Merchants	681	937		119	18	569
St. Louis	195	563		254	30	296
Exchange	251	520	16	41	39	325

Liabilities

Bank	*Capital*	*Circulation*	*Deposits*
State Bank	2,383	2,880	766
Southern	454	695	349
Farmers	626	1,390	216
Mechanics	413	798	327
Merchants	418	962	617
St. Louis	305	522	585
Exchange	365	610	246

By the end of 1859 the state seemed fairly well supplied with banking offices. St. Louis now had eight banks of issue with a combined capital of $12,500,000, twelve savings banks, and twenty-one private bankers. Although many of the other towns had private banks, the chartered banks of issue were rapidly extending their branch systems. Branch offices had been opened as follows: [1]

Branch Offices of the Chartered Banks of Issue of Missouri

State Bank of St. Louis:

Arrow Rock	Palmyra
Canton	St. Joseph
Chillicothe	Louisiana
Fayette	Springfield
Jefferson City	Cape Girardeau

[1] Sutherland and McEvoy, *Mo. State Gazetteer*, 1859 and 1860.

Southern Bank of St. Louis:

Independence	St. Charles
Gallatin	Warrensburg
Savannah	

Mechanics Bank of St. Louis:

Weston	Fredericktown
Warsaw	Osceola
Kansas City	

Union Bank of St. Louis:

Kansas City	Milan
Charleston	Richmond
La Grange	Warrensburg

Merchants Bank of St. Louis:

Osceola	Ste. Genevieve
Brunswick	

Western Bank of St. Joseph:

Fulton	Arrow Rock
Glasgow	Bloomington

Bank of St. Louis:

Boonville	Kirksville
Savannah	

Exchange Bank of St. Louis:

Columbia	Neosho
Glasgow	

Farmers Bank of Lexington:

Paris	Liberty

In general these branches had from $100,000 to $300,000 capital.

It was with this sort of a banking equipment that Missouri entered the Civil War. The country banks had never given up the policy of delaying redemption of their notes and, as a consequence, had experienced difficulty in keeping them in circulation. Also there had been enough fear of St. Louis banks to cause out-of-the-state bankers to demand specie wherever possible. This had meant a gradual lowering of their coin reserves.

Meanwhile the State Bank had been pursuing its regular course and taking such business as came its way. It now had more competition than before its issue monopoly was broken: but it was still the largest financial institution in the state and retained much of its former prestige. In 1858 it had again suspended because of fear of another panic, but after a few days resumed on its famous "Bankable Fund" basis. It has already been shown how this idea spread to the other banks. In its original form it was that the home office refused to pay gold for the notes of its own branches but offered to receive them on deposit or in payment for drafts at a discount of ¼ of 1 per cent.[1] This, of course, aroused much criticism, it being early recognized that the inaccessibility of the country banks meant, that if their notes were not redeemable in St. Louis, then for most purposes they were not redeemable at all. In 1859 R. A. Barnes, a wholesale grocer who had been a director for nineteen years, was elected president, but policies changed but little. From January 1st to November 1st the circulation of the bank was contracted from $1,350,00 to $715,000.[2] On January 1, 1859 its complete statement of condition for the St. Louis office was given out as follows:

[1] *St. Louis Democrat*, Aug. 7, 1858.

[2] *House Jour.*, 20th General Assembly Mo., 1859-60.

Resources		*Liabilities*	
Branch Capital	$760,380.00	Capital, State	$1,000,000.00
Discounts	818,105.83	Capital, Private	1,383,750.00
Exchange Matured ..	15,718.73	Deposits	523,734.25
Exchange Maturing .	1,086,314.93	Unpaid Dividends ...	3,374.38
Suspended Debt	36,187.62	Interest & Exchange	96,201.18
Due from Banks	66,014.58	Due to Banks	237,157.58
Furniture	18,734.63	Circulation	1,341,500.00
Notes of Other Banks	98,275.00	Contingent	81,095.35
Specie	545,956.42		
Circulation on Hand .	745,275.00		
Real Estate	100,000.00		
State Bonds	176,000.00		
	$4,666,962.74		$4,666,962.74

How it and the other banks of Missouri fared during the Civil War will next be considered.

CHAPTER XVII

Missouri Banking During the Civil War

The panic of 1857 and the subsequent depression, involving the extensive use of "bankable funds", left the banks of the state in a weakened condition to sustain the shock of the Civil War. Bank deposits were extremely small, amounting to only about $3,00 per capita.[1] *The Bankers Magazine* characterized Missouri banks along with those of Kentucky and Virginia as quite conservative when compared with Northern institutions;[2] but, in fact, their condition left much to be desired. Branch banking was the established practice; but the home offices were usually unable to control branch policies. The result was that the notes of the branches were below the standards of those of the mother banks and soon the latter began to pay out notes of distant offices. Saint Louis thus acquired a currency little better than that of Illinois and Wisconsin, and New York exchange rose to a permium of 1¾ per cent.[3] *The Merchants and Bankers Register of Philadelphia* for 1860 listed 43 chartered banks and branches in 33 Missouri towns. In addition it gave the names of 32 private banking houses, 17 of them in Saint Louis. The total capital was given as $11,910,400; circulation, $8,000,000; and specie, $5,000,-

[1] In 1860 population of state was 1,721,000 and bank deposits, $4,557,000; see Stephens, *op. cit.*, p. 536.

[2] December, 1860.

[3] *Banker's Magazine*, Mar., 1860, p. 246.

000.[1] *The Bankers Magazine* in August, 1860 reported a decrease of $4,000,000 in circulation since July, 1859.[2] It published the following consolidated comparative statement:

CONSOLIDATED STATEMENT MISSOURI BANKS (00,000 OMITTED)

	July, 1859	*August, 1860*
Capital	6.8	10.5
Deposits	3.2	2.9
Circulation	10.8	6.3
Due to Banks	1.2	.7
Loans	5.2	5.2
Domestic Exchange	7.0	9.3
Specie	4.5	4.2
Notes of Other Banks	1.2	.5
Due from Banks	.8	.4
Suspended Debt	.1	.3

The Bank of the State of Missouri shared in the general difficulty and did not always redeem its circulation.[3] Its condition, as reported in January, 1859, changed very rapidly.[4] *The Special Session Report of the Bank Committee* of 1860 showed discounts of $731,000; cash, $784,000, of which only $237,000 was gold and silver; deposits, $491,603; and a suspended debt account of $266,000. The report expressed great dissatisfaction with the existing condition of the bank and made lengthy comparisons with that of former days when the bank paper was convertible into gold on demand whether issued by the home office or by the most distant branch, and was actually preferred to gold in California and Oregon.[5] Considerable criticism was made of the conduct of the branches. At this time offices were in

[1] *Merchants and Bankers Register of Philadelphia*, 1860, p. 23 *et seq.*

[2] P. 162.

[3] *Banker's Magazine*, Apr., 1860, p. 825.

[4] See previous chapter.

[5] "Report of Bank Committee," pp. 1-7 of *Legislative Jour. of Mo.*, 1860 and *House Jour.*, 21st General Assembly Mo., 1860-61, p. 579.

operation in Fayette, Arrow Rock, Cape Girardeau, Palmyra, Springfield, Louisiana, Chillicothe, Canton, and St. Joseph.

The unsatisfactory condition of banking in the surrounding states added to Missouri's difficulties. In 1860 Arkansas had no banks at all. Iowa had thirteen and Illinois had seventy-two. Of the latter over half were banks of circulation only and transacted no business at their nominal locations.[1] Their notes circulated at 10-15 per cent discount, although sometimes they passed at much nearer par in small transactions.[2] Illinois, however, was planning reform legislation and it was expected that her currency would soon be better than Missouri's. In 1861 she passed a law providing for redemption of notes in Chicago and Springfield at a discount of ½ to ¾ of 1 per cent.[3] Previously they had been wholly inconvertible. Wisconsin was in a similar condition. Iowa currency had a considerably better standing, being quoted 4 per cent above Illinois notes in Chicago.[4] Although the Missouri banks had more specie than all the free banks of Illinois, Wisconsin and Indiana put together, their notes were more or less discredited.[5] In 1860 the State Bank Commissioner reported the discount as 1½ per cent below gold and 1 per cent below the notes of Indiana, Kentucky, Louisiana, and Ohio. Moreover, exchange on New York was 1½ per cent.[6]

With all their weakness the banks of Missouri were still able to render a considerable amount of war service. The

[1] *Banker's Magazine*, Jan., 1861, p. 585.

[2] *St. Louis Democrat*, Jan. 17, 1861.

[3] *Ibid.*, Feb. 14, 1861.

[4] *Ibid.*, Jan. 15, 1861.

[5] *Banker's Magazine*, Apr., 1860, p. 824.

[6] Dunbar, C. F., "State Banks in 1860" in *Economic Essays* (Sprague ed., New York, 1904).

local sentiment, however, was divided. Late in 1861 the State Bank Commissioner classified the Banks of St. Louis as to their political sympathies:[1]

Union		*Confederate*	
State Bank Merchants Exchange	Circulation, $3,411,000	Bank of St. Louis Mechanics Union Southern	Circulation, $3,086,000

On August 16, 1861 Major-General Fremont, officer in charge at Saint Louis, demanded that the banks lend his organization $250,000. The Exchange Bank handled the loan, but all the banks participated. The contributions were as follows:[2]

Bank	*Coin*	*Bankable Funds*
Bank of Missouri	$10,000	$42,000
Merchants	10,000	24,000
Mechanics	15,000	15,000
Union	10,000	None
Exchange	10,000	17,500
Southern	10,000	12,000
Bank of St. Louis	5,000	7,500
State Savings	10,000	14,000
Boatmen's	10,000	16,000
Franklin	None	2,000
German	10,000	7,600
Total	$100,000	$157,600

The next year this was repaid with ten per cent interest.[3] Other demands were made later. These were not always met gracefully, but in one way or another the government forced the banks to advance a great deal of money. It was, however, all repaid with interest. It is difficult to say how

[1] Stevens, W. B., *St. Louis the Fourth City* (St. Louis, 1909), p. 312.

[2] *Banker's Magazine*, Sept., 1861, p. 235.

[3] *Ibid.*, June, 1862, p. 970.

large the total borowings were. Stevens is authority for the following estimate:

State Bank	$291,000
Boatmen's	154,000
Exchange	141,000
Union	68,000
Southern	10,000
Merchants	75,000
Mechanics	36,000
	$775,000 [1]

Conrad, however, states that in all more than $2,000,000 was advanced before the close of the war.[2] At one time General Fremont seized all the specie in the vaults of the St. Louis office of the State Bank and issued a call to the branch offices to send what they had to him. His collections by this method were, however, extremely small. The Arrow Rock branch, being Southern in sympathy, buried its coin for a year and then secretly deposited it in a St. Louis bank where it remained until the close of the war.[3] United States bonds were purchased in large quantities. The State Bank alone had $599,000 in 1865.[4] There seems to be no record of the amount advanced to the Southern cause, but it was no doubt considerable. Large voluntary subscriptions were made to aid the families of soldiers on both sides. When the Western Sanitary Commission started such a fund the State Bank headed the list with a subscription of $5,000.[5]

Throughout most of 1860 the banks of Saint Louis at-

[1] Stevens, W. B., *St. Louis the Fourth City* (St. Louis, 1909), p. 312.

[2] Conrad, *Cyclopedia Mo. Hist.*, vol. i, p. 239.

[3] Napton, *Past and Present of Saline County* (1881), p. 476.

[4] 23rd Adjourned Sess., General Assembly Mo., 1865-66, *House Jour.*

[5] Conrad, *Cyclopedia Mo. Hist.*, vol. i, p. 239.

tempted to maintain par exchange and redemption of circulation. There was much talk of suspension, but the Merchants Bank in particular fought the idea. After a preliminary conference which accomplished nothing, its board of directors passed a resolution to petition the legislature to force the banks to pay out no currency or notes which they would not redeem at their own counters.[1]

On November 28, 1860 all the banks of Missouri except the Exchange Bank of Saint Louis suspended specie payments. Three days previously a bankers meeting had been held, attended by representatives of all the banks except the Exchange. At this meeting it was decided not to suspend. However, a second meeting, held on November 27th, reversed this action. It was a stormy session. The State Bank opposed suspension, having coin holdings equal to 70 per cent of its circulation, but finally gave in to the judgment of the meeting. The Merchants Bank, which had 72½ per cent coin against its notes, stood with the State Bank. The Exchange Bank refused to attend the conference. It had a very small circulation outstanding, and, due to its liberal policy of redemption, had little paper in the hands of brokers. Accordingly, it could afford to be independent and to take its own time for a decision. Little information is available as to the attitude of the private banking houses, but it is known that Barksdale and Anderson suspended. The action of the conference caused little surprise. It was expected and seems to have met with the approval of the local business men.[2]

In April, 1861 the Saint Louis banks came to an agreement to support one another's notes. This lasted until October when one of the banks announced a refusal of the

[1] *Banker's Magazine*, Apr., 1860, p. 824.

[2] *Ibid.*, Jan., 1861, p. 585.

notes of the Union Bank.[1] Later a new agreement was made between the State, Merchants, Union, and Southern Banks, whereby each agreed to accept and pay out the notes of all the others. By May, 1861 conditions were very bad. *The St. Louis Democrat* said the currency question was beyond all hope of settlement and spread a rumor that the credit of the state would be impaired by a default of the July interest on the bonded debt, the governor having planned to use the fund for other purposes. *The Evening News* vigorously denied this story.[2] *The New Orleans Crescent* had accused Saint Louis of leading in the race for suspension and had upbraided the banks for paying dividends while suspended.[3]

A demand was made that the legislature recognize actual conditions and legalize the action of the banks. On February 15, 1861 *The St. Louis Democrat* reported that the Senate had begun to discuss the question and would likely allow the expensive "bankable fund" system to be continued. A disposition of the chartered banks of issue to fight the savings institutions was noted. The savings banks had incurred the ill will of the country branches by demanding coin on all possible occasions, and it was this that caused the opposition. Meanwhile the House had passed a stay law, providing, as *the Democrat* said, "for the indefinite continuance of all notes not paid at maturity."[4] Finally the bank bill styled "An Act for the Relief of the Banks of Missouri" was passed by both houses and became effective March 18, 1861.[5] The House had previously passed an anti-bankable fund measure, but it had been rejected by

[1] Scharf, *Hist. of St. Louis City and County* (Philadelphia), 1883, p. 1379.

[2] Quoted in *Banker's Magazine*, May, 1861, pp. 915 and 940.

[3] Quoted in *St. Louis Democrat*, Jan. 24, 1861.

[4] *Ibid.*, Feb. 16, 1861.

[5] *Ibid.*, Mar. 6 and 9, 1861 and *Banker's Magazine*, Apr., 1861, p. 836.

the Senate.[1] This measure proposed to allow the banks to receive any sort of paper on deposit so long as they redeemed it in gold on demand. However, the banks announced that they would not receive deposits except on agreement not to demand redemption; so the law would probably have been a dead letter.[2]

The Relief Act undertook to do two things: (a) to remove the penalties for suspension and (b) to provide for the payment of the July interest on the state debt. It applied to the following banks: State, Merchants, Mechanics, Exchange, Southern, Union, St. Louis, Farmers, and Western. The more important provisions were as follows:

1. All provisions of the Act of March 2, 1857 which entailed forfeiture of charters for suspension were set aside until May 1, 1862.

2. Interest could not be charged on circulation during the period of suspension, and no notes of banks outside the state were to be paid out.

3. Notes of any Missouri bank affected by the act were made receivable for any debts due to such banks, provided that no branch notes were receivable at less than par.

4. The revenue bonds due June 1, 1861 were to be redeemed, and the July interest on the state debt paid. For the latter purpose Governor Jackson was authorized to raise the necessary funds by selling 3253 shares of the stock of the State Bank.

5. Any borrower, paying the interest and ten per cent of the principal of his loan, was to have the time extended for a period equal to that of the original loan upon giving proper security.

7. Any new circulation issued after the date of the act was to be stamped as suspended paper by the State Bank Commissioner.

[1] *St. Louis Democrat*, Feb. 28, 1861.

[2] *Ibid.*, Feb. 15, 1861.

9. The weekly statement heretofore required of St. Louis banks was discontinued.

11. The 6 to 7 per cent restriction on the interest rate was repealed, but the two to one limit on circulation was retained.

14. The banks were to lend $500,000 to the state government, assessments to be made on each bank in proportion to its capital. As security the governor was ordered to issue 9 per cent bonds, payable in three and five years for which the revenues of the state were pledged.[1]

The courts aided the policy of semi-suspension. In 1859 the Boatmen's Bank presented $54,840 notes of the Palmyra Branch of the State Bank and demanded gold. $1,190 of this amount was in denominations of $5.00, the rest $10.00's, $20.00's and $50.00's. The bank refused to pay unless it could consider each note a separate demand. It offered to pay each of the $5.00 notes in silver, and the others $5.00 in silver and the rest in gold. The Boatmen's Bank refused this offer and brought suit for the entire $54,840 in gold plus 20 per cent damages. The court said that the bank had the legal right to consider each $5.00 bill as a separate demand, but, under the Act of Congress of 1853 limiting the legal tender values of silver to $5.00, the bank could not tender silver coin for the larger notes. It, accordingly, ordered the bank to pay $53,650 in coin and $11,000 damages, also in coin.[2] Appeal was taken to the State Supreme Court. In 1863 a decision was handed down granting the bank the right to consider each note a separate demand, payable $5.00 in silver, the rest in gold.[3] The effect of this outcome on business can be imagined.

[1] *Banker's Magazine*, July, 1861, p. 24. The act was published in full as a state document. A copy is in the possession of the Boston Public Library.

[2] *Banker's Magazine*, Sept., 1860, p. 251.

[3] Sumner, W. G., *History of Banking in All the Leading Nations*, vol. i, p. 450, quoting 2 *Whittlesy* 497.

The banks took full advantage of the new law. The Union and City Banks soon became discredited, but most of the others continued to use "bankable funds" and accepted one another's notes. The Exchange Bank, however, persevered in its plan of action and refused to be a party to the agreement. The Mechanics, Merchants, Farmers, and Western announced that they would attempt early resumption. The Boatmen's Bank refused all notes except those of the State and Merchants Banks, while the Building and Loan Association (later the Bank of Commerce) refused them all. The Farmers Bank of Lexington had been thoroughly discredited, but, after burning $912, 680 of its notes, announcement was made that it had enough cash and assets to redeem all other notes outstanding, to pay its depositors, and to return the stock at par.[1] Part of its trouble had been due to robbery of specie by federal troops. Still its paper was generally refused. As a rule the notes of the stronger banks passed at ten per cent discount, but some of the banks kept separate accounts for each kind of notes.[2]

Fractional currency was forbidden by law, but in August, 1861 the Bank of Saint Louis began to issue small notes and the others soon followed its example. No attempt was made to enforce the law and the banks generally pledged their resources for their payment. Small change was so scarce that such notes were gladly accepted.[3]

It is somewhat difficult to get statements of condition of the various banks during the war. In January, 1861 all the banks except one declared their usual semi-annual divi-

[1] Letter from Mr. Aull, cashier, in *Banker's Magazine*, Nov., 1861, p. 395.

[2] *Banker's Magazine*, Nov., 1861, p. 394.

[3] *Ibid.*, Jan., 1863, p. 568 from *St. Louis Republic*, Dec. 16, 1862; and *Ibid.*, Aug., 1861, p. 156.

dends of five per cent.[1] In March, 1864 the State Savings Bank paid four per cent.[2] A consolidated statement for January, 1861 showed capital $13,178,000; specie, $4,160,000; and circulation, $8,000,000.[3] On July 1, 1862 the Saint Louis banks of issue reported their condition as follows:[4]

Bank	*Circulation*	*Deposits*	*Specie*	*Other assets (000 omitted)*
Western	$244	$244	$276	$101
Union	460	121	246	47
Southern	662	440	426	303
Mechanics	647	471	497	250
St. Louis	259	287	269	148
Merchants	608	836	529	611
Exchange	24	680	436	443
State	1,048	702	1,039	629
Total	$3,956	$3,784	$3,992	$2,536

The Boatmen's Bank, though not a bank of issue, was a strong institution. At this time it probably had $300,000 specie and as much more in "bankable funds".[5] In January, 1863 another consolidated statement was published showing in round numbers, capital $11,200,000; circulation, $4,000,000; deposits, $3,400,000; loans, $12,000,000; specie, $3,600,000; and notes of other banks, $1,300,000.[6] *The Bankers Magazine* in July, 1864 reported that the loans of Missouri banks had declined from $17,000,000 to $8,800,000 between January, 1861 and January, 1864, while in the same time the specie reserve had decreased from $8,000,000 to $2,000,000. In July, 1864 this latter was given

[1] *St. Louis Democrat*, Jan. 10, 1861.

[2] *Banker's Magazine*, Mar., 1864, p. 754.

[3] *Ibid.*, Feb., 1861, p. 660.

[4] *Ibid.*, Sept., 1862, p. 234.

[5] *St. Louis Democrat*, Mar. 4, 1861.

[6] *Banker's Magazine*, Jan., 1864, p. 506 statement for Jan., 1863.

as below $600,000.[1] A large number of the banks continued operations throughout the war period. The following list of chartered banks and branches with the capital of each as of October, 1863 shows that the state was not left without banking facilities, even though specie payments were suspended during a large part of the time:[2]

Banks of Issue	*Capital*
Merchants Bank, St. Louis	$1,200,000
Branch, Brunswick	200,000
Branch Ste. Genevieve	100,000
Merchants Bank, St. Louis	716,000
Branch Kansas City	107,000
Branch Warsaw	160,000
Branch Weston	134,000
Exchange Bank, St. Louis	750,000
Branch Glasgow	250,000
Branch Columbia	125,000
Bank of St. Louis, St. Louis	361,000
Branch Boonville	200,000
Branch Kirksville	78,000
Southern Bank, St. Louis	696,000
Branch Independence	200,000
Branch Savannah	87,000
Branch St. Charles	100,000
Union Bank, St. Louis	350,000
Branch Richmond	150,000
Branch Kansas City	100,000
Branch La Grange	83,000
Branch Warrensburg	100,000
Branch Charleston	87,000
Branch Milan	80,000
Third National Bank, St. Louis	1,049,000
State Bank, St. Louis	2,268,800
Branch Arrow Rock	100,000
Branch Canton	100,000
Branch Cape Girardeau	200,000

[1] *Banker's Magazine*, July, 1864, p. 74.

[2] *Executive Document* 50, 38th Cong. 1st Session, "Letter of Sec'y of Treas. giving Abstract of Bank Reports for Commissioner of Internal Revenue."

Branch Chillicothe	150,000
Branch Fayette	125,000
Branch Louisiana	200,000
Branch Palmyra	125,000
Branch Springfield	200,000
Branch St. Joseph	100,000
Western Bank, St. Joseph	244,000
Branch Bloomington	64,000
Branch Fulton	53,000
Branch Glasgow	250,000
Farmers Bank, Lexington	600,000
Branch Liberty	250,000
Branch Paris	150,000
First National Bank, Columbia	100,000

It will be noted from this statement that Missouri had only two national banks at this time. Her state banks were suspended, but were by ho means broken banks. The State Bank was probably the strongest of the group, but it was carrying on its business in accordance with the general rule. It was relatively sound, but was earning a low rate of return on its stock.

Here on the eve of the launching of the National Banking System it may be of interest to glance at the condition of the state banks nationally in comparison with those of Missouri. Most of the state experiments had ended in disaster. Vermont's state bank had closed as early as 1815. By 1830 Kentucky had seen two failures. The Indiana Bank, though successful, was now closed. Massachusetts and Illinois ventures had failed in the forties. Those of Georgia, Florida, and Arkansas had closed in 1842. Alabama had quit three years later leaving a debt of several million dollars. Louisiana had sold out, and Tennessee was now almost to the end. There were left only the Bank of Kentucky, the Farmers Bank of Delaware, the state banks of North and South Carolina, and the State Bank of Missouri. Delaware and the Carolinas were experiencing some measure of success aside from war disturbances. It was evident that the state systems had largely broken down before the national government came on the field.

Now as to the local conditions in Missouri. The list of state banks and branches in 1866 contained thirty names, but of these ten were closed or closing. Six of these represented offices of the Union Bank of St. Louis, which was liquidating. The State Bank had closed its Fayette Branch. There were in addition some fifty private and savings banks. Thirteen state banks had closed 1861-66, but of these most had either nationalized or become private banks.

Statements of the Bank of the State of Missouri were published in 1865 and 1867. They are extremely incomplete but are essentially as follows:

(000 OMITTED)

State Bank	*Sept. 30, 1865* [1]	*Dec. 31, 1865* [2]	*1867* [3]
Capital, Public		($3,379)	$1,086
Capital, Private		( )	2,305
Circulation		192	
Due to Banks		19	133
Deposits		1,240	946
Real Estate	$244	239	
Coin	868	156	
Notes of Other Banks	615	739	
State Bonds	408	400	
National Bonds	599		
Discounts	1,373	986	
Exchange	294	553	
Suspended Debt	592	715	
Liabilities of Directors		239	

[1] 23rd Adjourned Sess. General Assembly Mo., *House Jour.*, 1865-66.

[2] *Banker's Magazine*, May, 1866.

[3] 8th semi-annual Report Bank Commissioner Mo., Appendix, *Jour. of Mo. General Assembly* for 1867. A more complete analysis of the condition of the State Bank will be found in chap. viii.

CHAPTER XVIII

The Sale of the State Stock

As early as 1851 the question was raised as to the advisability of disposing of the public interest in the State Bank. It first came up in connection with the demand for increased banking facilities. The Senate Committee on Ways and Means suggested selling the state stock in order to get away from restrictions imposed by relations with the private stockholders. It was then proposed to start a new bank with $5,000,000 capital.[1] The matter was referred to a Bank Committee, of which Wayman Crow of Saint Louis was chairman. The report of this committee advised the sale of the state stock, but opposed any further public ownership of banking institutions. Mr. Crow took occasion to express forcibly his ideas on the superiority of private management. The essential features of the argument are here given:[2] "The committee concurs with the governor in the opinion that banks controlled by agents of the legislature are seldom, if ever, satisfactory. Bank management requires experience, capacity, honesty, and technical skill on the part of the directors. The legislature and the executive have not the opportunity of learning the qualifications of directors, but are compelled to rely on casual information from interested parties. The directors are thus

[1] *Banker's Magazine*, Mar., 1851, p. 700.

[2] *Ibid.*, p. 700 *et seq.* Adapted from the "Report of the Bank Committee, Senate of Mo.," Mar., 1851, Wayman Crow, Chairman.

often incompetent. But, even if competent directors could be secured, experience teaches that business organizations are not usually well managed unless private interest overlooks and controls their affairs. Such guaranties are wanting where the directors are appointed by the state. Experiences of our own and other states have proved these conclusions to be well founded; and that banks are rarely, if ever, well managed by such agents. So long as the state holds the present stock investment and is responsible for that of the University and Common School Funds, and so long as the disproportion of public to private stock remains as great as it is, it will be advisable to make no changes in the management. So long as the state owns so much stock, management could not safely be confided to private agents. Good policy then requires the state to cease to be a stockholder in the bank, and that at the first opportunity it can be accomplished without loss. Discussing the proper method of doing this, the committee presented the following plan: The charter still has six years to run, and the state has no power to abridge the term without the consent of the private stockholders. Even if the state had the power to cause the liquidation of the bank now, it could not be done without deranging business. Such results must be avoided and may be if certain fundamental steps are taken as follows: (1) the charter should be extended for a reasonable period in order to invite additional investment in the private stock; (2) the subscription books for private shares should be reopened; (3) a majority of the directors should be selected by the private stockholders; (4) as soon as an agreed amount of private stock has been taken, the bank or the private stockholders must purchase the state shares at not less than par; (5) the proceeds of the state sale should be deposited in the bank at 6 per cent interest; (6) in order to avoid legal difficulties incident to the constitutional requirement of reservation of one-half the stock for the state, such reservations could be made to become effective only upon order of the legislature. Such an order should not be given; (7) as a bonus the state should require an annual payment of ½ of 1 per cent on the capital stock; (8) in order to prevent over-issues of currency, the state auditor's signature should be required on each note, such signature to be withheld at the option of the auditor. The report argued that new stock could not be sold without an extension of the charter and, that if the bank were to be expected to buy the state stock, an increase of capital would be necessary. It concluded with the statement that the bank had failed to keep out the unsound currency of other states and that no other result could be expected so long as neighboring states continued their paper bank policies.

It is worth noting that the report did not bring specific charges against the management of the Bank of the State of Missouri, but merely presented the theory of Mr. Crow. The legislature evidently so accepted it, for there is no record of any further action.

The next legislature again took up the question and, on February 23, 1853, passed a law embodying many of the suggestions of the Crow Report. It authorized the sale of the state stock at not less than par, to be paid for in coin or state bonds. The proceeds were to be deposited in the bank at 6 per cent interest, and the vacant places on the board of directors were to be filled by the private stockholders. It was not, however, to become effective until ratified by the holders of a majority of the private shares.[1] There is no record that this assent was secured, and the law became a dead letter.

The fact was that the demand for a change had not yet

[1] *Banker's Magazine*, July, 1853, p. 76.

become strong enough to force action. The bank was still doing a satisfactory business. In February, 1854 it reported combined deposits and circulation of $3,800,000 and cash reserves of $1,200,000.[1] The Panic of 1857 and the consequent restriction of business was to turn the demand toward expansion of banking capital, and so the problems of state ownership were lost in the consideration of larger issues. Little more was heard of the Crow Recommendations. However, in 1857 *The St. Louis Democrat* attempted to revive the question, arguing that much of the circulation had surely been lost through twenty years of use and therefore would not be presented for redemption, and that this together with the established reputation of the bank would insure the sale of the state stock at a large premium. But it was not able to create much interest, and the outbreak of the war in 1861 postponed all discussion of internal fiscal affairs.

The passage of the National Bank Act with its ten per cent tax on the issues of state banks put a different face on the matter. It was not yet supposed that a bank could be really prosperous without the right of issue. To nationalize the bank and still retain state stock opened up too many chances for conflict with the federal power. Moreover, it was coming to be generally felt that the mission of the bank had been accomplished. It had provided standards of banking honor at a time when private institutions were too weak to do so; but now the chartered banks were vigorous institutions, and it looked as if the State Bank had become a mere competitor on a level with the rest. It was expected that many of the chartered banks would wish to nationalize and that federal control would likely bring efficient regulation. It looked as if the state could retire from the banking business without causing state business to suffer.

[1] *Banker's Magazine*, Feb., 1854, p. 636.

There was another powerful reason for selling the state stock. Profits had declined until the state's share of the dividend was not sufficient to pay the interest on the bonds issued to pay for the stock. In his report for 1865 the state auditor made a careful analysis of the situation.[1] He pointed out that, although the charter of 1837 had provided for an authorized capital of $5,000,000, one-half to be taken by the state, the whole amount had never been subscribed, and at the time of the reorganization in 1857 the state actually owned about two-thirds of the stock.[2] Under the new charter the state had been required to subscribe for $1,000,000 of the $3,500,000 authorized stock, but had actually taken $1,086,300 out of a total of $3,426,403.06. Included in the state investment were the following funds:

School Fund	$661,967.96
Seminary Fund	100,000.00
Sinking Fund	15,558.54
Subscription in her own right	308,773.50

The sources of these funds were as follows: (a) the School Fund representing the proceeds of the saline lands and other gifts from Congress, including the Surplus Revenue apportionment, and was paid over to the bank in gold; (b) the Seminary Fund resulting from the sale of the Seminary Lands granted by Congress, and was controlled by the curators of the University. A $23,000 payment on this had been made in gold to the Chillicothe Branch; (c) the Sinking Fund, due to an amendment to the bank charter made February 12, 1839, which provided that the excess dividends after paying the interest on the state bonds should be accumulated and used to pay the principal of the state debt: (d) the ownership of stock in her own

[1] *Report Mo. Auditor*, 1865, Appendix, pp. 77-80.

[2] State stock, $963,490.10; private stock, $511,015.00.

right which came about because the state did not have enough school funds to pay for her $1,000,000 subscription, and so had issued bonds for the remainder. These bonds had matured in 1863 and had been replaced by new twenty-year bonds. Although $362,000.00 of bonds had been issued, the stock received for them amounted to only $308,773.50. The bonds had been marketed below par, the loss aggregating $53,226.50. Thus interest had to be paid on a considerably larger amount than that on which dividends were received. The interest rate on the bonds was 5½-6 per cent but really amounted to more as it was payable in New York, and Eastern exchange was at a considerable premium. The auditor's estimate was

$21,425.00	interest and exchange
9,263.20	annual dividend.
$12,161.80	loss

He considered this alone reason enough for the state to dispose of its stock.

However, he did not favor throwing the stock on the open market, but thought liquidation of the bank preferable. Dividends had lately averaged a bare three per cent a year while the chartered banks of Saint Louis were paying twenty to twenty-five per cent. He argued that the market price depended largely on the earning power and offered as proof that Saint Louis bankers were bidding only 60 for the stock while its book value was 106½.

He arrived at the book value in this manner:

STATEMENT OF JULY 1, 1865

Assets

Real Estate	$243,780.28
Coin and Bullion on Hand	167,657.25
Coin and Bullion in New York, London, and Montreal	708,223.28
Notes and Currency	600,551.35
United States Bonds	600,000.00
Undivided Profits	298,420.58
State Bonds	408,000.00
Loans	1,580,436.17
Maturing Exchange	307,732.61
Due Otherwise	204,768.26
Charged Off	572,248.56
	$5,701,818.84

Liabilities

Circulation	$292,326.00
Due to Banks	79,831.06
Deposits	1,106,895.93
	$1,479,052.99

Total Assets	$5,701,818.84
Liabilities to Customers	1,479,052.99
Excess to be divided among Shareholders	$4,222,765.85
Capital	3,426,403.06
Excess over Capital	$796,362.79
Suspended Debt Which is Partly Good	572,248.56
Net excess	$224,114.23
Capital	$3,426,403.06
Net excess	224,114.23
Stockholders Equity in Bank	$3,650,517.29

ro 106.54 per cent of capital stock. On this analysis he argued that the proper procedure was a receivership.

The new state constitution of 1865 instructed the General Assembly at its first session under the new organic law to enact legislation enabling any of the existing chartered banks to take out national charters, and to provide for the sale of all state bank stock on such terms as might be established by law. It further ordered that the proceeds of the sale of the state stock should be invested in the bonds of the United States.[1]

The Twenty-third General Assembly proceeded to carry out the constitutional instructions. A computation, based on the statement of September 30, 1865, showed net assets in excess of capital stock and liabilities to outside parties of $86,000. This was somewhat less favorable than the auditor's July report, but was arrived at in a slightly different way. Only two-thirds of the suspended debt was charged off, but deduction of $102,000 was made to cover losses on state bonds sold at a discount. A resolution was introduced in the House, providing that on the above showing it would be unwise to sell stock below par, but that it would be better to liquidate the business and invest the proceeds in United States bonds, under the constitutional provisions. This did not meet with favor, and a bill permitting the bank to nationalize and then arrange for the purchase of the state stock was substituted for it. This passed the House by a vote of 102 to 6, and was at once sent to the Senate. Here it was referred to the Committee on Banks and Banking, which reported favorably, and the bill was passed 22 to 0. It was signed by the governor on March 5, 1866.[2]

The state at once asked for bids on its stock. A Saint Louis syndicate headed by James B. Eads made an offer of

[1] *Constitution of Mo.*, 1865, art. viii, sec. 3 and art. xix, sec. 6.

[2] See *Banker's Magazine*, June, 1866, p. 987 and *House Jour.*, 23rd Adjourned Session, General Assembly Mo., 1865-66 *passim*.

$1,178,635.50 and was accepted.[1] The contracts were signed on June 14 and 18, 1866. Payment was made in government bonds, and those of the Pacific, North Missouri, and Iron Mountain Railways. The proceeds were assigned to the different funds as follows:

Seminary Fund	$108,364.45
School Fund	717,337.90
Sinking Fund	16,860.92
General Revenue	334,600.70
Expenses of the Sale	1,471.53
	$1,178,635.50

For the first time since 1837 the state was out of the banking business.

[1] See *Report Mo. Auditor*, 1867, p. 26 *et seq.* for a further discussion of the sale of the state stock.

PART IV

THE FINAL PERIOD

CHAPTER XIX

THE NATIONAL BANK OF THE STATE OF MISSOURI

THE sale of the state stock marked the end of public bank operation in Missouri. It also marked a vital change in the character of the institution. Henceforth, it was to be essentially speculative rather than conservative, although there appeared a pronounced tendency to carry on the speculations under cover of the reputation for conservatism which had come down to it from the days of state ownership. Many of the officers and employees had seen long terms of service and they were retained where possible. Every effort was made to capitalize their loyalty. The subsequent career of the bank left a blot on its record. It was to do a "plunger" type of business for about eleven years and then to go down in the depression following the panic of 1873. Though not properly a part of the state experiment in banking, it has seemed best to carry the record to the end.

By the close of 1865 the Eads syndicate was in undisputed control of the assets of the bank. Robert A. Barnes, the retiring president, had lost the struggle with Eads. He became angry, purchased stock for spite, forced the new management to buy him out at a high price, and generally threw his influence against the bank.[1] Aside from this incident, the new institution started in great favor. The decision was made to nationalize it, but to keep the old name as nearly as possible. Acordingly it was rechartered as the National Bank of the State of Missouri and opened for

[1] *St. Louis Times*, June 21, 1877.

business on January 1, 1866. The authorized capital was $5,000,000 of which $3,410,000 was paid up.[1] This gave it a capital far larger than that of any Western bank, and left it the undisputed leader of Missouri banking affairs. If the prestige of the old bank could be maintained, the future seemed bright. J. H. Britton of the Third National Bank of Saint Louis became president, and the former cashier, Mr. A. S. Robinson, was retained. New York connections were made with the National Bank of Commerce.

Although by far the largest bank in the state, it was not without competition. In July, 1867 there were national banks in nine Missouri towns, reporting a total capital of $7,459,000.[2] Some of its Saint Louis competitors were comparatively large institutions. The Third National had a capital of $1,049,000; The Merchants National, $700,000; Saint Louis National, $535,000; Union National, $500,000.[3] In addition there were a large number of banks operating under state charters and a great many private banking houses. Some of these were of considerable size. Between the time of organization and the failure of the National Bank of the State of Missouri, the banking power of the state grew rapidly; and, while the National Bank of the State of Missouri continued as the outstanding institution, its lead was steadily diminished. In January, 1868, sixteen national banks reported a capital of $7,500,000; circulation, $3,300,000; deposits including those of other banks, $9,300,000; and a cash reserve of 24.2 per cent.[4] The specie holdings were generally low. In 1869 out of $4,222,000 reserves, reported by eight Saint Louis banks, $3,476,000 re-

[1] *Banker's Magazine*, Dec., 1866, p. 472.

[2] *Ibid.*, July, 1867, p. 56.

[3] *Ibid.*, Sept., 1865.

[4] *Ibid.*, Jan., 1868, pp. 544 and 556.

presented legal tender notes and New York City deposits.[1] By 1871 there were 29 national banks in the state.[2] There were still many state and private institutions, but the larger ones had shown a tendency to take out national charters. The Boatmen's Bank was the one outstanding example of a big bank that preferred to remain under state control. As early as 1864 *The St. Louis Democrat* had advocated a general law, allowing any state bank to nationalize without a special act of the General Assembly.[3] The increasing concentration of reserves in the East was causing not a little worry; and in 1866 the Saint Louis banks took the lead in a conference in Chicago condemning the requirement of redemption in New York, Philadelphia, or Boston.[4] The figures here given serve to indicate something of the sort of banking field entered by the newly nationalized state bank.

Information relative to its operations prior to the panic of 1873 is difficult to obtain. It was merely one of a group of Saint Louis banking houses, and the statistics given are usually of the nature of consolidated statements. Such information as is available is mostly the result of disclosures at the time of the failure. It remained the chief depository for the state of Missouri and a sub-depository for Illinois.[5] It undertook the task of retiring the currency of the old State Bank and by October, 1870 only $535.00 was left outstanding.[6] In 1867 E. P. Curtis was elected cashier, succeeding A. S. Robinson. J. H. Britton remained president. On this date the surplus was given as $353,000 and

1 *Banker's Magazine*, Jan., 1869.

2 *Ibid.*, Sept., 1871, p. 168.

3 *Ibid.*, Jan., 1864, p. 594, copied from *St. Louis Democrat*.

4 *Ibid.*, Oct., 1866, p. 305.

5 Stephens, *op. cit.*, p. 508.

6 *Banker's Magazine*, Sept., 1871, p. 168.

deposits, $1,673,000. A five per cent dividend was declared in July, 1867.[1] During this year large loans were made to the city of Saint Louis for current expenses. The borrowing was necessary due to a change in the assessment laws.[2] In 1868 it took a leading part in the organization of the local clearing house. There were 39 members. Clearings averaged about $2,000,000 a day. For January, 1869 the total was $56,000,000. Balances were paid in drafts.[3] This year also marked its first great venture into speculation. It purchased $1,000,000 of the Saint Louis Water Bonds at 92½, $800,000 on its own account, and $200,000 for its New York correspondent, The National Bank of Commerce. The rest of the issue was sold in Europe and to other Saint Louis banks.[4] From this time on one speculative deal followed another in rapid succession. The North Missouri Railroad, the Eads Tunnel and Bridge project, the Eads Jetties, and the Merchant's Exchange were all financed. Expensive real-estate transactions were undertaken. Desiring to move uptown a lot was purchased at the corner of Fourth and Olive Streets for $154,000. This was never used, for the New Exchange Building was projected and the bank was authorized by the Comptroller of the Currency to take stock in it. Quarters were provided in this building.[5] It was the established policy of the bank to bid on all state, county, and city loans. Deposits of public funds were secured whenever possible. Throughout these years of reckless expansion small dividends were paid regularly and, outside of banking circles at least, its reputation for conservatism seemed unimpaired. Many in-

[1] *Banker's Magazine*, Aug., 1867, p. 141.

[2] *Ibid.*, Jan., 1867, p. 964.

[3] *Ibid.*, Feb., 1869, p. 665.

[4] *Ibid.*, Apr., 1868, p. 832.

[5] *St. Louis Democrat*, June 21, 1877.

fluential men who had long been customers of the old State Bank remained on its books. As the successor of the State Bank it had a reputation difficult to destroy. Then came the panic of 1873 with its consequent shrinkage of values. Even loans that before had appeared to be fair business risks became dangerous overnight. The officials of the bank were well aware of the extent of the depreciation and, in an effort to write off losses, reduced the capital to $2,500,000.[1] At the same time the circulation was cut down from $1,645,531.00 to $50,000 by the retirement of United States bonds. Part of this contraction was due to the desire to escape heavy taxation. In lieu of all taxes the government required the following semi-annual payments: ½ of 1 per cent on the average circulation, ¼ of 1 per cent on the average deposits, and ¼ of 1 per cent on the capital in excess of bond holdings.[2] This of course was only the federal tax. By these drastic steps failure was avoided in 1873, but the bank had received a blow from which recovery was impossible. Clearing-house certificates had been used during the panic, but not a single bank closed its doors. The full effects of the trouble were not to become evident for several years.

[1] *St. Louis Democrat*, June 21, 1877.

[2] *St. Louis Times*, June 21, 1877, quoting *Revised Statutes* U. S., par. 5214.

CHAPTER XX

The Failure of the Bank

It had been a matter of common knowledge for some time among the bankers of the city that the National Bank of the State of Missouri was weak and constantly growing weaker. However, they had tried to protect it at least to the extent of saying nothing, and The Third National Bank had offered substantial aid by rediscounting several hundred thousand dollars of selected paper. The statement call for April 14, 1877 disclosed the following condition:[1]

Resources

Loans and Discounts	$3,787,352.23
U. S. Bonds to Secure Circulation	50,000.00
U. S. Bonds to secure U. S. Deposits	106,000.00
Other Stocks, Bonds and Mortgages	510,095.50
Due from Approved Reserve Agents	211,365.52
Due from Other National Banks	9,185.16
Due from State Banks	9,574.81
Real Estate, Furniture, etc.	281,713.44
Expenses and Taxes Paid	82,667.21
Checks and Cash Items	48,767.46
Exchanges for the Clearing House	78,256.14
Bills of Other Banks	71,008.00
Fractional Currency	999.05
Specie	11,431.00
Legal Tender Notes	268,000.00
U. S. Certificates of Deposit for Legal Tender	10,000.00
Redemption Fund	2,250.00
	$5,538,665.52

[1] *St. Louis Democrat*, June 20, 1877.

Liabilities

Capital Paid In	$2,500,000.00
Surplus	248,775.52
Undivided Profits	24,297.87
Circulation	44,860.00
Unpaid Dividends	10,919.00
Deposits	973,077.56
Demand Certificates of Deposit	14,008.81
Time Deposits	623,844.85
Certified Checks	1,595.80
Cashiers Checks	3,261.95
Due to National Banks	80,914.60
Due to State Banks	546,605.38
Rediscounts	336,504.18
Bills Payable	130,000.00
	$5,538,665.52

This was not a strong statement but it might have passed muster if it had not been known that many of the investments held were worth far less than par. At least this was known by the other bankers. For some months it had been common practice to present large checks for immediate payment without waiting for the regular clearings.[1]

After the publication of the April statement somebody became alarmed and wrote to the Comptroller of the Currency demanding an investigation of the bank. William P. Watson, a representative of the Treasury Department and an expert examiner, was sent down from Chicago to make a thorough examination of the books. He reported early in May that the bank had much dead paper and that in his opinion forty per cent of the capital was gone. He said a previous examination made by him had been found incorrect as to the character of the cash items and the amount of past-due paper in the portfolio.[2] He also found

[1] Statement of a competitor made after the failure in *St. Louis Democrat*, June 21, 1877.

[2] *Reply of Comptroller of Currency to Letter of W. H. Bliss*, St. Louis District Att'y (1879, Washington).

that no elections of directors had been held for three years, but that this was not due to negligence of the officers, for regular calls had been issued each year at the proper time, but a quorum had never responded. Instead of closing the bank, the Comptroller ordered an election of directors for May 29, 1877 and made plans for a fuller investigation.

About $600,000 of the stock was owned in Saline, Howard, Boone, Pike, Marion, Cape Girardeau, Greene, and Cooper Counties. When the national charter was taken out, the holders of the stock of the Old State Bank branches were merely given an equal amount of stock in the new bank. Although holding nearly one-fourth of the stock they had remained singularly indifferent as to their interests and had not been represented on the board of directors. Quotations on the stock had declined from above par to around 60, but the panic had caused such widespread depreciation in securities that this alone did not seem to stir the country members to action. They had received their dividends regularly and had asked few questions. However, when it was announced in January that the regular dividend would be passed and that likely none would be paid in july, interest began to be aroused. It was quite evident that the election called for May 29th would not go by default. The Saline, Howard, Boone, and Cooper County stockholders agreed to vote for H. S. Mills, who had been cashier of the Arrow Rock Branch of the State Bank from 1857 to 1864 and who now owned $20,000 stock. The Pike, Marion, Cape Girardeau, and Greene County men proposed Ex-United-States-Senator John B. Henderson of Pike County, a former cashier of the Louisiana Branch Bank. He was not a stockholder, but bought 25 shares in order to qualify.[1]

[1] The National Bank Act required only 10 shares, but it had been raised to 25 in this case by the by-laws.

The two combinations planned to vote for each other and thus to get two country directors. The attempt was successful. Two new members were elected from St. Louis, W. M. Samuels and N. S. Chouteau, Members re-elected included President Britton, Vice-President Barton Bates, James B. Eads, J. S. Walsh, and C. F. Burns.[1]

Henderson immediately demanded to see the books. There was no opposition. At the first meeting of the new board he introduced a resolution asking the president to appoint an examining committee. It was adopted, and Chouteau, Mills, and Henderson were appointed with President Britton and Vice-President Bates as assisting members.[2] The committee at once undertook to make a thorough examination and, after working ten days and nights and going over every note or other investment separately, reported that in their opinion the bank was hopelessly insolvent. President Britton and Cashier Curtis gave every assistance during the examination. Liabilities exclusive of capital were given as $2,387,000 and assets at face value, $5,000,000. Such examination as they could give, the report continued, led to the conclusion that the depreciation was so great as to demand the immediate closing of the bank.[3] The board went into session at 10 a. m. Tuesday the 19th of June and, after debating the report all day, admitted insolvency and passed the following resolution by an unanimous vote:[4]

1. Reasonable profits can no longer be expected.

2. The interests of the creditors can best be served by a receivership.

[1] A complete account of the election is given in *The St. Louis Republic*, June 21, 1877.

[2] *St. Louis Democrat*, June 21, 1877.

[3] *St. Louis Republic*, June 21, 1877.

[4] *St. Louis Daily Times*, June 20, 1877.

3. Two directors should be appointed to correspond by wire with the Comptroller of the Currency and report at 10 a. m. tomorrow.

4. In case the Comptroller should refuse a receivership, voluntary liquidation is recommended.

Pursuant to instructions from the Comptroller, the bank was closed for purposes of liquidation Wednesday, June 20, 1877; and two days later Mr. Walter S. Johnston was named receiver.[1]

There was comparatively little excitement and no run on the other banks of the city. Just before the passage of the resolution several new accounts were offered, but were refused. After its passage no more business was transacted. A reporter for the *St. Louis Democrat* visited the bank and found only six people in the lobby. Several of them had checks, but were told by Mr. Curtis that no funds could be paid out. There was some excitement in financial and commercial circles, but no great alarm on the Exchange. Few members of the Exchange were customers of the bank. Its depositors were chiefly corporations, country banks, executors, guardians, and men who had done business with the State Bank in other days. It also held city and county funds and was the official depository of the bankruptcy court.[2] On June 23rd *The Democrat* was able to report the money market placid and the effects of the failure gone. But these were the superficial effects.

The newspapers tried to make the best of the situation and said no other banks and no business houses would be affected. The country banks which had funds on deposit were offered assistance by the other banks of the city, and

Letter to the author from W. G. Fowler, Deputy-Comptroller of Currency, June 22, 1921 (see appendix for a copy of his letter).

[2] *St. Louis Democrat*, June 21, 1877.

arrangements were made to protect their outstanding checks. *The Democrat* on June 21st published a list of the country accounts and the banks that would honor their checks. The Boatmen's and Saint Louis National Banks were especially active in this work. They also offered to carry the city government for current needs, and announced that individual depositors who presented certificates of claims would be advanced 40-50 per cent of their face value at current interest rates. The Saint Louis National Bank advanced $100,000 to take care of the necessary payments of the bankruptcy court.[1]

All of the Saint Louis newspapers contained very full accounts of the failure. On June 20th *The Democrat* printed the following editorial. It represents a first reaction before any investigation was made:

This is the largest failure since the first days of the panic when Jay Cooke and Henry Clews went over. There had been some comment before the failure, but people thought a $2,500,000 capital and government supervision was pretty good protection for depositors. We are told the depositors will ultimately be paid in full. Confidence in the bank management is, however, shaken. The directors are men who commanded esteem and who had ample outside means; yet in ten years the capital is gone, and the richest and oldest bank west of the Mississippi River is gone. Stockholders must learn to watch their bank. The directors had full control. Latterly they had not even gone thru the form of being elected. The English requirement of a full statement to the stockholders' meeting should be used here. Rumors were current yesterday afternoon. Yesterday morning the directors voted to stop business and protect the creditors. There has been a terrible shrinkage of values since 1873. For some weeks there has been a pressure to sell stock in

[1] Dacus, J. A. and Buel, J. W., *A Tour of St. Louis* (St. Louis, 1878).

the open market. Questions were asked, "What is the matter with the old State Bank?" Somebody wants to sell, but the question remained unanswered.[1]

A preliminary statement of the accounts was given out on June 20th essentially as follows: deposits about $2,-400,000 including $240,000 city funds and $130,000 to the credit of assignees, registers, and masters in chancery. These latter and the city funds were secured by bonds.[2] Official state deposits were only $3,000, but the bank admitted holding $500,000 state money on a sub-contract from a St. Joseph, Missouri bank.[3] Country banks had large accounts.

The report that stock had been offered for sale in large blocks just previous to the failure gave color to the charge of fraud. Over five hundred people were reported to have sold stock during the last few months. The receiver took notice of this and announced that he intended to institute suits to set aside the transfers, on the ground that the sellers knew of the condition of the bank. Ex-President Barnes was reported to have sold a large part of his stock and to have invested the proceeds in county bonds.[4] It seemed difficult to get action. The receiver, Mr. Johnston, wrote to the comptroller that a grand jury investigation was expected, yet the fall term of 1877 and the spring term of 1878 came and went without it. At the fall term of 1878 an inquiry was demanded, but was opposed by the district attorney. Indictments were finally returned against Britton, Bates, and Curtis.[5] At least the agitation caused the names of the owners of record, as of August 1, 1876, to be made

[1] *St. Louis Democrat*, June 20, 1877 (Adapted).

[2] *Ibid.*, June 20, 1877.

[3] *St. Louis Republic*, June 21, 1877.

[4] *Ibid.*

[5] *Reply of Comptroller*, etc., *op. cit.*

public. There were 25,000 shares of par value $100 each. In 1876 they had been assessed at $70 by the county assessor, but were quoted at 59-60 just before the suspension. James B. Eads, the largest stockholder, had 2702 shares; President Britton, 1,542; Barton Bates, 1,175; and J. A. Ubsdell, 1,150. The other holdings were much smaller. The Aetna Insurance Company had 200; University of Missouri, 230; National Bank of Commerce, New York, 70; and H. S. Mills, 200. Aside from Britton, Bates, and Mills the holdings of the other directors were very modest —barely enough to qualify. Fifty stockholders had as many as 100 shares. The complete list included 485 names.[1]

Whatever may be said about the conduct of the bank previous to the election of the new board of directors, it was generally conceded that Henderson, Mills, Chouteau, and Samuels were standing for an honest settlement; and it is to the credit of the president and cashier that they placed no obstacles in the way. In fact the city government had been given to understand that it would not be to its best interests to largely increase its balance, although the bank could probably have received at least $500,000 from this course, and its officers knew that to refuse it meant certain suspension. After conditions became desperate the officials seem to have at least tried to stop where they were.

The causes of the failure have been indicated in the previous chapter. The Comptroller's office records three major causes: fraudulent management, excessive loans to officers and directors, and depreciation of securities.[2] Five directors, chiefly Bates, Britton, Eads, and Curtis owed the bank $800,000.[3] Eads paid at least a part of his indeb-

[1] *St. Louis Democrat*, June 21, 1877.

[2] Letter from Deputy-Comptroller Fowler, *op. cit.*

[3] *Banker's Magazine*, July, 1877, p. 70.

tedness and was given his notes, thus securing exemption from prosecution. This, however, was done on an order from a competent court.[1] The comptroller charged the officers with paying unearned dividends and making false reports, but seemed loath to press the prosecution. The receiver had written him that the cashier, Mr. Curtis, was a man of natural moral excellence and fine business habits, that he was familiar with all details and in the process of liquidation gave more assistance than any one except the equally guilty assistant cashier. Many items were listed with the depreciated securities. In 1871 the North Missouri Railroad was reorganized as the Saint Louis, Kansas City, and Northern. The bank made a large loan on the stock as collateral on a basis of valuation of $80 a share. It paid 2-3 per cent dividends for several years but they were forced, and the stock soon declined to 60.[2] It was quoted at 20-25 at the time of the failure. Heavy loans had been made on the Eads Bridge and Tunnel. This stock had sold for 150 and was now nearly worthless. The Olive Street corner once purchased for a building site had cost $154,000, and the bank had refused later to sell at $180,900. Now, $100,000 was offered for it. Likely the total real-estate holdings of the bank had depreciated $250,000 in the last two or three years.[3]

The Saint Louis Democrat secured a large number of interviews both with parties directly concerned and with representative financial interests. These statements contain much of interest relative to the condition of the bank and the state of public opinion. President Britton was first asked for an interview. The reporter said he found

[1] *Reply of Comptroller, op. cit.*

[2] *St. Louis Democrat*, June 21, 1877.

[3] *St. Louis Times*, June 20, 1877.

Colonel Britton leaning on a counter talking earnestly to a man. He asked him to come back to see him in the evening. He went back to the bank at 7 p. m. and found the Colonel with two watchmen waiting for him. He said he had decided not to be interviewed until the federal examiner had made his report, but in spite of this statement he continued the conversation. He said he was confident that the bank would pay all its debts and he hoped it could resume. In fact he had opposed the suspension, but had yielded to the judgment of the board and voted to close. He assigned as causes, general stagnation and shrinkage of securities. Among the more important losses were the bridge and jetties advances but he thought this money would come back with interest. He denied that the bank held any stock in the North Missouri Railroad, but admitted having made personal loans to it which he thought were safe. He said the Chamber of Commerce loan of $50,000 was wholly gone. The cashier refused to make any statement whatever.

Mayor Overstolz stated that the city deposits were protected by a special bond of $500,000 signed by President Britton, Barton Bates, John Jackson, James B. Eads, and J. S. Walsh. The balance in the bank was given as $244,-953.63. Only $12,923.29 cash was available in the city hall vaults, but other banks in the city had offered to supply current needs. The Fourth National Bank had been selected as city depository. The County Treasurer refused to tell the amount of the county deposit, but said he had some funds in three other banks. President Britton and Mr. Henderson both estimated this account at about $80,000. At the office of the City Auditor the reporter listened to a tirade against the bank by General Shields. He called the officers thieves and said they should be sent to jail for life. He accused the bank of receiving $1,100 water collections after the resolution to close had been passed. The

Water Board had over $12,000 on deposit. The School Board had nothing, having checked out $131,000 state fund apportionment two weeks before.

The examiner, Mr. Howenstein, was next interviewed. He expressed surprise that the bank had closed at all. He said he had examined it the night before and found plenty of money there, that the depositors would lose nothing, and that a 25 to 50 per cent dividend might be expected very soon. The other examiner, Mr. Barnard, was inclined to discuss the various investments of the bank and to commend the officers for their public spirit in making public advances in time of need. He cited a $1,000,000 loan made to the city in 1875.

The reporter then sought to get an expression from various competitors. R. J. Lackland, President of the Boatmen's Bank, was first visited. He talked in a guarded fashion, but said that the low figure of the recent stock quotations indicated that the failure had been anticipated. He thought no other banks and little business would be involved, as the bank was still a sort of government institution and had comparatively few commercial accounts. At any rate he thought most of the banks were unusually well supplied with funds. He indicated that his bank had not been friendly toward the failed institution, and that he knew little about its affairs. At the Manufacturer's Bank it was stated that the bank had been carrying too much real estate and was doing too little business to make profits on its big capital. They did not expect to see any business failures, as few business men carried their accounts there. At Bartholomew Lewes & Co. he was told that every bank in the city had been expecting the failure for a year, and that it was common knowledge that it had made no loans lately. The Valley National Bank also professed no surprise at the failure. The Commercial Bank said their organization would lose nothing, for they made it a policy to get ready for things which they expected.[1]

However much the suspension may have been looked for by the bankers, it was a surprise to the average man about town. *The Democrat* said it created universal surprise outside of financial circles.[1] *The Times* called it a "thunder clap" and said the many "I told you so's" were not heard yesterday.[2] The fact that so many public accounts and accounts of country banks were on the books indicates that the failure was not generally expected.

Bank Examiner Howenstein at once made a complete audit and reported that the capital stock was very largely gone. Walter S. Johnston, the receiver, was a well qualified man and unembarrassed by any Saint Louis acquantance. He liquidated the business with signal success. In 1879 the Comptroller of the Currency was able to report that 70 per cent dividends on all the approved claims had been paid. The cash disbursements totaled $1,500,000.[3] After serving until 1885 Mr. Johnston resigned and Edgar T. Welles was appointed in his place. An assessment of 25 per cent was levied and finally all proved claims were paid with interest. There remained $63,676.85, which amount was turned over to Mr. Welles as agent for the shareholders. The affairs of the bank were not finally closed until June 16, 1887.[4]

It had been stoutly maintained that no other banks would be affected, but it was soon found that the lack of excitement and run did not mean that the trouble was over. On July 10th the German Bank suspended with liabilities of $200,000. Four days later the Butchers and Drovers Bank,

[1] These interviews were published in *The St. Louis Democrat*, June 21, 1877.

[2] *St. Louis Times*, June 20, 1877.

[3] Letter of Comptroller, *op. cit.*

[4] Letter from Deputy-Comptroller, *op. cit.*

The North Saint Louis Savings Association, and the Bank of Saint Louis closed their doors. On July 16th The Bremen Savings Association failed. The runs continued. As the smaller banks began to close, everybody became frightened. In sixteen months Saint Louis loans dropped from $42,-000,000 to $29,000,000; deposits from $38,500,000 to $27,-000,000; and the number of banks from forty-six to thirty-two.[1] The country banks seem to have escaped the trouble, but the excitement spread to Kansas City, and the following January The Maston and First National Banks suspended. The latter bank had deposits of $350,000.[2] It is, of course, not to be maintained that all the trouble was due to the failure of the National Bank of the State of Missouri. These banks had also been taking speculative risks on their own account. However, it is known that most of these institutions were among its creditors, and the excitement relative to its closing, no doubt, had much to do with starting runs on the other banks.

This marks the end of one of America's great banks, although its period of usefulness had ended with its nationalization in 1866. Since that time it had been a great corporate speculator rather than a bank. This last chapter of its history should not lead to forgetfulness of its great service. The Bank of the State of Missouri played a major rôle in the financial development of Missouri and of the whole Mississippi Valley. Its prime function had been to set standards. It had taught the lesson of sound and conservative banking at a time when honor and responsibility were not commonly found in the banking business. In the face of this great service it may well be excused for

[1] Stephens, *op. cit.*, p. 508 (altogether there were 25 failures in the state. Of these 20 paid their depositors in full).

[2] *Banker's Magazine*, Mar., 1878, p. 740.

often failing to care for the legitimate needs of its customers. Private banks were, at least in some measure, able to remedy this fault, but they could not have set standards. It is to the State Bank that Missouri's unusual banking record is chiefly due. It is to be greatly regretted that its last days as a national bank did not measure up to its record while under state control.

BIBLIOGRAPHY

American State Papers, 5 vols., Finance (1789-1828), (Washington, 1832-59).

Banker's Magazine (Boston, 1848-54; New York, 1855-1878).

Bay, W. V. M., *Bench and Bar of Missouri*, art. on "Henry Shurlds" (St. Louis, 1878).

Benton, Senator Thomas H., "State of the Currency," address before U. S. Senate, Jan. 20, 1832.

Berkeley, W. A., *The Money Question* (Grand Rapids, 1876).

Boonville Herald (copied in *Mo. Intelligencer*).

Bourne, E. G., *History of the Surplus Revenue of 1837* (New York, 1886).

Bulletin American Institute Bank Clerks

Palmer, Paul G. of National Bank of Commerce, St. Louis, "Banking in Louisiana Purchase," Nov. 15, 1904.

Plehn, C. C., articles in issues of June 1, 1903, June 15, 1903 and July 1, 1903.

Bullock, C. J., *Essays on Monetary History of the U. S.* (Boston, 1907).

Callender, Guy Stevens, *The Economic History of the U. S.* (Boston, 1909).

Campbell, R. A., *Gazetteer of Missouri* (St. Louis, 1875).

Carr, Lucien, *Missouri, A Bone of Contention* (Boston, 1888).

Catterall, R. C. H., *The First Six Years of the Second United States Bank* (Ph.D. thesis, University of Chicago, 1902).

——, "Successes and Failures of the First and Second United States Banks" in *Proc. Academy Political Science*, vol. i, no. 2, January, 1911.

Cincinnati Gazette.

Clarion, The (copied in *Mo. Republican*).

Conference on Resumption, proceedings of an adjourned meeting of delegates of various banks, City Hall, New York, April 11, 1838.

Comptroller, Deputy (W. G. Fowler), Letter to author 1921. See Appendix.

Coman, Katherine, *Economic Beginnings of the Far West*, 2 vols. (New York, 1912).

Conant, C. A., *History of Modern Banks of Issue* (New York, 1896).

Conrad, H. L., *Encyclopedia of Missouri History*, 4 vols. (St. Louis), article on "Saint Louis Banking."

Cox, James, *The Old and New in Saint Louis* (St. Louis, 1894).

Crow, Wayman, "Report of the Bank Committee, Senate of Missouri" in *Banker's Magazine*, March, 1851.

Dacus, J. A. and Buel, J. W., *A Tour of St. Louis* (St. Louis, 1878).

Darby, *Personal Recollections* (St. Louis, 1880).

Davis, W. B. and Durrie, D. S., *History of Missouri* (St. Louis, 1876).

Dean, Sydney, *History of Banking and Banks* (Boston, 1884).

Dewey, D. R., *State Banking Before the Civil War*, National Monetary Commission.

Douglas, R. S., *History of Southeast Missouri* (Chicago, 1912).

Dowrie, G. W., *Development of Banking in Illinois* (University of Illinois Studies in the Social Sciences, vol. ii, no. 4, Dec., 1913).

Dunbar, C. F., "State Banks in 1860" in *Economic Essays* (Sprague edition, New York, 1904).

Edwards, R. and Hopewell, M., *The Great West* (St. Louis, 1860).

Eliason, "Beginnings of Banking in Minnesota" in *Minnesota Historical Society Collections*, vol. xii, 1905-08.

Financial Register (Philadelphia).

Gallatin, Albert, *Considerations on Currency and Banking in the United States* (1831).

Garnett, C. H., *State Banks of Issue in Illinois*, H. H. Harris Prize Essay, University of Illinois Studies, 1898.

Geyer, H. S., *Digest of Laws of Missouri* (St. Louis, 1818).

Gilbart, J. W., *History of Banking in America* (London, 1837).

Goddard, T. H., *General History of Banks of Europe and United States* (New York, 1831).

Gouge, Wm. M., *Short History of Paper Money and Banking in the United States* (New York, 1833).

Green, Duff, *Facts and Suggestions* (New York, 1866).

Hadden, C. B., "History of State Banks and Early Banking Systems of Wisconsin," in *Wisconsin Academy of Sciences*, vol. x.

Hazard's Register (Philadelphia, vol. iii (1840-41)), U. S. Commercial and Statistical Register.

Hepburn, A. B., *The Contest for Sound Money* (New York, 1903).

Hildreth, Richard, *History of Banks* (Boston, 1837).

——, *Banks, Banking and Paper Currencies* (Boston, 1840).

Holdsworth, J. T., "Lessons of State Banking Before the Civil War" in *Proc. Acad. Political Science*, vol. i, no. 2, Jan., 1911.

Houck, Louis, *History of Missouri* (Chicago, 1908), vol. iii.

Iowa, Charter State Bank of (Muscatine, Iowa, 1858).

Jeffersonian Republican (copied in *Mo. Intelligencer*).

Jones, Breckenridge, article "A Hundred Years of Banking in Missouri," in Centennial number of *Missouri Historical Review*, Jan., 1921.

Journal of Banking (Philadelphia), July, 1841-July, 1842.

Kargan, E. D., *Mercantile, Industrial and Professional St. Louis* (St. Louis, 1904).

Kentucky, Memorial of President and Directors of Bank of, to Kentucky House of Representatives (State Printer, Frankfort, 1841).

Knox, J. J., *History of Banking in the United States* (New York, 1903).

Laughlin, J. Laurence, *Report Indianapolis Monetary Commission*, 1898.

Lucas' Letters 1815-1836 (St. Louis, 1905), published by his grandson, J. B. C. Lucas.

McClure, C. H., "Early Opposition to T. H. Benton in Missouri" in *Missouri Historical Review* (Columbia, Missouri), April, 1916.

McCulloch, A. J., *The Loan Office Experiment in Missouri, 1821-36, University of Missouri Bulletin*, vol. xv, no. 24, Social Science Series, Aug., 1914.

Merchants and Banker's Register (New York, 1857-1871).

Missouri Argus (St. Louis). Established in 1831, under the name of *Workingmen's Advocate*, a democratic daily from 1835-41. In politics it favored the State Bank and opposed everything that was advocated by its competitor, *The Missouri Republican*. The file is owned by the St. Louis Historical Society. See especially 1835-39.

Missouri Courier.

Missouri Documents

Auditor of Missouri, Report of State, 1830-65. The Missouri Historical Society (Columbia, Missouri) has complete file. See especially 1840, 1844, 1846, 1849, 1850, 1853, 1854, 1856, 1859, 1861, 1863, 1865.

Report Missouri Auditor, 1865, appendix.

Report Missouri Auditor, 1867.

Bank of Missouri, 1856, Report of Committee to Examine.

Banking Laws of Missouri, 1837.

Banks of Missouri, Act for Relief of, March 18, 1861 (St. Louis, 1861).

Bonds, *Report of Committee of 1838 to whom was Referred the Sale of the State* (pamphlet in New York Public Library).

Laws of Missouri, 1804-24 (State Printer).

Laws of Missouri, 1845.

Laws of Missouri, 1804-1867. Official Publications. File in possession of Missouri Historical Society (Columbia, Missouri). See especially 1836, 1838, 1840, 1841, 1843, 1845, 1856, 1857.

Legislative Journals, House and Senate, General Assembly of Missouri, 1820-1877. Official State Records in possession of Missouri Historical Society (Columbia, Missouri). Fullest use was made of this file for all of this period.

Missouri Gazette (St. Louis), 1808-1809.

Missouri Intelligencer. Established at Franklin, Howard County, as *Missouri Intelligencer and Boone's Lick Advertiser* by Patten and Holliday, April 23, 1819. It was removed to Fayette in 1826 and to Columbia in 1830. It supported the U. S. Bank and was against a state institution. The Missouri Historical Society at Columbia, Missouri has an almost complete file. Extensive use was made of this for the period, 1819-35. It is unusually valuable for its reflection of financial conditions in the rural districts. It still survives as the present *Herald-Statesman* of Columbia, Missouri.

Missouri Republican (St. Louis). Established 1809 as *Missouri Gazette*, later the *St. Louis Republic*. It consistently supported the U. S. Bank and opposed the state banking plan. A complete file is in the possession of the St. Louis Historical Society, St. Louis, Missouri. Use was made of it chiefly for the years, 1837 and 1877.

Missouri Republican. Annual Review, January 10, 1854.

Münch, *Der Staat, Missouri* (St. Louis, 1859).

Napton, W. B., *Past and Present of Saline County* (1881).

Niles Register (Baltimore).

Palmyra Courier (copied in *Missouri Intelligencer*).

Peters. 4 Peters U. S. 410; 11 Peters U. S. 257; 11 Peters U. S. 348.

Pope, Jesse, address, "Part which Banks of Missouri have Played in Commercial Development of State" in *Proceedings Missouri Bankers' Association*, 1905.

Rader, Perry S., *History of Missouri* (Columbia, Missouri, 1898).

Reaves, L. O., *St. Louis the Future Great City*. Biographical edition (St. Louis, 1875).

——, *ibid.*, Centennial edition, 1904.

Ridgely, W. B., "Early Banking in the West," address before Missouri Bankers' Association (1904). Reprinted in *Trust Companies* (New York, June, 1904).

Royall, W. L., *History of Virginia Banks Prior to Civil War* (New York, 1907).

St. Louis

Anonymous—*Historical and Descriptive Review of St. Louis* (St. Louis, 1891).

Anonymous—*Thoughts About the City of St Louis* (St. Louis, 1854).

Chamber of Commerce, Proceedings St. Louis (St. Louis, 1842) in relation to improvement of navigation of Mississippi.

Chamber of Commerce of St. Louis, Report of Committee appointed by—on "Trade, Commerce and Manufacturing, 1852," also 1842.

City Directory of St. Louis. 1816, 1817, 1818, 1819, 1821, 1829, 1834, 1837, 1838, 1839, 1844, 1847, 1850, 1853, 1857, 1863.

St. Louis Democrat, B. Gratz Brown, editor. Files were consulted for 1855 to 1858 inclusive, 1861 and 1877.

St. Louis Republic, Centennial edition, July 12, 1908.

St. Louis Times, 1877.

St. Louis Gas Light Company, Report Directors, 1848.

Scharf, J. T., *History of St. Louis City and County*, 2 vols. (Philadelphia, 1883).

Shepard, E. H., *History of St. Louis and Missouri* (St. Louis, 1870).

Simons, A. M., *Social Forces in American History* (New York, 1911).

Skillman, W. D., *The Western Metropolis* (St. Louis, 1846).

Spaulding, E. G., *One Hundred Years of Banking* (Buffalo, 1876). Address.

Stephens, Lon V., address "Banking and Resources of Missouri" at World's Congress of Banks and Financiers (Chicago, 1893).

Stevens, W. B., *St. Louis the Fourth City*, 2 vols. (St. Louis, 1909).

——, *History of St. Louis* (St. Louis, 1905). Earlier edition of *St. Louis the Fourth City*.

Sound Currency, published by Sound Currency Committee, Reform Club, New York.

L. C. Root, April 15, 1895, "The States as Bankers."
May 15. 1897. "Tax on State Bank Notes."
L. C. Root, Sept. 1, 1897, "The Second United States Bank."
Dec. 1, 1897, "Wild Cat State Banking."

Sumner, W. G., *History of Banking in All the Leading Nations*, vol. i, United States (New York, 1896).

Sutherland and McEvoy, *Missouri State Gazetteer 1859-60*.

Taylor, J. N. and Crooks, M., *Sketch Book of St. Louis* (St. Louis, 1858).

Turner, F. J., *Rise of the New West* (New York, 1906).

United States Government Documents

Report of T. Cadwalader, investigator for U. S. Bank in "Petition for a Branch Bank in St. Louis," March 17, 1827.

Congressional Report. House of Representatives, April 13, 1830. (Report of President Cheves and McDuffie to Committee of Ways and Means).

Comptroller of the Currency and of the Receiver of the National Bank of the State of Missouri, *Reply of to Letter of W. H. Bliss*, U. S. District Attorney at St. Louis (1879, Washington).

Comptroller of Currency, Report of 1876.

21st Congress, 1st session, *House Document 263*.

——, *House Document 358*. Report of Committee on Ways and Means.

22nd Congress, 1st session. *House Report 460*. "Bank of United States," April 30, 1832.

——, 2nd session, *House Document 8*. Letter of Secretary of Treasury, Dec. 11, 1832.

23rd Congress, 1st session, *House Document 498*. "Condition of State Banks in 1834."

——, 2nd session, *House Document 27*. Report of Secretary of Treasury of U. S. on "Public Money," Dec. 15, 1834.

——, ——, *Senate Document 17*, Dec. 18, 1834.

24th Congress, 2nd session, *House Document 65*. "Letter of Secretary of Treasury Relative to Condition of State Banks," Nov. 21, 1835.

25th Congress, 2nd session, *Senate Bulletin 211*. "Statement St. Louis Branch U. S. Bank," June 30, 1837.

34th Congress, 3rd session, *Executive Document 87*. "Condition of Banks Thruout the Union."

38th Congress, 1st session, *Executive Document 50*. "Letter of Secretary of Treasury giving Abstract of Bank Reports for Commissioner of Internal Revenue."

Utley, H. M., "Wild Cat Banking System of Michigan," in *Michigan Pioneer Collections*, vol. v, 1882.

Violette, E. M., *History of Missouri* (New York, 1918).

Wetmore, *Gazetteer of Missouri* (St. Louis, 1837).

Wildman, M. S., *Money Inflation in United States* (New York, 1905).

APPENDIX

Letter from W. J. Fowler, Deputy-Comptroller of the Currency, relative to the liquidation of The National Bank of the State of Missouri.

Treasury Department
Washington
June 22, 1921.

Mr. J. Ray Cable
The University of Oklahoma
Norman, Oklahoma

Sir:

Your letter of June 15th, is received with reference to the Bank of the State of Missouri.

You are advised that the records of this office show that The National Bank of the State of Missouri in St. Louis, Missouri, was declared insolvent and placed in the hands of a receiver on June 23, 1877, Walter S. Johnston being the receiver appointed.

Mr. Johnston subsequently resigned and Mr. Edgar T. Welles was appointed to succeed him on January 31, 1885. The receivership paid dividends aggregating one hundred per cent and interest to creditors who proved their claims as required by law; and the affairs of the receivership were finally closed and a shareholders' agent elected to whom the remaining assets of the bank, aggregating $63,676.85 were turned over. Mr. Edgar T. Welles was elected shareholders' agent on June 16, 1887.

The cause for the failure of the bank was fraudulent management, excessive loans to officers and directors and depreciation of securities.

Respectfully,
W. J. Fowler
Deputy Comptroller.

Bei Fragen zur Produktsicherheit wenden Sie sich bitte an:
If you have any questions regarding product safety,
please contact:

Walter de Gruyter GmbH
Genthiner Straße 13
10785 Berlin
productsafety@degruyterbrill.com